QUANTITATIVE PLANNING OF ECONOMIC POLICY

QUANTITATIVE PLANNING

of

ECONOMIC POLICY

A Conference of the Social Science
Research Council Committee on Economic Stability

Bert G. Hickman, *Editor*

Henri Theil
Karl A. Fox and Erik Thorbecke
Jati K. Sengupta
Etienne S. Kirschen and Lucien Morissens
C. A. van den Beld
Willem Hessel
Bernard Cazes
Shuntaro Shishido
Tsunehiko Watanabe
Charles C. Holt

The Brookings Institution • Washington, D.C.

Library of Congress Catalogue Card Number 65-18314

THE BROOKINGS INSTITUTION is an independent organization devoted to nonpartisan research, education, and publication in economics, government, foreign policy, and the social sciences generally. Its principal purposes are to aid in the development of sound public policies and to promote public understanding of issues of national importance.

The Institution was founded December 8, 1927, to merge the activities of the Institute for Government Research, founded in 1916, the Institute of Economics, founded in 1922, and the Robert Brookings Graduate School of Economics and Government, founded in 1924.

The general administration of the Institution is the responsibility of a self-perpetuating Board of Trustees. The Trustees are likewise charged with maintaining the independence of the staff and fostering the most favorable conditions for creative research and education. The immediate direction of the policies, program, and staff of the Institution is vested in the President, assisted by the division directors and an advisory council, chosen from the professional staff of the Institution.

In publishing a study, the Institution presents it as a competent treatment of a subject worthy of public consideration. The interpretations and conclusions in such publications are those of the author or authors and do not purport to represent the views of the other staff members, officers, or trustees of the Brookings Institution.

Foreword

THE PAPERS INCLUDED IN THIS VOLUME are the outcome of an international conference held at the Brookings Institution on August 19-24, 1963. The primary purpose of the conference was to inform economists and policy-makers about some of the leading developments in the field of quantitative policy planning in recent years and to provide an objective appraisal of the contribution of quantitative research techniques to the planning and implementation of economic policy in three of the countries which have pioneered in their use—France, Japan, and The Netherlands. A special effort has been made by the authors to provide authoritative expositions of their respective topics without the use of advanced mathematics.

The conference was sponsored by the Social Science Research Council Committee on Economic Stability, with financial support made available to the Council by the Ford Foundation. The planning committee consisted of Karl A. Fox, Bert G. Hickman, Charles C. Holt, and Erik Thorbecke. Jati K. Sengupta and Erik Thorbecke served as discussion rapporteurs, and Mr. Hickman has relied heavily on their notes in the preparation of his introduction. Sheau-eng Lau drew several of the charts. Kathleen Sproul edited the final manuscript and saw it through the press. Charlene Semer prepared the index. The book is a product of the Economic Studies Division, which is under the direction of Joseph A. Pechman.

The opinions and views expressed are those of the authors and do not purport to represent the views of the trustees, officers, or other staff members of the Brookings Institution, the Social Science Research Council, or the Ford Foundation.

Robert D. Calkins
President

January 1964
The Brookings Institution
1775 Massachusetts Avenue, N.W.
Washington, D.C.

Contents

ix

Authors' Tables and Figures

1

Introduction

BERT G. HICKMAN[1]

THE PAPERS INCLUDED IN THIS VOLUME were presented at an international conference held at the Brookings Institution in August 1963. Together they comprise an authoritative appraisal of the principal techniques of quantitative policy planning and of the specific application of such techniques to macroeconomic policy problems in three of the countries which have pioneered in their use. Although not designed to provide an exhaustive survey of this vast subject, the papers will nevertheless serve to inform the nonspecialist about a number of the leading developments in the field of quantitative policy planning during the past ten or fifteen years. Some of these developments concern highly technical aspects of the theory of economic policy and of econometric model building; these are, however, discussed without recourse to advanced mathematics, in order to reach as wide an audience as possible. But the reader who finds that his intellectual appetite is whetted by the numerous delicacies of the feast set before him has only to consult the references given in the papers for more rigorous or detailed presentations.

Both economic theory and empirical technique receive due recognition in the following pages for their contribution to the formulation of quantitative economic policy. These technical contributions would, however, be sterile indeed, were there no organizational means to reach a consensus on the instruments and objectives of economic policy and to implement the resulting decisions. The institutional and political aspects of formulating and executing economic policy therefore also receive a large share of attention in the papers dealing with the actual planning experiences of France, Japan, and The Netherlands.

A paper-by-paper summary would serve little purpose as an introduc-

[1] Member of the Senior Staff, Economic Studies Division, The Brookings Institution.

tion to the contents of the volume, since each paper amply speaks for itself. Thus, I will discuss here several topics that cut across the papers, to highlight some of the key concepts and issues and to indicate similarities and differences in the various planning approaches. Finally, I will briefly summarize the suggestions made in the papers and in the conference discussions concerning profitable directions for further research on the techniques of policy planning and implementation.[2]

THEORY OF ECONOMIC POLICY

The basic logic of the theory of quantitative economic policy is set forth with admirable clarity in Henri Theil's paper. The policy problem is viewed as analogous to the theory of rational consumer choice, in which the consumer is assumed to maximize his utility, subject to the budget constraint given by his income and the prices of goods and services. Thus to solve the problem of consumer choice, it is necessary to specify (1) a utility or indifference function, (2) a budget constraint function, and (3) a conditional maximization procedure. In the same way, to solve the policy problem it is necessary to specify (1) a preference function for the decision-maker, (2) a model of the economy setting forth the constraints facing the decision-maker, and (3) a conditional maximization procedure.

Now, in the pure theory the preferences and constraints can be given exact mathematical expression, and exact procedures exist for finding the maximum. In actual practice, the precision implied by the pure theory may possibly never be attained, but it is certainly a goal worthy of serious and diligent pursuit. Moreover, by laying bare the logical structure of the problem, the pure theory provides an indispensable set of concepts for systematic thinking about the methods and procedures of quantitative policy planning.

To give the theory operational content, Theil specifies a linear econometric model of the economy and a quadratic preference function. The econometric model describes the quantitative relationships estimated to exist between the economic variables under the control of the decision-maker (such as tax rates, government expenditure, and central bank holdings of government securities) and the noncontrolled variables which he is interested in affecting by policy actions (such as employment,

[2] Space limitations made it necessary to omit the conference discussions from this volume.

the consumer price level, and the balance of payments). In this respect—the use of a linear econometric model of the economy—Theil's approach closely resembles the pioneering work of Jan Tinbergen, and the similarities and differences are worth noting.[3]

In Tinbergen's nomenclature, the controlled variables are the policy *instruments* and the noncontrolled variables representing policy objectives are the *targets*. Two other classes of variables also appear in a complete econometric model representing the macroeconomic structure of an economy. These are the exogenous variables or *data* which are taken as given by the policy-maker and those noncontrolled endogenous variables which are *irrelevant* to the policy decision even though they may be directly or indirectly affected by it. (See the diagrammatic representation of Tinbergen's system in Figure 3-1 of the paper by Karl A. Fox and Erik Thorbecke.)

In policy applications neither Tinbergen nor Theil works with the complete structural model of the economy. Instead, they eliminate the irrelevant endogenous variables by algebraic manipulation until they are left with a set of equations equal in number to the target (noncontrolled) variables, where each equation contains only one target variable and all other variables are therefore either instruments (controlled variables) or data.[4]

At this point the two men part company, since Tinbergen eliminates the maximization problem as such and instead assumes that the decision-maker has specified a fixed value for each of the target variables. The equations are then solved simultaneously for the set of values of the instrument variables which is consistent with the fixed targets and the given data. These are the values at which the decision-maker should set the instruments in an attempt to attain the specified targets, given the information at his disposal.

This procedure does not guarantee, of course, that the target values will actually be realized even if the instruments are set at the specified values. In the first place, the exogenous data are given, in the sense that they are not determined by the model, but they must often be forecast instead of being known with certainty. Secondly, the coefficients relating the instrument and target variables must either be estimated by statistical probability techniques or established by other empirical methods or

---

[3] J. Tinbergen, *On the Theory of Economic Policy* (North-Holland, 1952; 2d ed. 1963), and *Economic Policy: Principles and Design* (North-Holland, 1956).
[4] The data variables are absorbed in the constant term of the model equation used in the simplified examples given by Theil in the present paper.

a priori assumption; hence they are also not known exactly in any given application.[5] As C. A. van den Beld and Tsunehiko Watanabe show us, both sources of error have proved troublesome in the policy planning experience of The Netherlands and Japan, and this is doubtless true in other countries as well. One of the virtues of econometric policy analysis, of course, is that it remorselessly exposes such errors, so that their causes can be analyzed and efforts can be made to reduce them.

Other salient characteristics of the Tinbergen approach may be summarized as follows:

1. The approach lays particular stress on the structural interrelationships of the economic system, thus driving home three important lessons: a change in one instrument variable will in general affect the values of all target variables; a particular target variable may be importantly affected by a change in an instrument variable with which it is related only indirectly through other endogenous variables, so that the best policy attack is often an indirect one; and a rational economic policy requires coordination of all important policy instruments in a unified program.

2. The approach reveals whether a specified set of fixed targets is *compatible*—in the sense that all the target values can be achieved simultaneously with the given set of instruments. *Incompatibility* can arise for two reasons. One, if there are fewer instruments than targets, the number of unknowns (instrument variables) in the policy equations is smaller than the number of equations, and a solution is impossible except by coincidence. Within the Tinbergen framework, this situation can only be corrected by increasing the number of instruments or reducing the number of targets until there is an equal number of each in the equation system. Two, even when a unique solution is possible because the number of instruments and targets is equal, it may turn out that one (or more) of the *boundary conditions* placed on the values of the instrument variables has been violated. Such boundary conditions constrain the permissible values of the instrument variables within certain ranges: e.g., tax rates cannot be increased more than x percent or government expenditure varied by more than y percent within a particular time span. Boundary conditions may be imposed for technical, institutional, or political reasons. No matter what the reason for imposing it, if one of the instrument boundary conditions is violated in the original solution, it is necessary to modify the original set of targets, usually by substituting the violated boundary condition for one of the original targets, so that the former instrument itself becomes a target, and then to re-solve the system for a consistent set of instruments and targets. It may be necessary to try several modifications of the system before a consistent solution is found.

3. Should the number of instruments exceed the number of targets, the

---

[5] In this approach the coefficients of the policy model will usually be derived from those of the structural model instead of being estimated directly, but the same remarks apply to the structural coefficients.

number of unknowns will exceed the number of policy equations, and an infinite number of solutions will usually be possible. In this case, arbitrary values can be chosen for a selected set of "excess" instrument variables and the system can then be solved for the remaining instrument values. This situation provides great flexibility insofar as instrumental choice is concerned, since it permits experimentation with alternative combinations of instrument values to attain the given set of targets.

Let us now return to the point at which Theil and Tinbergen parted company. Theil, instead of assuming a set of fixed targets, specifies a decision-maker's preference function that includes all instrument (controlled) and target (noncontrolled) variables, but does not depend on fixed values of the instruments or targets. Rather it is specified in terms of deviations of the unknown values of the instruments and targets from their stipulated desired values. Moreover, each deviation variable is weighted to show the relative importance attached by the decision-maker to a deviation of that particular variable from the level which would be desired for it unconditionally—i.e., if its attainment did not affect the other targets or instruments. The preference function is then maximized subject to the constraints given by the set of equations showing how the instrument and target variables are related in the econometric model of the economy. The solution gives the best attainable combination of target and instrument values, when account is taken both of the decision-maker's preferences with respect to goals and of the limits placed on his ability to achieve these goals within the economic system represented by the econometric model.

It may at first be thought strange that desired values of the instruments enter the preference function along with the desired target values. It must be remembered, however, that some instrumental variables also partake of the nature of policy objectives or targets in their own right. An obvious example is government expenditure, which may be desired for its direct contribution to well-being, in addition to its indirect effects on private investment, employment, and other potential target variables. Moreover, even when a particular instrument has no direct welfare connotations, to restrain its movements may be desirable for political reasons or because of economic considerations that are not directly incorporated in the macroeconomic model. Incidentally, worth noting is that Tinbergen's procedure of imposing boundary conditions on the values to be taken by the instruments is analogous in important respects to the inclusion of weighted deviations of the instrument variables from their desired values in the preference function and can accomplish much the same results.

Several conceptual advantages may be cited for the preference-function approach over the method of fixed targets. First, a unique solution is obtainable irrespective of whether the number of instruments exceeds, equals, or falls short of the number of targets. Second, the substitution of flexible for fixed targets not only adds realism to the specification of policy objectives but makes it possible to find an optimal decision without disregarding any of the targets, whereas under the Tinbergen approach one or more targets must sometimes be dropped to obtain a consistent solution. Third, when a quadratic preference function is specified, the important problems of uncertain predictions and of decision-making under dynamic conditions are easily handled, as Theil's paper will show.

The simplicity of the approach as set forth by Theil is admittedly largely a result of the assumption of a quadratic form for the preference function. It is this assumption that permits use of the certainty equivalence theorem and results in simple linear decision rules for the maximizing policy strategy. The principal conceptual deficiency of the quadratic form is that it treats positive and negative deviations from the desired values as equally undesirable, whereas asymmetric preferences are doubtless realistic for some targets and instruments—the decision-maker must surely prefer, for example, that the employment target be missed on the high side rather than on the low side. Any particular mathematical specification of the preference function can of course only approximate reality; therefore, on an operational level, the important question is whether the quadratic approximation is more appropriate than other workable alternatives, and this can only be discovered by systematic empirical research.

POLICY MODELS AND APPLICATIONS

For rigorous application of either the fixed-target or preference-function approach, a complete econometric model must be built, in which all relevant target and instrument variables are included and all coefficients are numerically estimated. The 36-equation model currently used by the Dutch Central Planning Bureau and discussed in the van den Beld and Fox-Thorbecke papers is an excellent example. It is an annual model, designed for short-term macroeconomic forecasting and the planning of short-term stabilization policy.

Although it is true that great progress has been made in the improvement of such models since the pioneering efforts of Tinbergen in the early 1930's, this is still an active research area with many stimulating challenges. Much of the progress is due to the development of Keynesian economics, which provided an ideal basic framework for these short-term models, relying as they do so heavily on aggregative variables drawn from the national income accounts. By the same token, however, the Keynesian concepts would be largely empty of empirical content were it not for the great strides that have been made in the definition and measurement of national income and product within a consistent and increasingly elaborate social accounting system. Another vital contribution has come from the elaboration and refinement of sophisticated methods for the specification and estimation of functional relationships in econometric models—a difficult technical field which the complementary papers by Jati K. Sengupta and by Fox and Thorbecke ably survey. Finally, the modern electronic computer has reduced the computational cost of estimating and manipulating large equation systems to practicable proportions in both time and money.

In contrast to The Netherlands, both France and Japan have focused their planning procedures primarily on long-term development objectives rather than short-term stabilization goals. There is a corresponding difference in the principal techniques of quantitative economic analysis. Instead of the closed, short-term macro-econometric model that is the central feature of Dutch planning, the French and Japanese planning bureaus rely principally on long-term projections and input-output tables for the empirical analysis of economic constraints.

The principal characteristics of the long-term (five- or ten-year) projections, which provide the basic framework for the French and Japanese plans, are discussed in the papers of Bernard Cazes and Shuntaro Shishido. The general approach is to project GNP and its components for several alternative potential growth rates and to examine the feasibility of the alternatives in the light of the constraints involved on both the demand and production sides, after which one of the alternative projections is selected to serve as the planning framework. Again, we find heavy reliance on the Keynesian income-expenditure theory and the national income and product accounts, just as in short-term macroeconomic models. In contrast to the short-term models, however, in which the existing size of the labor force is usually the only specified production constraint, it is necessary in projecting long-term development paths to give explicit attention both to the availability of labor, capital, and materials inputs over time and to the rate of productivity advance.

The functional relationships in these long-term projection models are generally simple in form and are not as a rule estimated by sophisticated statistical techniques. Numerical values are assigned to the parameters by such devices as historical trend analysis, average observed saving propensities and capital-output ratios, input-output tables, and estimates of informed persons or firms about particular sectors. This is not a static intellectual field, however, and examples are given in the papers by Cazes, Shishido, and Watanabe of the constant search for better structural specifications and improved methods of parameter estimation and consistency analysis.

Apart from the foregoing distinctions concerning short-term and long-term models and planning objectives, there is an important difference between the policy uses to which quantitative economic models are put in The Netherlands and those in France and Japan. The Netherlands Central Planning Bureau follows the Tinbergen approach, in which, it will be recalled, a policy model is derived from the complete structural model of the economy by eliminating the irrelevant endogenous variables. The equations of the policy model are then solved for the unknown instrument values which would achieve a specified set of target values under the forecasted economic conditions. If a conditional-maximization, preference-function approach were followed instead, the unknowns in the final set of policy equations would include the values of the flexible targets as well as those of the instruments. In either case, the fundamental purpose of the policy analysis is to use the econometric model, in combination with information about the decision-maker's preferences, to solve for an explicit set of quantitative governmental actions designed to achieve certain quantitatively specified policy objectives.

In contrast, the French and Japanese projections are used primarily to discover the physical and financial conditions which must be met if a certain growth rate is to be realized, rather than to design an explicit quantitative policy to achieve that objective. That is, from a planning point of view, the principal unknowns are the sectoral investment and production targets which are implied by, and consistent with, the macrostructure and input-output relationships of the economy and the exogenously specified rates of increase of labor input and GNP (or labor input and productivity) and exports. Once these investment and production targets are determined, their achievement is left largely to the private initiative of businessmen, modified or conditioned by the use of the financial and regulatory powers of the state. Such powers involve the use of policy instruments, of course, but the important point in the present context is that the decision regarding their use is not the subject of investigation within the economic model.

However, policy variables are not completely neglected in the long-term models. In the Japanese development model described by Shishido, for example, there are five policy parameters: the share of government purchases in GNP, the share of transfer payments in GNP, the indirect tax ratio on GNP, and the direct tax ratios on wage and nonwage income respectively. These last two tax ratios are treated endogenously, but the other ratios are exogenous. It is interesting to note also that the government surplus is treated as an exogenously fixed target, because of a traditional policy of adherence to a balanced budget. As Shishido shows, the model can be used to study the macroeconomic implications of quantitative variations in the exogenously given policy instruments, external conditions, and limiting factors. In this way, the model can be used to search for a consistent set of macroeconomic instruments and targets by successive approximations, and the approach is therefore akin in spirit to that of Tinbergen, although methodologically less direct than his.

Apart from the wealth of information about economic models contained in the conference papers, the reader will find much material concerning that other cornerstone of economic policy—preferences and the preference function. Preferences receive a good deal of attention, for example, in the survey that Etienne S. Kirschen and Lucien Morissens present of the objectives and instruments of postwar economic policy in nine Western countries. The purpose of these authors was not to formulate a quantitative preference function, but their qualitative investigation of policy objectives and instruments contains many suggestive insights for such an attempt. These insights include their distinction between the measurable objectives of economic policy and the higher-order aims the objectives are meant to serve, their classification of short-term and long-term objectives, and—most enlightening of all—their tabulation of the dominant preferences of the major political and interest groupings and their analysis of the relative influence of various policy-making groups, both inside and outside of government, in pursuit of selected objectives. These last findings serve as a healthy reminder to the economist, if there was need for one, that the determination of desired values of targets and instruments in the preference function, and of the weights to be attached to them, is essentially a political problem.

Much the same point is made by C. A. van den Beld in his authoritative paper on short-term planning experience in The Netherlands, where he notes that the mathematical approach to the decision problem has never been applied in practice owing to the difficulty of attaching weights to the variables in the welfare or preference function, but that the Dutch system of advisory councils and committees has provided a pragmatic way out of this difficulty. Another author, Willem Hessel, writes of Dutch policy-making from the perspective of his experience as a member of the principal advisory organ, the Social Economic Council (SEC), which is comprised of employers' and workers' representatives and independent experts. His paper evaluates the quantitative guidelines concerning budget, monetary, and wage policy adopted at different times by the government and discusses the comprehensive, compromise-policy programs recommended by the SEC in 1957 and 1959. He makes clear, both explicitly and by example, that quantitative specification of policy preferences through the committee device is essentially a bargaining process, subject to the realities of the political situation, in which the preferences of the members influence one another not necessarily in a convergent manner.

EFFECTIVENESS OF PLANNING TECHNIQUES

It is difficult to generalize about the influence of quantitative planning on either the economic policies or the economic experience of our small sample of countries. The closest link between quantitative economic analysis and actual policy decisions is clearly to be found in The Netherlands. There the short-term macroeconomic model is used not only to make forecasts on the assumption of unchanged policies but also to predict the policy outcomes associated with proposed action programs or to predict the instrumental combinations needed to achieve specified targets.

It is apparent from both papers on Dutch planning, moreover, that the quantitative estimates of the Central Planning Bureau do indeed importantly affect the actual decisions concerning wage and fiscal policies, although having less to do directly with monetary policy. Hessel points out, however, that the margin of action on wage and fiscal policies in 1957 and 1959 was smaller than the margin of unforeseen changes, in the sense that the predicted changes in important target variables (as a result of the policy actions taken) were smaller than the differences between the forecasts incorporating the policy actions and the actual performance of the economy. In similar vein, C. A. van den Beld notes that the procyclical fiscal and monetary actions of the early and mid 1950's are partly to be explained by forecasting errors. But he also notes improvement after 1958 in both the forecasts and the policy actions with regard to stabilization goals, and he stresses that some of the earlier destabilizing policy actions resulted partly from political considerations affecting the choice of target and instrument values. Finally, both authors allude briefly to the acute labor market tensions and large wage increases developing late in 1963, which highlight the difficulties of reconciling competing claims on the national income with the achievement of stable full employment growth without inflation.

As already mentioned, the French system of "indicative planning," although quantitative in character, is only indirectly concerned with specific governmental decisions about quantitative economic policy. Instead, its primary purpose is to estimate consistent four- or five-year quantitative growth targets for both the private and public sectors. As Cazes points out, the achievement of the planning goals is left largely to the phenomenon of "self-fulfilling prophecy," according to which "a belief is verified to the degree to which it is held by a sufficient number of people." This process is doubtless facilitated by the intricate network of government agencies and private commissions and working groups which is utilized in the preparation of each plan, since this institutional framework assures that the major decision-making groups participate closely in the determination of the plan's objectives. The result is that the objectives are probably more internally consistent than would otherwise be true and that the action groups are more favorably disposed psychologically to act on the basis of the plan.

Far from complete reliance, however, is placed on individual initiative to attain the goals of the plan. Again as mentioned earlier, the considerable financial and regulatory powers of the French government are used to reduce private deviations from the plan wherever possible. Moreover, although the plan does not represent a four-year budget in which the global allocation and the distribution of public expenditures are rigidly determined, the annual budgets are nevertheless articulated with the plans. Since public investment accounts for about one third of all fixed capital formation in France, the control of public expenditure in itself affords the government great leverage over the accomplishment of the plan's general objectives.[6]

[6] For a comprehensive English-language discussion of French planning, see John and Anne-Marie Hackett, *Economic Planning in France* (George Allen & Unwin, 1963).

In Japan, as in France, the principal emphasis is on indicative planning for long-term growth, rather than on the quantitative analysis of short-term policy decisions. Neither of our writers on Japanese planning claims an intimate relationship between the formal quantitative projections and actual governmental policies, and Watanabe in particular expresses skepticism about the effectiveness of national quantitative planning insofar as actual economic performance is concerned. On a technical level, the quantitative projections have regularly underestimated actual performance and there appear to be serious internal inconsistencies in the present ten-year plan. Watanabe also stresses the smaller political influence of the Economic Planning Agency relative to that of other key government agencies—a situation which he believes has sometimes resulted in policy decisions inconsistent with the overall national plan. Finally, both Shishido and Watanabe refer to the failure to achieve a sufficient growth of social overhead capital, such as transportation, water, and sewage facilities. They attribute the shortage of such facilities to inadequate projections of the need, rather than to failure to implement the planned volume of public investment.

Needless to say, a balanced summary of the effectiveness of quantitative planning techniques in the various countries is difficult to encompass within a few brief paragraphs, and the reader is referred to the detailed appraisals offered in the papers themselves so that he may form his own impressions and judgments. I believe that enough has been said, however, to show that the authors are thoroughly aware of the weaknesses as well as the strengths of existing methods for the planning and implementation of quantitative economic policy. This double awareness was also evident in the round-table discussions of the papers during the conference, in which a constantly recurring theme was the need to develop better techniques at every stage of the decision-making process.

Thus, to conclude the volume with Charles C. Holt's reflections on the current status of and future need for research on various aspects of quantitative-decision analysis as it relates to national economic policy seems especially appropriate. He places particular stress on the need to develop quantitative knowledge about welfare objectives and their relative importance in the preference or social welfare function, since this is presently the area of greatest ignorance. He does not, however, neglect the search for better technical methods for handling the statistical decision problem under conditions of dynamic uncertainty or for improving the estimation of economic relations, and he concludes by distinguishing a fourth problem area of a less technical nature, though of equal or greater importance than the others. This is the problem of relating the professional advice of the economist to the political-decision process so that the economist's quantitative analysis may be of maximum effectiveness and use to the responsible decision-makers. In this connection, and also with regard to preferences, Holt stresses that the skills, techniques, and theory of other social science disciplines and the legal profession need to be brought to bear on problems which cannot be solved with the economist's tool kit alone.

RESEARCH SUGGESTIONS

Holt's paper provides a cogent basic agenda for the sort of multi-pronged attack that would be required for full development of the promise implicit in current techniques of quantitative-decision analysis. It may be useful to supplement his presentation with a brief summary of some of the research suggestions made in the other papers (and during the conference discussions), without attempting to establish priorities or implying that every conferee would agree with every suggestion.

With regard to the preference function, agreement was general on the great importance of quantifying welfare objectives and the trade-offs between them. One line of approach would be quantitative studies of the welfare losses corresponding to different degrees of unemployment, inflation, rates of economic growth, and other major policy goals. The purpose would be to provide a more objective basis for the formulation of social value judgments about policy targets and instruments. Other suggestions concerned the direct collection of data on preferences, as by questionnaires and interviews, and the inference of revealed preferences of policy-makers from empirical analysis of their actual decisions. Isolated examples of all these approaches can be found in the literature, but the area has nevertheless been comparatively neglected and deserves much more systematic attention than economists have given it to date.

Another profitable line of investigation is to find the sensitivity of the optimal policy solutions for a given economic model to different types of preference functions. If the optimal solutions are rather sensitive to small variations in the weights or form of the preference function, the decision-maker could be presented with several alternative solutions derived under different preference assumptions and could choose among them on the basis of his evaluation of the preferences. An example of an experimental sensitivity analysis is given in Theil's paper.

Research on the preference function may encounter some knotty identification problems in realistic situations. One difficulty is that preferences, while in principle independent of the constraints expressed in the economic model, may in practice be related to them. That is, the interpretation placed on the constraints, and the uncertainty discounts attached to them, may be influenced by the policy-maker's preferences. Conversely, his preferences may be influenced by what is thought possible of achievement under the constraints; hence the preferences may change as the constraints do. Indeed, this is virtually certain to happen (or appear to happen) if only a few policy objectives are made explicit at a given time, as is amply demonstrated in the historical examples given in the country papers of shifts in the principal targets in response to the changing economic situation. Such observed changes *may* represent a movement to a new position along a stable preference function, but in practice it may be impossible to distinguish such movements from shifts to new preference functions.

Another kind of interdependence is to be found in committee situations where there is bargaining over the weights to be attached to the variables in a collective preference function. Individual preferences may be deliberately misrepresented to establish bargaining positions, and stated preferences may therefore depend on estimates of the likely positions to be taken by other participants and of their "true" preferences. In general, the sociological, group-dynamic, and game-theoretic aspects of the administrative interactions involved in the determination of policy objectives, are indicative of important problems for theoretical and empirical research in an essentially interdisciplinary field.

With regard to model building, the problems of better specification of structural relationships and of improvements in statistical data received the bulk of attention at the conference, partly because so much progress has already occurred in the development of refined techniques of parameter estimation. The most obvious, but albeit also the most important, suggestion of this character is that explicit attention be given to policy problems in future attempts to improve econometric models. Models without explicit policy variables and parameters may be of some use for forecasting purposes, but to be of real assistance in decision-making, a model must include relevant instrumental variables.

This precept has been kept at the forefront, incidentally, in the quarterly econometric model of the United States economy which was constructed by an interuniversity team under the sponsorship of the

Social Science Research Council Committee on Economic Stability. This model, which is now undergoing further development and testing at the Brookings Institution under the supervision of Lawrence R. Klein and Gary Fromm, includes many more governmental and financial equations than have previous efforts of this type and offers great promise for investigation and simulation of the effects of quantitative fiscal and monetary policies on economic stability.[7] In view of the substantial importance attached to the instruments of monetary policy in all Western countries (see the paper by Kirschen and Morissens), the monetary sectors of most econometric models appear surprisingly rudimentary, even after allowing for the inherent difficulties of establishing the relevant relationships within financial markets and between financial and real variables.

With the increasing attention being devoted to growth problems even in industrialized countries, further development of econometric growth models may confidently be expected. Thus Cazes reports that, to provide the basic framework for parliamentary debate on the Fifth Plan, the French are using a global econometric model in which the growth rate of GNP is an endogenous variable dependent on specific assumptions about resource development and productivity change, in sharp contrast to the methods and assumptions employed in the earlier plans. The Japanese are also experimenting with long-term models taking explicit account of technical progress and capital-labor substitution, and capable of projecting the intermediate paths to be taken by a limited number of basic indicators throughout the ten-year planning period (see the paper by Shishido). Similar work is now underway in United States academic circles.

It is still uncertain how closely short-term and long-term models can be integrated. Quarterly or even monthly models may be necessary for full understanding of the business cycle and for purposes of short-term forecasting and the planning of stabilization policy, and they offer the further advantage of reducing simultaneous structural interdependence, with its attendant difficulties of estimation and causal interpretation (see the Fox-Thorbecke and Sengupta papers). Such models must necessarily emphasize short-term decisions and relationships which are inconse-

    [7] The Brookings-SSRC model is briefly discussed in the Fox-Thorbecke paper. For further details, see *The Brookings-SSRC Quarterly Econometric Model of the United States*, edited by James S. Duesenberry, Gary Fromm, Lawrence R. Klein, and Edwin Kuh, which is scheduled for publication by Rand McNally (Chicago) and North-Holland (Amsterdam) in early 1965.

quential for long-term development, however. It is probable that for some time to come it will be necessary to maintain separate models for different purposes, as in the Japanese scheme of a quarterly (or annual) short-term model, a long-term (5-10-year) model, and a perspective (10-20-year) model. All the same, the links among such models will doubtless be strengthened by the elaboration of production functions and the inclusion of endogenous variations in the capital stock and the labor force.

Another suggestion which found favor at the conference was to improve communications among econometric institutes and planning agencies around the world. A principal purpose would be to improve the forecasting of world exports and the world price level. Such forecasting has been a weak point in each of the countries surveyed herein, and a greater degree of international cooperation would facilitate a systematic comparison and improvement of internal and external forecasts in each country. A related point was greater standardization of input-output tables at the international level, since it is sometimes necessary to make intercountry comparisons of such data.

Several suggestions were made about data collection and preparation. Models are based on data which contain error components. To avoid misunderstanding and misinterpretation of the meaning of basic data, it is important for model builders to study how the basic data are prepared in various agencies and the assumptions on which they are based. This does not imply, however, that efforts should necessarily be made to eliminate all errors in data, since the additional cost of data preparation must be weighed against the benefits to be derived from more accurate estimates. (See the Fox-Thorbecke paper for discussion on this point, which also applies to other sources of error.) Stress was also placed on the need for developing and collating appropriate data for analyzing the economic problems of regions and localities within larger countries. It can be observed that the systematic study of developmental and stabilization problems through quantitative models is continually uncovering new data needs and giving purposeful direction to the evolution of national accounting systems.

The last research area to be discussed concerns the institutional framework and its relationship to the policy analysis. In policy matters, for example, it may be invalid to accept the going framework as given and to set about applying the model, since political parties and pressure groups are constantly attempting to alter the institutional environment—a point which is particularly relevant for long-term models but which may also be overlooked in short-term models with occasionally destabilizing consequences. Finally, there was general agreement that a comparative study of how economic policy decisions are actually made within the different institutional setups of various countries, and of the extent to which policy models are used at different stages of the decision process, would be an important contribution.

2

Linear Decision Rules for Macrodynamic Policy Problems

HENRI THEIL[1]

THIS IS AN EXPOSITORY ARTICLE on the methodology of macroeconomic policy. It is not concerned with such problems as the merits of a welfare state, the virtues of free competition and free trade, which are, to a large extent, "qualitative" problems. Nor will it have any pretensions with respect to such once-and-for-all projects as building a large dam in an underdeveloped country. Rather, it focuses on the day-to-day problems of keeping employment at a satisfactory level, watching the balance of payments, keeping the price level constant or at least preventing a runaway inflation, ensuring a satisfactory increase of per capita income in successive years, watching the distribution of income among wage earners and capitalists, among the rural and the urban parts of the population, and so on. In simple (though perhaps oversimplified) terms: its focus is growth and stability with respect to a certain number of key variables, all of which are measured quantitatively.

THE PROBLEM

That there is a problem is due to the fact that not all of these variables are under the complete control of one single authority. Under these circumstances a macroeconomic decision-maker has to take measures which affect his country's economy indirectly—for example, taxation measures. There is also a direct effect (the tax-rate changes themselves), but if the measures are taken with a view of reducing the number of unemployed, say, their primary objective is indirect. The difficulty is then: should such measures indeed be taken, or will the number of unemployed

[1] Director, Econometric Institute, Netherlands School of Economics.

18

diminish satisfactorily without them? If it will not, which tax rates are to be changed—or perhaps should something else be done? What is the appropriate time for taking the measures? And how large should they be (how large the tax-rate reductions)? In other words: what, when, and how much?

THE METHODS

The standard practice of Western countries is to attack this problem very informally. When there are difficulties (as to employment, balance of payments, etc.), one takes measures which, hopefully, will lead to a more satisfactory state of affairs. Intuition and "feeling" are frequently the most important ingredients of the procedure. The apparatus of economic theory will usually be employed, of course, but the difficulty is that this theory gives little guidance as to the quantitative impact of the measures taken.

From the standpoint of economic analysis this situation is not satisfactory, and the present article is written under the assumption that analysis has something to offer. The starting point is that the procedure should be based on two cornerstones, one of which is the decision-maker's desires regarding the development of his economy. Under certain general conditions it is possible to specify such desires by a preference function of which the key variables mentioned above are the arguments. (We do not consider here the problem of the relationship between his desires and those of the people whom he is supposed to represent.) The other cornerstone is the mechanism of the economy: how do the key variables which are not controlled react when the decision-maker changes certain variables which he does control? How do these key variables react to outside forces? Under certain conditions it is possible to specify the mechanism of an economy by a set of algebraic equations—an econometric model.

If we succeed in specifying desires by means of a preference function and the economy's mechanism by means of an econometric model, we can in principle apply a conditional maximization procedure. The argument which follows will show that there is a lot to be said about this; first, however, it is worthwhile to emphasize that this kind of approach is very common in economic theory. The consumer, for example, is supposed to have certain desires which can be described by a utility function. He is supposed to maximize this function, but not unconditionally; there is the budget constraint which he has to face, since his income is fixed and the prices are given for him. Similarly, a manufacturer may want to produce cattle feed at minimum cost; the feed should, however, satisfy certain constraints regarding protein content, water content, and so on. In all such cases we have a conditional maximization or minimization problem.

Frisch and Tinbergen are two well-known names in the development of the theory of economic policy. Tinbergen, in particular, works with a very simple representation of the decision-maker's preferences.[2] His decision-maker sets "target values" for those key variables which are not controlled; the procedure is then to find the values which the controlled variables should take in order that the other variables take their target values. This approach has the great virtue of combining separate policies (wage-price policy, fiscal policy, etc.) in one coherent system. It is also very simple when the econometric model is completely linear and when the two groups of variables (controlled and noncontrolled) are equally numerous. It offers no solution for the problem of uncertainty, which is an important aspect, for there exists no econometric model which guarantees perfect predictions. Also, we shall wish to take account of dynamic features. The approach which will be described here—that of a quadratic preference function which is to be maximized over time subject to linear constraints—has been developed by the present author[3] and P. J. M. van den Bogaard and C. van de Panne in the Netherlands and by C. C. Holt, F. Modigliani, J. F. Muth, and H. A. Simon in the United States.[4]

QUADRATIC PREFERENCES AND LINEAR CONSTRAINTS

Let us start with the simplest possible case: that of a decision-maker who controls one variable (his "instrument"), who is interested in one other variable which he does not control (his "noncontrolled variable"), and who considers only one period, say one year. To give things names,

[2] J. Tinbergen, *Economic Policy: Principles and Design* (North-Holland, 1956), Vol. 11 of *Contributions to Economic Analysis*.

[3] H. Theil, *Economic Forecasts and Policy* (2d ed.; North-Holland, 1961), Vol. 15 of *Contributions to Economic Analysis*. The material in this present article is largely taken from my more recent book, *Optimal Decision Rules for Government and Industry* (North-Holland and Rand McNally, 1964), Vol. 1 of *Studies in Mathematical and Managerial Economics*. For the convenience of readers, the bibliography used in the 1964 book is reprinted at the end of this article.

[4] Holt, Modigliani, Muth, and Simon, *Planning Production, Inventories, and Work Force* (Prentice-Hall, 1960).

let the instrument x be government expenditure and the noncontrolled variable y be GNP. Let GNP be a linear function of government expenditure:

(1) $$y = a + bx.$$

This equation represents in our simple case the mechanism of the economy. It is one of the cornerstones of the procedure, for it is the constraint which the decision-maker has to take into account: on January 1 he must decide on the level of government expenditure of that year, and the value of GNP is then automatically determined by (1).

For the other cornerstone, the preference function, we shall work with a quadratic function, which will be specified in two steps. First, the decision-maker is supposed to have certain "desired values" in mind, η for GNP and ξ for government expenditure. For example, he may wish a 5 percent increase of GNP, compared with last year, and a 3 percent increase of government expenditure (in view of defense considerations, road building, normal salary increases of civil servants, etc.). In general we shall find that such desires cannot be realized, because they are contradicted by the constraints. In our example, $\eta \neq a + b\xi$ in general, compare (1). This, however, is not serious, since ξ and η are only desires. The second step is then relevant, which implies that the decision-maker formulates a quadratic form in the deviations between desires and the corresponding actual values. For example:

$$h(x - \xi)^2 + k(y - \eta)^2.$$

This weighted sum of squares is to be minimized. Then, by adding a minus sign to obtain a function which is to be maximized, we have the following preference function:

(2) $$w(x, y) = - h(x - \xi)^2 - k(y - \eta)^2.$$

The problem can now be formulated as follows. The decision-maker must decide, on January 1, on the level of government expenditure of that year. He is interested both in this variable and in GNP of that same year. This interest is formalized by saying that he wants to maximize the quadratic preference function (2). He cannot do so unconditionally, however, because he must take account of the constraint (1). Carrying out this conditional maximization problem is a small mathematical exercise. The result is:

(3) $$x^0 - \xi = \frac{kb}{h + kb^2} (\eta - a - b\xi).$$

The left-hand side contains the optimal decision x^0, measured as a deviation from the desired level of government expenditure, ξ. The expression in parentheses on the right is the difference between the desired level of GNP, η, and the GNP level that would be realized if the decision-maker would decide to set government expenditure at its own desired level, $a + b\xi$. We can therefore regard this expression in parentheses as a measure for the "inconsistency" of the decision-maker's desires: he wishes ξ for his instrument and η for his noncontrolled variable, but if he decides on ξ he does not get η, he gets $a + b\xi$, which is in general different.

The formula shows that he should *not* decide on ξ if η differs from $a + b\xi$. He should decide on x^0. The value ξ is the best instrument value when this variable is considered in isolation; but x^0 is optimal in a more complete sense, namely, when account is also taken of the impact of the instrument on the noncontrolled variable as well as of the preferences regarding this variable. The equation shows further that the difference $x^0 - \xi$ is proportional to the "inconsistency" just mentioned. If we take h, k, and b all positive (which is certainly realistic), we find that if the desired GNP level, η, is above the level implied by the desired level of government expenditure, $a + b\xi$, the optimal decision, x^0, is above the latter desire, ξ. This is a plausible result. Note finally that (3) is a complete mixture of the coefficients of constraint and preference function. It contains both a and b—belonging to the constraint (1)—and ξ, η, h, k—belonging to the preference function (2). This feature, the mixture of preferences on the one hand and the actual mechanism of the economy on the other hand, is something one will always find in this kind of analysis.

Our example is, of course, very simple; a much more elaborate analysis along the same lines has been carried out by P. J. M. van den Bogaard and A. P. Barten for the Dutch economy. They considered four noncontrolled variables:

> employment,
> price level of consumer goods,
> share of wages in national income,
> surplus on the balance of payments;

and five instruments:

> wage rate,
> tax rates, indirect taxes,
> tax rates, income taxes for wage-earners,
> tax rates, income taxes for nonwage-earners,
> government expenditure on goods and services.

(It may seem strange that the wage rate is taken as a government instrument, but this was actually true in The Netherlands in the period considered, to the extent that government consent for wage increases was required.) Each of the four noncontrolled variables was expressed in terms of the five instruments by means of an econometric model. These equations formed the constraints subject to which a quadratic preference function was maximized. Actually, three alternative preference functions were used, one representing the standpoint of a typical employer, one the standpoint of a typical trade unionist, and one a "neutral" standpoint. It goes without saying that the algebra of this application is more complicated than that of our present example (matrix algebra is required, though not of a very advanced kind), but it does not lead to essentially different situations. We shall come back to this application later on.

UNCERTAINTY, EXPECTED UTILITY, AND CERTAINTY EQUIVALENCE

Whether we have only one constraint containing only two variables, such as (1), or several constraints containing any larger numbers of variables, in all cases we shall be faced with the problem that such constraints give no more than an imperfect description of the mechanism of the economy. The simplest way to take account of this is to assume that the constraint is subject to random shifts. Consider, for example, equation (1); the idea is that the influence of government expenditure on GNP is correctly described by the multiplicative coefficient b, but that there are other factors influencing GNP besides government expenditure (trivially true in this example!), which imply that the constant term a is not really constant but a random variable. This assumption is of course weaker than the one which works with a truly constant coefficient a.

This change has important implications, which can be read directly from equation (3). If a is a random variable (whereas ξ, η, h, k, b remain fixed as before), the optimal decision x^0 becomes a linear function of a random variable and is, therefore, random itself. Hence, whether a particular, numerically specified, decision is optimal depends now on the outcome of a chance mechanism! Clearly, this does not carry us very far. To solve the problem we shall change our criterion: instead of maximizing the preference function subject to the constraint, we shall now maximize the *expectation* of the preference function subject to the constraint, the latter being interpreted stochastically (i.e., with a random coefficient a).

This is completely in line with the expected-utility hypothesis which was formulated by Von Neumann and Morgenstern.[5] These authors showed that if a person has to make decisions in uncertain situations, he will behave (under certain, rather weak, conditions) as if he maximizes expected utility. That is, there exists a preference or utility function describing this person's preferences such that the maximization of the expectation of this function leads to the best decision from his point of view, given the uncertainty which he has to face.

In what follows we shall assume that, when a decision-maker faces stochastic constraints, such as equation (1) when a is random, his objective is to maximize the expectation of a quadratic preference function, such as equation (2), subject to these constraints. There is a theorem which considerably facilitates the actual computation of the decision which maximizes the expectation. It is known as the "certainty equivalence theorem" and runs as follows: this decision is precisely the same as the decision that would be made if all uncertainty would be disregarded right at the beginning by replacing the random coefficient a by its own expectation. How this works is easily illustrated with the aid of (3). That equation specified the optimal decision x^0, which maximizes the preference function itself subject to the constraint as it actually is. We are now interested in the decision which maximizes the expectation of the preference function subject to the stochastic constraint. The certainty equivalence theorem states that this decision can be computed in the old way, provided only that a is replaced by its expectation. It is therefore equal to ξ plus the right-hand side of (3), except that a is replaced by $\mathcal{E}a$. That is all.

The theorem of course holds only under certain conditions. One is that the variance of a should be independent of the instrument x. Another is that the preference function should indeed be quadratic. A pragmatic reader who likes simple procedures might be tempted to use this as an argument in favor of quadratic preference functions. This is really not satisfactory, but it is appropriate in this context to point to the procedures of minimum-variance estimation in statistics and mean-square error minimization in engineering, which derive their popularity

[5] J. von Neumann and O. Morgenstern, *Theory of Games and Economic Behavior* (3d ed.; Princeton University Press, 1953).

mainly from considerations of mathematical convenience. A more profound argument in favor of quadratic preference functions is that the procedure allows us to have decreasing marginal rates of substitution. Linear programming is much less flexible in this respect, its marginal rates of substitution being always constant; also, the subject of linear programming under uncertainty is far more difficult. But it must be admitted that the present approach is not able to handle inequality constraints under conditions of uncertainty.[6]

THE DYNAMIC APPROACH: STRATEGIES AND
FIRST-PERIOD CERTAINTY EQUIVALENCE

Our example above was oversimplified, not only because a low number of variables entered into the problem, but also because we considered only one period. This will now be generalized. We shall suppose that GNP depends both on government expenditure in the current year and on government expenditure in the preceding year:

$$(4) \qquad y_t = a_t + b_0 x_t + b_1 x_{t-1}.$$

Clearly, it is now necessary to "date" our variables: the subscripts t and $t-1$ refer to the years t and $t-1$, respectively. Note that the constant term has also a time subscript, a_t. This is because its random variability leads to different values in different years.

We shall extend the problem further by assuming that the decision-maker is interested, not in just one year, but in two consecutive years.[7] Let us indicate these years by 1 and 2; then this alteration will be made more specific by assuming that the preference function (2) is replaced by

$$(5) \qquad \begin{aligned} w(x_1, x_2, y_1, y_2) = & -h[(x_1 - \xi_1)^2 + (x_2 - \xi_2)^2] \\ & - k[(y_1 - \eta_1)^2 + (y_2 - \eta_2)^2], \end{aligned}$$

where ξ_1 and ξ_2 are the desired levels of government expenditure in years 1 and 2, respectively, and similarly for η_1, η_2. Hence our objective is again the minimization of a weighted sum of squares of dis-

---

[6] For our simple example the certainty equivalence theorem can be derived in a straightforward manner; substitute the constraint (1) into the preference function (2), take the expectation, and minimize with respect to x.

[7] There is no necessary connection between the two years here and the two years of x in (4). We just take the simplest generalization in both cases.

crepancies between desires and corresponding realizations, but these
discrepancies refer now, of course, to two years instead of one.

Let us first solve this generalized problem for the case in which there
is no uncertainty. We write the constraint (4) for the two years, $t = 1$
and $t = 2$, separately:

$$(6) \qquad\qquad y_1 = a_1 + b_0 x_1 + b_1 x_0,$$

$$(7) \qquad\qquad y_2 = a_2 + b_0 x_2 + b_1 x_1.$$

It will prove useful to introduce, on the analogy of the procedure of
the preceding section, the inconsistency of the decision-maker's desires.
There are now two such inconsistencies, one for each year:

$$(8) \qquad\qquad i_1 = \eta_1 - (a_1 + b_0 \xi_1 + b_1 x_0),$$

$$(9) \qquad\qquad i_2 = \eta_2 - (a_2 + b_0 \xi_2 + b_1 \xi_1).$$

(Note that x_0, the level of government expenditure in the year preceding
the first, is given from the past.) After some algebra, one finds the optimal decisions x_1^0 and x_2^0, which maximize the preference function (5)
subject to the constraints (6) and (7). They are:

$$(10) \qquad\qquad x_1^0 - \xi_1 = \frac{(b_0^2 + h/k)b_0 i_1 + b_1(h/k)i_2}{A},$$

$$(11) \qquad\qquad x_2^0 - \xi_2 = \frac{-b_0^2 b_1 i_1 + (b_0^2 + h/k)b_0 i_2}{A},$$

where

$$(12) \qquad\qquad A = (b_0^2 + h/k)^2 + b_1^2 h/k.$$

As in the one-period case, we find that the optimal decisions coincide
with the corresponding instrumental desires, ξ_1, ξ_2, when there is no
inconsistency, $i_1 = i_2 = 0$. This is not the general case, of course; and
as soon as the inconsistencies do not vanish, they determine the discrepancies $x_1^0 - \xi_1$ and $x_2^0 - \xi_2$ linearly. Note that such a discrepancy
does *not* vanish when there is no inconsistency in the corresponding
year. That is, when i_1 vanishes but i_2 does not, the optimal decision x_1^0
nevertheless deviates from the instrumental desire ξ_1; and similarly for
the second year, *mutatis mutandis*. Hence there is a clear interaction
between the decision processes of the two successive years. This is not
the case when $b_1 = 0$; i.e., when GNP is independent of government
expenditure of the year before. In that special case the formulas (10)
and (11) are both equivalent to (3), as is easily verified.

Next, we consider our two-period problem under conditions of uncertainty. As in the one-period case, we shall concentrate on the random

variability of the constant terms of the constraints, a_1 and a_2. We see from (8) and (9) that they affect the inconsistencies i_1 and i_2 linearly; and since these occur linearly, too, in the optimal-decision equations (10) and (11), we conclude that x_1^0 and x_2^0 are both linear functions of the random variables a_1 and a_2 and hence random themselves. Again, we turn to the expected-utility hypothesis. Does it lead to the same convenient certainty equivalence result?

Not quite, but almost. The point is that, in general, a two-period decision problem under conditions of uncertainty is essentially different from a one-period decision problem. The latter is characterized by a decision which is to be made now, at this moment, and that is all. The former problem has a decision of this moment, which is followed by a complete period during which certain information is received, after which the second decision is to be made at the beginning of the second period. It is clear that the decision-maker can use this information when formulating his second-period decision. For example, consider equation (6). At the beginning of the first period he does not know a_1; he knows that it is a random variable and he may know its expectation and its variance, perhaps its complete distribution, but he surely does not know the precise value which this chance mechanism is going to produce. One period later, however, he may know more. Let us write (6) in the form

$$(13) \qquad a_1 = y_1 - b_0 x_1 - b_1 x_0.$$

The coefficients b_0 and b_1 are assumed to be fixed and given. Hence a_1, as it is actually realized, depends on three values: x_0, which is given from the past; x_1, which is the decision made at the beginning of the first period and which, of course, is known to the decision-maker at the beginning of the second period; and, finally, y_1, which is the realized value of the noncontrolled variable during the first period. It is clear that when the decision-maker's information service is of sufficient quality, he should be able to know y_1 at the beginning of the second period. When this is the case, a_1 is no longer random but completely known at the moment when the second-period decision has to be made. Hence this decision can be made dependent on the knowledge of a_1. In addition, a_2 (though still future) is "nearer in time" at the beginning of the second period than at the beginning of the first, so that the decision-maker's ideas regarding the distribution of a_2 may have changed. This, too, is additional information received during the first period, which can be used for the formulation of the second-period decision.

In the "static" one-period case, it is our task to find that numerical value of the level of government expenditure which maximizes the expectation of the preference function subject to the constraint. In the "dynamic" two-period case, we need two levels: one for the first year, one for the second. It is therefore our task to find, for each year, that level which maximizes expected utility subject to the constraints, *given* the information which is available when the decision must be made. It follows from the argument of the preceding paragraph that we are really looking for a *function* of available information which maximizes expected utility, rather than for a numerical value as in the static case. Such a function which specifies what is to be done depending on the available information, whatever the contents of this information may be, is called a "strategy" or a "decision rule." Hence we are interested in the *maximizing strategy*, which (by definition) maximizes expected utility subject to the constraints.

The first-period decision of any strategy has the special characteristic that it cannot be made dependent on the content of the information that becomes available in the course of time (for trivial reasons). This does not mean, however, that the first-period decision of the maximizing strategy is unaffected by the fact that such information will become available later on and that it will be possible to react to this information. On the contrary, one can find simple examples which show that this can easily happen. But when we have a quadratic preference function whose expected value is to be maximized over time subject to linear constraints, a very convenient result emerges, known as "first-period certainty equivalence." Under some minor additional conditions (which amount to assuming that the decision-maker is unable to influence the chance mechanism which generates the a's), the first-period decision of the maximizing strategy is precisely the same as the first-period decision that would be made if all uncertainty would be disregarded right at the beginning by replacing the coefficients a_1 and a_2 by their expectations.

This is exactly the same result as in the static case except that it now applies to the first-period decision only. If we want to apply it to our two-period example, we have to go back to (10), which deals with the optimal first-period decision x_1^0 when there is no uncertainty. In the uncertainty case, i_1 and i_2 are random variables, since they depend linearly on a_1 and a_2. Replacing a_1 and a_2 by their expectations then amounts to replacing the inconsistencies by their expectations. In other words, the first-period decision (government expenditure in the first year) of the maximizing strategy is equal to ξ_1 plus the right-hand side of (10), except that i_1 and i_2 are replaced by $\mathcal{E}i_1$ and $\mathcal{E}i_2$, respectively. Hence our decision rule specifies the first-period decision as a linear function of $\mathcal{E}i_1$ and $\mathcal{E}i_2$ and, therefore, of $\mathcal{E}a_1$ and $\mathcal{E}a_2$ (which explains the term "linear decision rule").

We observed that the certainty equivalence theorem in the dynamic case applies to the first-period decision only. It is therefore not true that we can find the second-period decision of the maximizing strategy by applying the same procedure to (11). However, this is not really serious. The second-period decision has to be made at the beginning of the second period. At that moment the first period belongs to the past, so that the second period has become the first. We can therefore apply exactly the same first-period certainty equivalence result to find the second-period decision. This will be illustrated later.

FORECASTING FUTURE ACTIONS
AND THEIR CONSEQUENCES

The ideas of the above section are somewhat more abstract than those of the earlier sections, so that it is tempting to consider an illustration. But we shall resist this temptation, because it is worthwhile to pursue the line of thought a little further. We shall consider how the decision-maker can forecast his own future actions, how he can forecast the consequences of these actions in terms of values to be taken by the non-controlled variables, and how he revises these forecasts each period, to incorporate the new information he has received in the meantime.

Let us start with our first, simple one-period case. We have seen that if the coefficient a is random rather than fixed and if the decision-maker's objective is to maximize expected utility, his decision can be read from equation (3) in the following manner: it is ξ plus the right-hand side of that equation, except that a is replaced by $\mathcal{E}a$. The decision-maker is *not* able to say what the corresponding GNP level, y, will be. This is because y is equal to $a + bx$, according to (1), and a is unknown. But let us substitute for x the value just mentioned:

$$(14) \qquad y = a + b \left[\xi + \frac{kb}{h + kb^2} (\eta - \mathcal{E}a - b\xi) \right].$$

Clearly, the random coefficient a occurs only once in this expression—immediately behind the equation sign. Since it occurs linearly we see that, if we consider the expectation of y ($\mathcal{E}y$) rather than y itself, the right-hand side of (14) remains as it is except that the a just mentioned becomes $\mathcal{E}a$. It follows that the decision-maker can compute $\mathcal{E}y$, for $\mathcal{E}a$ is known to him (since he needs $\mathcal{E}a$ for his decision anyhow). But $\mathcal{E}y$ can be regarded as a forecast of y and the forecast error, $\mathcal{E}y - y$, has obviously zero expectation. We can therefore say that the decision-maker is able to formulate an unbiased forecast of the GNP level that will be realized, given that he has decided on the level of government expenditure which maximizes expected utility.

In the dynamic case, the situation is similar, but the scope of forecasting is extended considerably. One new feature is that the decision-maker can forecast his own future actions. More precisely, he can formulate unbiased predictions of the later-period decisions of the maximizing strategy. We had stated earlier that it is not possible to use equation (11) to find the second-period decision. It is, nevertheless, worthwhile to make this computation, because it enables the decision-maker to obtain a *forecast* of that decision one year before the decision must actually be made. This is certainly convenient, since he can take some preliminary measures if necessary. When the decision-maker takes a larger horizon into account than the two years of our example, he will be able to forecast over a longer period. Needless to say, the mere fact that it is possible to forecast unbiasedly does not mean that the forecast errors are small. One should normally expect that these errors become larger and larger (on the average) when the period predicted is farther away.

Forecasting future instrument values is a new feature compared with the one-period case. In the latter case, we have only forecasts for the noncontrolled variables; and this, of course, is also possible in the dynamic case. Such forecasts are obtained by substituting the predicted instrument values into the constraints; the result is a set of forecasts of future noncontrolled values, which are unbiased, too, in view of the linearity of the constraints. In addition to all this, such forecasts are regularly revised in the light of new evidence. To show how this works, we consider a decision-maker who has a horizon of three years (1, 2, and 3) in mind. At the beginning of year 1 he computes the decision to be made for that year (the level of government expenditure, say). At the same moment he also computes forecasts for the decisions to be made in years 2 and 3, as well as forecasts for the values to be taken by the noncontrolled variables in years 1, 2, and 3. One year later he stands at the beginning of year 2. He then computes the decision to be made for that year and also a new forecast for the decision to be made in year 3. This forecast is indeed new—i.e., it is in general different from the forecast of the same decision made one year earlier—because it is based on the information which the decision-maker has received during the first year. There are similar revisions of the forecasts made for the noncontrolled variables. This is illustrated in the following section.

AN APPLICATION

Our one-period and multi-period examples were oversimplified, since only one instrument and one noncontrolled variable were considered. To give an impression of how the method really works in practice we should take a larger example. The one taken here is the study (mentioned earlier) by van den Bogaard and Barten with five instruments and four noncontrolled variables. The application is based on conditions in The Netherlands in the three-year period 1957-59. The decision-maker is supposed to have a constant horizon of three years in mind: that is, at the beginning of 1957 he plans until the end of 1959; at the beginning of 1958 until the end of 1960; and at the beginning of 1959 until the end of 1961. These are the three dates that will be considered here. Similar computations have also been made for the case in which the attention is confined until the end of 1959 (which remains so until the very end), but these will be disregarded.

The constraints are derived from an econometric model consisting of about forty equations (of which twelve are behavioral equations). The uncertainty in these constraints (corresponding with the coefficients a, a_1, a_2 of our simple examples) is due partly to the presence of disturbances in the behavioral equations, partly to the presence of exogenous variables in the model which are beyond the decision-maker's control (such as the price level of imported goods). It is *not* assumed, as was assumed in the preceding pages, that everything is known as soon as it belongs to the past. For example, we found earlier that a_1 can be determined as soon as y_1 is known—see equation (13)—and we assumed that y_1 is known as soon as it is realized, namely, at the end of the first period. This is frequently not realistic, since statistical information of past values may lag behind the event. It is therefore assumed here that only estimates are available, which are revised every year.

It was mentioned in the discussion of quadratic preferences that three alternative preference functions are used: one representing the standpoint of a "typical" employer, one the standpoint of a "typical" trade unionist, and one a "neutral" standpoint. Consequently, we shall have three sets of outcomes, each of which describes a "world" of its own. For example, the results for the employer specify how economic conditions in The Netherlands would have been if his preferences, together with the uncontrolled forces, had ruled the country; similarly, the results for the trade unionist show how things would have been if his preference function (and the uncontrolled forces) had been in command. Note that the differences between the three sets of outcomes are entirely due to the differences in preferences; the constraints (which deal with the impact of the decisions made and of the development of the uncontrolled forces) are the same for all. The three preference functions are all quadratic but more complicated than the ones considered in our previous examples. They contain, for instance, the sum of squares of the successive differences of the instrument values to ensure that the instruments do not behave too wildly over time.

As an example let us take the trade unionist's decisions and forecasts of decisions, regarding the wage rate (one of the five instruments). A convenient presentation of the results is by way of a rectangular array whose columns refer to the years in which the decisions are made and whose rows refer to the years in which the computations are made. The result for the wage rate (measured as a percentage change compared with the level of the preceding year) is then as follows (the figures in italics represent the decisions which are actually to be made; all other figures are forecasts of future decisions):

	1957	1958	1959	1960	1961
1957	*8.30*	4.41	3.81		
1958		*3.32*	4.12	4.20	
1959			*4.55*	4.36	4.32

The first row shows that at the beginning of 1957 the following computations are made: the wage rate is to be raised by 8.30 percent in 1957 (compared with the 1956 level) and it is predicted that there will be another 4.41 percent increase in 1958 and also a 3.81 percent increase in 1959. One year later, at the beginning of 1958, another series of computations is made and 1958 is now the first year. The result is that the wage rate increase to be applied in that year is 3.32 percent, i.e., slightly less than the 4.41 percent that was predicted one year earlier. Also, the 3.81 percent prediction for 1959 is now revised to a slightly larger value (4.12 percent), and an entirely new prediction is made

—a 4.20 percent increase for 1960. This prediction is "entirely new," because 1960 was not forecast at all one year before. In the same way, there is a new series of computations at the beginning of 1959; the results show that that year's decision is a 4.55 percent increase (still larger than the revised prediction made at the beginning of 1958), while the predicted increases for 1960 and 1961 are of the same order of magnitude.

The results of the noncontrolled variables have a slightly different form because they involve imperfect estimates of past realizations. A comparison of forecasts with actual values therefore requires that we consider the most recent statistical data, which in this case amounts to data available in the spring of 1962. As an example we take the employer's forecasts of the number of employed (also measured as a percentage change compared with the level of the preceding year):

	1957	1958	1959	1960	1961
1957	2.66	2.41	2.52		
1958	0.55	2.72	2.20	2.71	
1959	1.08	0.05	4.24	3.79	3.55
1962	*1.19*	*−0.19*	*1.94*		

The first row shows that at the beginning of 1957 employment was predicted to increase by 2.66 percent in that year, by 2.41 percent in 1958, and by 2.52 percent in 1959. At the beginning of 1958 the 2.66 percent prediction was reduced to only 0.55 percent. This is no longer a forecast but an estimate of a past realization, since the figure refers to 1957 while the computation is made at the beginning of 1958. Evidently, the 0.55 percent estimate was too low, because it was revised to 1.08 percent at the beginning of 1959 and the most recent estimate (of 1962), which is considered as "actual" or "true" here (and therefore italicized), is an increase of 1.19 percent. In the same way we see that the 1957 forecast for 1958 is revised in an upward direction (from 2.41 to 2.72), then drastically in a downward direction (to 0.05), after which the final estimate turns out to be negative. And so on. For 1960 and 1961 no "final" estimates are given because these years are too close to 1962.

A complete survey is presented in Table 2-1, from which the reader can draw his own conclusions. As to the units employed, wage rate, employment, and the price level of consumer goods are expressed as percentage changes compared with the level of the preceding year. For the share of wages in national income the following procedure is adopted. If the share is 65.1 percent this year and 66.2 percent next

TABLE 2-1. *Forecasts, Estimates, and Realizations of Instruments and Noncontrolled Variables for Three Strategies in The Netherlands, 1957-1959*[a]

Computations Made the Beginning of	Trade Unionist					Neutral					Employer				
	1957	1958	1959	1960	1961	1957	1958	1959	1960	1961	1957	1958	1959	1960	1961
INSTRUMENTS															
Wage rate (percent)[b]															
1957	*8.30*	4.41	3.81	4.20	4.32	*5.91*	2.24	1.93	2.45	2.63	*6.16*	2.71	2.20	1.49	1.73
58		*3.32*	4.12	4.36			*0.75*	1.46	2.74			*0.80*	1.15	1.60	
59			*4.55*					*2.16*					*1.68*		
Indirect taxes (billions of guilders)[c]															
1957	*-0.11*	-0.05	-0.01	0.04	-0.01	*0.03*	0.06	0.05	0.01	-0.03	*-0.02*	0.02	0.02	-0.03	-0.05
58		*0.12*	0.10	-0.02			*0.04*	0.02	-0.05			*-0.04*	-0.05	-0.10	
59			*0.02*					*-0.06*					*-0.12*		
Direct taxes on wage income (billions of guilders)															
1957	*-0.04*	-0.06	-0.04	-0.03	-0.03	*-0.03*	-0.04	-0.03	-0.01	-0.00	*-0.08*	-0.08	-0.06	-0.07	-0.07
58		*-0.04*	-0.01	-0.02			*-0.05*	0.01	-0.00			*-0.14*	-0.06	-0.09	
59			*0.02*					*0.01*					*-0.09*		
Direct taxes on nonwage income (billions of guilders)															
1957	*0.99*	0.95	0.97	-0.47	-0.53	*0.33*	0.19	0.15	0.03	-0.02	*-0.11*	-0.17	-0.16	-0.11	-0.10
58		*0.05*	-0.35	-0.45			*-0.14*	-0.07	-0.12			*-0.26*	-0.19	-0.13	
59			*-0.05*					*-0.05*					*-0.17*		
Annual change in government expenditure on goods and services (billions of guilders)															
1957	*0.14*	0.22	0.24	0.13	0.21	*-0.02*	0.01	0.09	0.20	0.25	*0.09*	0.07	0.07	0.22	0.22
58		*-0.12*	0.04	0.16			*0.03*	0.09	0.28			*0.22*	0.20	0.29	
59			*0.04*					*0.23*					*0.33*		

Employment (percent)[b]

1957	2.61	1.61	2.05	3.23	4.44	2.36	1.73	2.18	2.52	3.57	2.66	2.41	2.52	2.71	3.55
58	0.50	1.10	1.90	3.98		0.24	1.82	1.86	3.63		0.55	2.72	2.20	3.79	
59	1.03	−1.42	3.67			0.77	−0.85	3.89			1.08	0.05	4.24		
62	*1.14*	*−1.66*	*1.35*			*0.88*	*−1.09*	*1.59*			*1.19*	*−0.19*	*1.94*		

Price level of consumer goods (percent)[b]

1957	2.34	0.73	−0.07	2.12	1.61	1.96	0.30	−0.61	−0.33	−0.42	2.56	0.69	−0.18	−0.99	−0.93
58	6.31	1.70	2.98	1.57		5.94	−0.64	−0.31	−0.68		6.52	−1.45	−0.80	−1.66	
59	4.30	2.94	1.19			3.94	0.68	−1.59			4.51	−0.13	−2.15		
62	*3.50*	*1.71*	*1.38*			*3.14*	*−0.55*	*−1.41*			*3.71*	*−1.36*	*−1.97*		

Shares of wages in national income (billions of guilders)

1957	1.27	0.19	0.70	0.09	0.93	1.06	0.02	0.55	0.39	1.12	0.73	−0.11	0.45	0.22	0.98
58	0.20	0.61	0.61	0.22		−0.01	0.33	0.88	0.46		−0.35	0.15	0.78	0.35	
59	0.47	−0.17	0.74			0.27	−0.40	0.81			−0.08	−0.58	0.70		
62	*1.93*	*0.88*	*−0.23*			*1.72*	*0.65*	*−2.24*			*1.38*	*0.47*	*−2.35*		

Surplus on the balance of payment (billions of guilders)

1957	0.30	1.72	2.28	0.71	0.71	0.44	1.44	1.67	0.08	0.14	0.31	0.97	1.24	−0.54	−0.39
58	−0.48	1.22	1.34	1.14		−0.33	0.47	0.49	0.22		−0.47	−0.22	−0.16	−0.43	
59	−0.68	1.84	1.26			−0.53	1.20	0.28			−0.67	0.51	−0.39		
62	*−0.52*	*1.90*	*2.01*			*−0.37*	*1.26*	*1.08*			*−0.51*	*0.68*	*0.41*		

[a] The italicized figures represent true values; all other figures are either forecasts of future values or preliminary estimates of past realizations.

[b] Percentage changes compared with the level of the preceding year.

[c] One guilder is almost 30 dollar cents.

year, then the increase 1.1 is recorded—i.e., the change in the percentage share. All other variables are in billions (10^9) of guilders. (A guilder is almost 30 dollar cents.) For the three tax variables a procedure was developed to transform tax-rate changes into amounts of tax received, which can be described as follows. In general, taxes, T, are levied on something, say income, Y, and the relation in linearized form is $T = \alpha + \beta Y$, where β stands for the marginal tax rate in the relevant area. When tax rates are changed this affects both α and β but (in the Dutch experience) α much more than β. Here the β changes are neglected and the table specifies the α change induced by the tax rate changes.

CONCLUDING REMARKS

1. As stated at the end of the section on "Uncertainty, Expected Utility, and Certainty Equivalence," it is undoubtedly true that the use of quadratic preference functions is restrictive. But they are not necessarily as simple as the weighted sum of squares which was used in our examples. We may have a complete quadratic form containing cross-products as well, so that the marginal utility of each variable depends then in principle on all variables. In fact, the application shown in Table 2-1 goes in this direction, because its preference functions contain squares of successive differences of certain variables. This means that the marginal utility of such a variable in a given year depends on the values which this variable takes in the preceding year and in the succeeding year. In that case it is no longer true that the three-year decision problem can be split up into three independent one-year decision problems as soon as current noncontrolled variables are independent of previous instrument values (see the discussion of the case $b_1 = 0$, on page 26).

2. The linearity of the constraints is another restrictive assumption. In addition, we assume that the multiplicative coefficients (the b's) are fixed and given. This is of course not really true in general, since econometric models are generally estimated rather than determined. In principle, one can get around this difficulty by adopting a Bayesian point of view. The decision-maker then fixes the b's at certain numerical values which measure his "prior beliefs."

3. The limitations as to the restrictive character of the assumptions have to be weighed against the advantages of the method in case the assumptions are (approximately) satisfied. The method is able to handle the uncertainty problem, both in a static and in a dynamic context, for

arbitrary numbers of controlled and noncontrolled variables. It is possible to compute the loss (= utility reduction) in case a suboptimal decision is made. (This loss turns out to be a quadratic form in the decision error.) In general, the suboptimality of a decision made is due to an imperfect specification of constraints and preference function. Constraint errors are generally due to specification errors of the model used. This means that it is possible, *via* the decision made, to compute the loss caused by specification errors of the model, which in turn leads to certain suggestions as to which aspects of the model should be investigated further. Also, the application of the method is not confined to macroeconomic decision problems. The work of Holt and others (see footnote 4 above) deals with cost minimization of a paint factory and is characterized by such problems as sales forecasting and cost coefficient estimation.

BIBLIOGRAPHY*

ARROW, K. J. *Social Choice and Individual Values.* Cowles Commission Monograph No. 12. John Wiley and Sons, Inc., New York; Chapman and Hall, Ltd., London. 1951.

ARROW, K. J., S. KARLIN and P. SUPPES (editors). *Mathematical Methods in the Social Sciences, 1959.* Stanford University Press, Stanford. 1960.

BANBURY, J., and J. MAITLAND (editors). *Proceedings of the Second International Conference on Operational Research.* English Universities Press, Ltd., London. 1961.

BOGAARD, P. J. M. VAN DEN. "On the Static Theory of Certainty Equivalence." Report 6010 of the Econometric Institute of the Netherlands School of Economics. March 28, 1960.

BOGAARD, P. J. M. VAN DEN, and G. ARNAIZ. "On the Sensitivity of Committee Decisions under Alternative Quadratic Criteria." Report 6107 of the Econometric Institute of the Netherlands School of Economics (also Report No. 7 of the International Center for Management Science). May 30, 1961.

BOGAARD, P. J. M. VAN DEN, and A. P. BARTEN. "Macroeconomic Decision Rules for The Netherlands, 1957–1959." Report 5915 of the Econometric Institute of the Netherlands School of Economics. June 15, 1959.

BOGAARD, P. J. M. VAN DEN, A. MONREAL LUQUE and C. VAN DE PANNE. "Étude sur les implications des horizons alternatifs dans la programmation quadratique dynamique." *Revue de la Société Française de Recherche Opérationnelle,* Vol. 6 (1962), pp. 163–183.

BOGAARD, P. J. M. VAN DEN, and H. THEIL. "Macrodynamic Policy-Making: An Application of Strategy and Certainty Equivalence Concepts to the Economy of the United States, 1933–1936." *Metroeconomica,* Vol. 11 (1959), pp. 149–167.

BOGAARD, P. J. M. VAN DEN, and J. VERSLUIS. "The Design of Optimal Committee Decisions." *Statistica Neerlandica,* Vol. 16 (1962), pp. 271–289. [An abbreviated version of this article was published under the title "The Design of Socially Optimal Decisions" in *Proceedings of the Second International Conference on Operational Research,* edited by J. BANBURY and J. MAITLAND. English Universities Press, Ltd., London. 1961.]

BOWMAN, E. H. "Consistency and Optimality in Managerial Decision Making." *Management Science,* Vol. 9 (1963), pp. 310–321.

BURGER, E. "On Extrema with Side Conditions." *Econometrica,* Vol. 23 (1955), pp. 451–452.

CHERNOFF, H., and N. DIVINSKY. "The Computation of Maximum-Likelihood

* Reprinted from H. Theil, *Optimal Decision Rules for Government and Industry* (North-Holland and Rand McNally, 1964).

Estimates of Linear Structural Equations." Chapter X of *Studies in Econometric Method*, edited by W. C. HOOD and T. C. KOOPMANS. Cowles Commission Monograph No. 14. John Wiley and Sons, Inc., New York; Chapman and Hall, Ltd., London. 1953.

CHURCHMAN, C. W., and M. VERHULST (editors). *Management Sciences, Models and Techniques*. Two Volumes. Pergamon Press, Oxford, London, New York and Paris, 1960.

DEBREU, G. "Definite and Semidefinite Quadratic Forms." *Econometrica*, Vol. 20 (1952), pp. 295–300.

DEBREU, G. "Representation of a Preference Ordering by a Numerical Function." Chapter XI of *Decision Processes*, edited by R. H. Thall, C. H. COOMBS and R. L. DAVIS. John Wiley and Sons, Inc., New York; Chapman and Hall, Ltd., London. 1954.

FISHER, W. D. "Estimation in the Linear Decision Model." *International Economic Review*, Vol. 3 (1962), pp. 1–29.

FRISCH, R. "Numerical Specification of a Quadratic Preference Function for Use in Macroeconomic Programming." Mimeographed report of the University Institute of Economics, Oslo. 1957.

FRISCH, R. "A Complete Scheme for Computing All Direct and Cross Demand Elasticities in a Model with Many Sectors." *Econometrica*, Vol. 27 (1959), pp. 177–196.

GORMAN, W. M. "Separable Utility and Aggregation." *Econometrica*, Vol. 27 (1959), pp. 469–481.

HARSANYI, J. C. "Cardinal Welfare, Individualistic Ethics, and Interpersonal Comparisons of Utility." *Journal of Political Economy*, Vol. 63 (1955), pp. 309–321.

HICKS, J. R. *Value and Capital*. Second Edition. Oxford University Press, London. 1946.

HOLT, C. C. "Decision Rules for Allocating Inventory to Lots and Cost Functions for Making Aggregate Inventory Decisions." *Journal of Industrial Engineering*, Vol. 9 (1958), pp. 14–22.

HOLT, C. C. "A General Solution for Linear Decision Rules." Mimeografed report of the Carnegie Institute of Technology, Pittsburgh, Pennsylvania. 1960.

HOLT, C. C. "Linear Decision Rules for Economic Stabilization and Growth." *Quarterly Journal of Economics*. Vol. 76 (1962), pp. 20–45.

HOLT, C. C., and F. MODIGLIANI. "Firm Cost Structures and the Dynamic Responses of Inventories, Production, Work Force, and Orders to Sales Fluctuations." *Study of Inventory Fluctuations and Economic Stability*, Congress of the United States, Joint Economic Committee. 1961.

HOLT, C. C., F. MODIGLIANI and J. F. MUTH. "Derivation of a Linear Decision Rule for Production and Employment." *Management Science*, Vol. 2 (1956), pp. 159–177.

HOLT, C. C., F. MODIGLIANI, J. F. MUTH and H. A. SIMON. *Planning Production, Inventories, and Work Force*. Prentice-Hall, Inc., Englewood Cliffs, N.J. 1960.

HOLT, C. C., F. MODIGLIANI and H. A. SIMON. "A Linear Decision Rule for

Production and Employment Scheduling." *Management Science*, Vol. 2 (1955), pp. 1–30.

HOOD, W. C., and T. C. KOOPMANS (editors). *Studies in Econometric Method.* Cowles Commission Monograph No. 14. John Wiley and Sons, Inc., New York; Chapman and Hall, Ltd., London. 1953.

HOUTHAKKER, H. S. "Additive Preferences." *Econometrica*, Vol. 28 (1960), pp. 244–257.

KALMAN, R. E., L. LAPIDUS and E. SHAPIRO. "The Optimal Control of Chemical and Petroleum Processes." Pages 6–17 of *Proceedings of the Joint Symposium on Instrumentation and Computation in Process Development and Plant Design*, published by The Institution of Chemical Engineers, London. 1959.

KLEIN, L. R. *Economic Fluctuations in the United States, 1921–1941.* Cowles Commission Monograph No. 11. John Wiley and Sons, Inc., New York; Chapman and Hall, Ltd., London. 1950.

KOOPMANS, T. C., and W. C. HOOD. "The Estimation of Simultaneous Linear Economic Relationships." Chapter VI of *Studies in Econometric Method*, edited by W. C. HOOD and T. C. KOOPMANS. Cowles Commission Monograph No. 14. John Wiley and Sons, Inc., New York; Chapman and Hall, Ltd., London. 1953.

KOYCK, L. M. *Distributed Lags and Investment Analysis.* Vol. IV of Contributions to Economic Analysis. North-Holland Publishing Company, Amsterdam. 1954.

MANSFIELD, E., and H. V. WEIN. "Linear Decision Rules and Freight Yard Operations." *Journal of Industrial Engineering*, Vol. 9 (1958), pp. 93–98.

MARSCHAK, J. "Rational Behavior, Uncertain Prospects, and Measurable Utility." *Econometrica*, Vol. 18 (1950), pp. 111–141.

MARSCHAK, J. "Elements for a Theory of Teams," *Management Science*, Vol. 1 (1955), pp. 127–137.

NAGEL, E., P. SUPPES and A. TARSKI (editors). *Logic, Methodology and Philosophy of Science—Proceedings of the 1960 International Congress.* Stanford University Press, Stanford. 1962.

NEUMANN, J. VON, and O. MORGENSTERN. *Theory of Games and Economic Behavior.* Third Edition. Princeton University Press, Princeton. 1953.

PANNE, C. VAN DE, and G. J. AEYELTS AVERINK. "Imperfect Management Decisions and Predictions and Their Financial Implications in Dynamic Quadratic Cost Minimization." *Statistica Neerlandica*, Vol. 15 (1961), pp. 293–318.

PANNE, C. VAN DE, and P. BOSJE. "Sensitivity Analysis of Cost Coefficient Estimates: The Case of Linear Decision Rules for Employment and Production." *Management Science*, Vol. 9 (1962), pp. 82–107.

RADNER, R. "Team Decision Problems." *Annals of Mathematical Statistics*, Vol. 33 (1962), pp. 857–881.

REITER, S. "Surrogates for Uncertain Decision Problems: Minimal Information for Decision Making." *Econometrica*, Vol. 25 (1957), pp. 339–345.

ROTHENBERG, J. F. *The Measurement of Social Welfare.* Prentice-Hall, Inc., Englewood Cliffs, N.J. 1961.

ROTHENBERG, T., and C. T. LEENDERS, "Efficient Estimation of Simultaneous

Equation Systems." Report 6216 of the Econometric Institute of the Netherlands School of Economics. June 19, 1962.

SAMUELSON, P. A. *Foundations of Economic Analysis.* Harvard University Press, Cambridge. 1953.

SCHLAIFER, R. *Probability and Statistics for Business Decisions.* McGraw-Hill Book Company, Inc., New York, Toronto and London. 1959.

SIMON, H. A. "Dynamic Programming under Uncertainty with a Quadratic Criterion Function." *Econometrica,* Vol. 24 (1956), pp. 74–81.

STROTZ, R. H. "The Empirical Implications of a Utility Tree." *Econometrica,* Vol. 25 (1957), pp. 269–280.

THEIL, H. "Econometric Models and Welfare Maximization." *Weltwirtschaftliches Archiv,* Vol. 72 (1954), pp. 60–83.

THEIL, H. "A Note on Certainty Equivalence in Dynamic Planning." *Econometrica,* Vol. 25 (1957), pp. 346–349.

THEIL, H. *Economic Forecasts and Policy.* Second Edition. Vol. XV of Contributions to Economic Analysis. North-Holland Publishing Company, Amsterdam. 1961.

THEIL, H. "Alternative Approaches to the Aggregation Problem." Pages 507-527 of *Logic, Methodology and Philosophy of Science—Proceedings of the 1960 International Congress,* edited by E. NAGEL, P. SUPPES and A. TARSKI. Stanford University Press, Stanford. 1962.

THEIL, H. "On the Optimal Management of Research: A Mathematical Approach." Report 6212 of the Econometric Institute of the Netherlands School of Economics (also Report No. 17 of the International Center for Management Science). May 10, 1962.

THEIL, H. "On the Symmetry Approach to the Committee Decision Problem." *Management Science,* Vol. 9 (1963), pp. 380-393.

THEIL, H., and J. C. G. BOOT. "The Final Form of Econometric Equation Systems." *Review of the International Statistical Institute,* Vol. 30 (1962), pp. 136-152.

THEIL, H., and E. KAPTEIN. "The Effect of Forecasting Errors on Optimal Programming of Production-Inventory and Anti-Depression Policies." Report 5906 of the Econometric Institute of the Netherlands School of Economics. February 25, 1959. [An abbreviated version of this article was published under the title "The Effect of Forecasting Errors on Optimal Programming" in *Management Sciences, Models and Techniques,* Vol. 1 (pp. 295-322), edited by C. W. CHURCHMAN and M. VERHULST. Pergamon Press, Oxford, London, New York and Paris. 1960.]

THEIL, H., and T. KLOEK. "The Operational Implications of Imperfect Models." Chapter 8 of *Mathmatical Methods in the Social Sciences, 1959,* edited by K. J. ARROW, S. KARLIN, and P. SUPPES. Stanford University Press, Stanford. 1960.

THRALL, R. M., C. H. COOMBS and R. L. DAVIS (editors). *Decision Processes.* John Wiley and Sons, Inc., New York; Chapman and Hall, Ltd., London. 1954.

TINBERGEN, J. *On the Theory of Economic Policy.* Second Edition. Vol. I of Contributions to Economic Analysis. North-Holland Publishing Company, Amsterdam. 1952.

TINBERGEN, J. *Economic Policy: Principles and Design.* Vol. XI of Contributions to Economic Analysis. North-Holland Publishing Company, Amsterdam. 1956.

VAN DE PANNE, C., *see* PANNE, C. VAN DE.

VAN DEN BOGAARD, P. J. M., *see* BOGAARD, P. J. M. VAN DEN.

VERDOORN, P. J., and C. J. VAN EIJK. "Experimental Short-Term Forecasting Models." Mimeographed report of the Central Planning Bureau, The Hague. 1958. [This report was a paper read at the Bilbao Meeting of the Econometric Society in 1958.]

VON NEUMANN, J., *see* NEUMANN, J. VON.

3

Specification of Structures and Data Requirements in Policy Models

KARL A. FOX[1] and ERIK THORBECKE[2]

THIS PAPER WAS DESIGNED to play a particular role in relation to the other conference papers. The intended role may be clarified with the aid of Figure 3-1, which is a visual representation of Tinbergen's theory of economic policy.

Professor Theil's paper includes in a highly condensed fashion all the elements of Figure 3-1. It concentrates on the selection of values of policy instruments, z_j, and policy targets, y_i, that will maximize a preference or objective function, W, the feasible combinations of values of instruments and targets being constrained by one or more equations embodying a "model" of the presumed or estimated structure of the economy. Exogenous factors, u_k, not subject to either direct or indirect control by the decision-maker, are subsumed in the additive constant terms in Professor Theil's equations. If for *ad hoc* reasons we regard some economic variables, x_s, as irrelevant for a given policy decision we can eliminate them from a complete model by algebraic means, leaving a set of equations containing only policy instruments and targets (plus the additive effects of the strictly noncontrollable variables).

Professors Kirschen and Morissens concern themselves with listings and classifications of the targets actually pursued in several countries, and the policy instruments employed in their pursuit. These are essentially the y_i and z_j of Figure 3-1. Target variables themselves are regarded as contributing to certain broad policy aims—security, social justice, and the like. These aims are not formally related by the authors to a preference function, but they reflect the attitudes of policy-makers from which

---

[1] Professor of Economics and Head of Department of Economics and Sociology, Iowa State University.
[2] Professor of Economics, Iowa State University.

43

FIGURE 3-1. *The Theory of Economic Policy*[a]

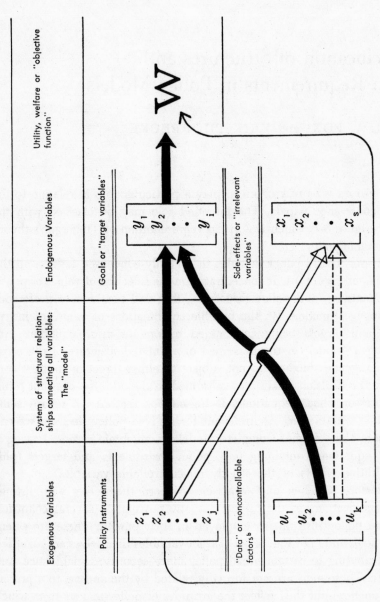

| Exogenous Variables | System of structural relation-ships connecting all variables: The "model" | Endogenous Variables | Utility, welfare or "objective function" |

Policy Instruments

z_1
z_2
$\bullet \bullet \bullet \bullet z_j$

"Data" or noncontrollable factors[b]

u_1
u_2
$\bullet \bullet \bullet \bullet u_k$

Goals or "target variables"

y_1
y_2 $\bullet \bullet \bullet y_i$

Side-effects or "irrelevant variables"

x_1
x_2 $\bullet \bullet \bullet x_s$

W

[a] Classification of variables based on J. Tinbergen.
[b] Not subject to control by the policy-maker or level of government that sets the goals and uses the policy instruments in question.

44

a preference function, W, might be derived. No explicit attention is given to quantitative economic models or equation systems connecting instruments and target variables, though at least intuitive knowledge of such models is implied in the cross-classification of objectives and the instruments employed to achieve or approach them.

Our paper is concerned with problems of "developing the physique" of a model of the economy; the selection of variables to be included, the classification of variables from the standpoint of economic policy, and the specification of the structural relationships among the variables. In much econometric literature the estimation of models of an economy has been treated as a problem primarily of probability theory and statistics. Assumptions about the joint probability distributions of disturbances in different equations and the large sample properties of different estimators can and should be stated rigorously. But the concept of the structure of an economy is independent of and logically prior to techniques for measuring that structure. Particular statistical techniques applied to aggregative economic time series by no means exhaust our knowledge of the economic system.

We will concentrate upon the economic and logical aspects of policy models. (In the complementary paper which follows this one, our colleague J. K. Sengupta is concerned with the statistical problems involved in specifying and estimating policy models.) The spirit of our endeavor is reflected in a statement by L. R. Klein:

> If econometric results are today more useful than in the past, this is only partly a result of the particular method of estimation, but much more significantly a product of painstaking research of a more pedestrian nature. The building of institutional reality into *a priori* formulations of economic relationships and the refinement of basic data collection have contributed much more to the improvement of empirical econometric results than have more elaborate methods of statistical inference. I look towards improvements in precision of econometric judgments of the order of magnitude of 50 percent as a result of a better knowledge of the functioning of economic institutions, through the use of new measurements on variables, and through the use of more accurate data. In contrast, I would expect marginal improvements of 5 or 10 percent through the use of more powerful methods of statistical inference. All routes to improvement must be followed since any gains, no matter how small, are precious, yet different contributions should be kept in proper perspective. The adoption of more powerful methods of mathematical statistics is no panacea.[3]

[3] L. R. Klein, "Single Equation *vs.* Equation System Methods of Estimation in Econometrics," *Econometrica*, Vol. 28 (October 1960), p. 867.

For concreteness, our discussion will proceed in terms of a mature economy. In certain sections we will draw directly upon problems and properties of the Brookings-SSRC model of the United States, in the development of which the senior author has participated along with some twenty other economists.[4]

THE STRUCTURE OF A NATIONAL ECONOMY

An econometric model of a national economy is composed of technical, behavioral, and institutional relationships and identities. As economic policy is concerned with the movement of the economy over time, the variables in a policy model will consist of economic time series. (This does not necessarily imply that the relationships between variables must be estimated from time series.)

Let us suppose that we have been assigned the task of developing a model of the United States economy with which to anticipate the effects of alternative sets of policies. We decide that the model should include at least 100 equations and 200 variables, consisting of time series of quarterly observations for the period 1947-62.

The number of possible combinations of explanatory variables, lagged and nonlagged, which might be included in equations for estimating the 100 endogenous variables is extremely large. If we are to do a workmanlike and defensible job of organizing the time series variables into structural equations with appropriate patterns of time lags, we must justify our specifications in terms of a very searching analysis of the economic institutions and decision-making processes which determine the course of economic activity in the real world.

At first thought, it may appear that our 200 time series contain a tremendous amount of information about the structure of the economy. But these series consist exclusively of national totals and averages, with no geographic breakdown. With 100 equations in all, we cannot subdivide the economy into more than 6 or 7 producing sectors—such as "durable manufactures" or "nondurable manufactures." Furthermore, the degree of intercorrelation among time series in an economy in which population, real income per capita, prices, and wages are all increasing is so high that multiple regression techniques sometimes give us esti-

[4] See especially pp. 81-85 below.

mates of structural coefficients which are demonstrably absurd when checked against cross-section studies or studies of individual firms and households.

If we intend to reflect in our model the technological structure, transactions patterns, and decision-making processes of the real world, we are not limited to the use of aggregative time series for the United States as a whole. For example, our knowledge of the functioning of the housing sector may be enhanced by studying time series on residential construction and related variables in each of a large number of metropolitan areas. Or we may examine family expenditure surveys for particular points in time as a basis for establishing consumption-income relationships. Input-output studies for particular years may help us to see why series on production and employment in two industries show certain relative amplitudes and turning point dates.

In brief, it is essential to supplement time series data with other information about the structure of the economy and to build some of this information into the policy model in the form of imposed coefficients (treated as exact numbers) or of coefficients which may vary within imposed upper and lower bounds (as in some "mixed estimation" procedures).

In the next few pages we will discuss aspects of the economic structure of a mature economy which cannot be inferred from time series but which strongly condition the feasibility and impacts of economic stabilization policies.

Interindustry (Input-Output) Relationships

Figure 3-2 shows a conventional input-output framework, with the format slightly altered to emphasize, first, the consistency of input-output analysis with the gross national product and income accounts and, second, the relationship of the cross-section structure of the economy to a pair of matrix equations. Total economic activity is divided into n categories. Final demand is divided into five categories: personal consumption expenditures, C; gross private domestic fixed investment, I; government purchases of goods and services, G; the increase in inventories in each industry where an increase occurs, ΔH_a; and gross exports E. Autonomous inputs are divided into eight categories: inventory depletions for those industries showing depletions, $-\Delta H_d$; gross imports, M; depreciation, D; indirect business taxes, T_b; wage and salary payments, W; interest, i; net rent, R; and before-tax profits, π.

The national income accounts incorporate the following identities:

$$GNP = C + I + G + (\Delta H_a - \Delta H_d) + (E - M) \tag{1}$$

$$= TG \text{ Output} - \Delta H_d - M - \sum_{i=1}^{n} \sum_{j=1}^{n} X_{ij},$$

$$GNI = D + T_b + W + i + R + \pi \tag{2}$$

$$= TG \text{ Outlay} - \Delta H_d - M - \sum_{i=1}^{n} \sum_{j=1}^{n} X_{ij},$$

and

$$GNI = GNP. \tag{3}$$

The double summation term in equations (1) and (2) represents the interindustry demands—flows of raw materials, semimanufactures, com-

FIGURE 3-2. *Input-Output Structure of an Economy*

Total Gross Output		Industry \ Industry	Interindustry Demands 1	2	3	· · ·	n		Final Demands C 1	I 2	G 3	ΔH_a 4	E 5
X_1		1	X_{11}	·	·	·	X_{1n}		f_{11}	·	·	·	f_{15}
X_2		2	·				·		·				·
X_3	=	3	·				·	+	·				·
·		·	·				·		·				·
·		·	·				·		·				·
X_n		n	X_{n1}	·	·	·	X_{nn}		f_{n1}	·	·	·	f_{n5}

+

Autonomous Inputs		1	2	3	· · ·	n
ΔH_d	1	S_{11}	·	·	·	S_{1n}
M	2	·				·
D	3	·				·
T_b	4	·				·
W	5	·				·
i	6	·				·
R	7	·				·
π	8	S_{81}	·	·	·	S_{8n}

=

Total Gross Outlay or Income	X_1	X_2	X_3	· · ·	X_n

ponents, and services—which are pronounced and relatively stable features of a mature economy. These intermediate flows are "netted out" in calculating gross national product (GNP) and gross national income (GNI), but they constitute an extremely important mechanism for transmitting changes in activity in a given industry into changes in output and employment in other industries. Whenever economic measures are adopted which stimulate consumption, investment, or exports or which increase government purchases of goods and services, this interindustry mechanism is called into play. It also operates when measures are taken to reduce final demands.

The input-output nexus between final demand and total gross output may be stated as follows:
Let

$$(4) \qquad a_{ij} = \frac{X_{ij}}{X_j}, \qquad i, j = 1, 2, \cdots, n;$$

so that $X_{ij} = a_{ij}X_j$. An increase of \$1.0 million in X_j (the gross output of Industry j) will *directly* require an increase of a_{ij} million dollars of inputs from Industry i. But the increase in output of Industry i will in turn call for an increase in inputs from Industry k, and the latter increase might call for additional inputs from Industry j.

To capture all of these first, second, third (and higher) order effects in a single calculation, we use the techniques of matrix algebra to solve for a set of coefficients

$$(5) \qquad \alpha_{ij} = \frac{X_{ij}}{F_j}, \qquad i, j = 1, 2, \cdots, n;$$

so that $X_{ij} = \alpha_{ij}F_j$, where F_j represents deliveries to final GNP demand components from Industry j.[5]

Consider for a moment some implications of equation (5). Suppose,

---

[5] Thus we write:
$$X = AX + F,$$
where X is a column vector of the n X_j's, A is an n by n matrix of the coefficients a_{ij}, and F is a column vector of the n F_j's (final demand components) where $F_j = C_j + I_j + G_j + (\Delta H_a - \Delta H_d)_j + (E_j - M_j)$. (For any given industry, either ΔH_a or ΔH_d will be zero.)
Then
$$(I - A)X = F,$$
where I is an n by n identity matrix, and
$$X = (I - A)^{-1}F,$$
where $(I - A)^{-1}$ is the n by n inverse matrix of $(I - A)$ with elements α_{ij}.

for concreteness, that our input-output model of the economy is divided into twenty sectors ($n = 20$). An increase in deliveries to final demand from Industry j will lead through the coefficients α_{ij} to specified increases in the outputs of each of the twenty industries. The coefficients α_{ij} include both direct and indirect input requirements to support a unit of deliveries to final demand from Industry j. If every one of the twenty industries derives inputs from at least one of the other nineteen, it appears intuitively that no α_{ij} can be zero, although some of them may be quite small.

Suppose we are in a position to determine F_1 for each of a succession of time periods (quarters or years). If the prescribed time path of F_1 were recorded on a revolving drum, we might visualize twenty tracing pens whose amplitudes of movement were related to movements in F_1 by the coefficients α_{i1}. If so, we would have a total of twenty-one lines recorded on the drum; each time series would correlate perfectly with each of the others. In the usual deterministic setting, this is the implication of an input-output matrix with constant coefficients.

If we were free to determine independently the time paths of each of the F_j's (as we might in a mobilization economy), we could make similar time series tracings of the net effects of changes in each F_j upon each of the 20 X_i's. Alternatively, we could arrange the 400 "net effect" tracings in another fashion, so that the net effects of each of the 20 F_j's upon (say) output from Industry 1 would be recorded on the same time series chart. If the 20 ordinates were summed, we would obtain a time series chart for X_1, and we could make similar charts for each of the other nineteen industries.

The above discussion assumes that the α_{ij}'s, and the a_{ij}'s from which they are derived, remain constant over the relevant time period. We know, of course, that this is not the case for any extended period. If we made a new input-output transactions matrix each year, we could recompute the corresponding α_{ij}'s annually. Or, as time flows continuously in our revolving drum example, we might conceive of continuous variations in each α_{ij} and a continuous adjustment in the amplitude of each of the twenty tracing pens in relation to a unit movement in the pen which records the policy-determined time path of F_j. The sources of change in the technical coefficients and the costs and benefits of frequent recomputation of the input-output matrix are considered in the next section.

Extent and Welfare Consequences of Changes
in Input-Output Coefficients Over Time

It is possible to use a disaggregated interindustry breakdown in connection with either a macroeconomic model built for short-run stabilization purposes or one constructed for long-run economic growth (development) purposes. Such an input-output scheme is essential in the latter case to follow through the implications of changes in GNP and final demand, F_j, on interindustry deliveries, the X_{ij}'s, and to test the consistency of the long-term model in terms of balance between the requirements for and availability of inputs. In the case of a stabilization model, where the planning horizon is short and the deviations of the variables from their initial values are smaller than in a growth model, the superimposition of an interindustry breakdown may be less essential. Nevertheless, policy instruments can have a differential impact on different industries and it is helpful to the policy-maker to be able to assess the sectoral—in addition to the global—consequences of the changes in these instruments. It is clear that a regional breakdown can be added to the interindustry matrix and that in a similar fashion the consequences of macroeconomic decisions can be followed through (conceptually) to whatever level of disaggregation is desired, down to the individual households and firms.

Most countries which have undertaken comprehensive input-output studies have made them at intervals of several years, and publication has lagged two or more years behind the year to which the data pertain. If under these circumstances an interindustry breakdown is used jointly with a macro-policy model, the extent to which the input-output coefficients, the a_{ij}'s, can be assumed to remain constant over time becomes an important consideration. Ideally, the policy-maker would want to know the time paths of all a_{ij}'s in addition to the time paths of the components of final demand, the F_j's, so that he can take into account the error—which, as will be seen, appears to be highly correlated with time—resulting from the use of noncurrent coefficients. Ultimately, the cost of preparing a new input-output matrix and of estimating the current a_{ij}'s will have to be weighed against the loss of welfare (in terms of a reduced value for W in the welfare function—see Figure 3-1) through either a lower level of attainment of the target variables, the y_i's, included in

W for a given set of values of instrument variables, or an increase in the variance of the frequency distributions of the target variables in the reduced form equations relating them to the exogenous variables 'for any given set of values of instrument variables, the z_j's.

The above conditions can be stated somewhat differently by saying that the revision of the input-output coefficients should be undertaken when the loss of welfare (measured in a "policy output" sense, i.e., lower levels for the stabilization goals, y_i's, and greater uncertainty of attaining these targets because of higher variance) *for a given set* of instruments is equal to the cost of preparing a new set of estimates for the a_{ij}'s. It is, of course, obvious that there exists the inherent difficulty in the above calculus of measuring the welfare benefits and the computational and statistical costs of better parameters in comparable units.

It appears, however, that once the major stabilization goals are specified and the policy-maker has postulated their relative contributions to welfare, W, as well as their barter terms, the equivalence between a marginal change in the level of attainment of each stabilization target and GNP can be established "grosso modo."[6] The combined reduction in the level of GNP resulting from points one and two above could then be expressed in money terms and weighed against the easily computable dollar costs of more current or improved structural parameters. It is, of course, obvious that the same general principles could as well be applied to the structural and behavioral parameters of a macroeconomic model.

It seems relevant to examine the main changes which can occur in the input-output coefficients, the a_{ij}'s, over time and determine the impact of each type of variation on the error term, which, following Sevaldson,[7] can be defined as the difference between the observed X_i's arrived at on the basis of the $\bar{a}_i$'s derived from the "same" set of observations as the $\bar{X}_i$'s and $\bar{F}_i$'s (observed values are denoted by a bar) and the calculated X_i's representing estimates on the basis of a given (perhaps concurrent) matrix of a_{ij}'s and the same observed final demand set of $\bar{F}_j$'s.

In the first case we obtain:

$$(6) \qquad \bar{X}_i = \sum_{j=1}^{n} \bar{a}_{ij}\bar{F}_j, \qquad i = 1, 2, \cdots, n;$$

[6] See, for instance, C. J. van Eijk and J. Sandee, "Quantitative Determination of an Optimum Economic Policy," *Econometrica*, Vol. 27 (January 1959), pp. 1-13.

[7] Per Sevaldson, "Changes in Input-Output Coefficients," Chap. 16 in Tibor Barna, ed., *Structural Interdependence and Economic Development* (St. Martin's Press, 1963).

and in the second case,

$$(7) \qquad X_i = \sum_{j=1}^{n} \alpha_{ij} \bar{F}_j, \qquad i = 1, 2, \cdots, n.$$

Subtracting (7) from (6) we have the set of errors in model estimates:

$$(8) \qquad u_i = \bar{X}_i - X_i, \qquad i = 1, 2, \cdots, n.$$

Likewise another set of deviations can be defined:

$$(9) \qquad k_{ij} = \bar{a}_{ij} - a_{ij}, \qquad i, j = 1, 2, \cdots, n.$$

In the case of an open model, u_i will be a function of k, α_{ij}, and $\bar{F}_j$. An evaluation of the quality of the input-output model must be based on the imputed welfare loss resulting from the u_i's, whereas the stability of the coefficients is dependent on the individual k_{ij}'s, and the u_i's in turn are generated by the k_{ij}'s.

Very briefly, Sevaldson distinguishes between a number of factors which influence k_{ij} (and u_i) and which seem appropriate to the present analysis. These components are a trend factor, a function of the level of production in the receiving sector, a function of factors exogenous to the model, a function of other variables of the model such as prices and their changes over time, a term representing errors of observations, and a residual term:

$$(10) \qquad k_{ij} = {}_1k_{ij}(t) + {}_2k_{ij}(x_j) + {}_3k_{ij}(Z) + {}_4k_{ij}(X) + {}_5k_{ij}(0) + {}_6k_{ij}.$$

It should be clear that a purely additive decomposition of k_{ij} into six components is a simplification of the "true" relationship between these variables. One would, for instance, expect a substantial amount of interaction to exist between all or some of the components in their combined effect on k_{ij}. It can be argued, for instance, that the trend factor, ${}_1k_{ij}(t)$, is highly correlated with (and thereby reinforces) the impact of the level of output in the receiving sector ${}_2k_{ij}(x_j)$ on k_{ij}. Technological change is often a function of the interaction between the above two components.

The impact of ${}_1k_{ij}(t)$ on the a_{ij}'s has been analyzed for a number of industries and the conclusion which seems warranted is that these changes are quite gradual in mature economies even when important input-saving techniques become available. The adoption of new techniques is slowed down by a number of constraints—for example, fixed capital which might not be scrapped until price falls below average variable cost in the existing (old) plant. Even though the incremental technical coefficients are often substantially different from the average coefficients, the relatively slow rate of adoption of best-practice techniques tends to keep the input-output coefficients relatively stable.[8] (The a_{ij}'s can be interpreted as weighted averages of coefficients associated with the different techniques actually used in the industries.) A rapid rate of increase of output in expanding industries will therefore tend to alter the structural coefficients more rapidly, through the faster adoption of new (best-practice) techniques, than relatively slower (or even negative) rates of increase in declining industries. Likewise, it appears that industries utilizing capital intensive techniques with a short life expectancy will be able to generate a higher annual rate of replacement capital than other industries and thereby shift more rapidly to new techniques.

The second additive component of k_{ij} is $_2k_{ij}(x_j)$, which measures the extent to which the coefficients depend on the level of output of the various industries. The assumption of input/output proportionality is more valid for some industries than others (as, for instance, in the case of certain purely chemical processes). For certain industries the level of output is an important determinant of the a_{ij}'s. Capacity limitations will customarily affect the coefficients. On the whole, if some allowance is made for the impact of capacity ceilings on the a_{ij}'s, the assumption of direct proportionality appears tenable for short-run stabilization models as indicated by the empirical evidence presented below.

The next two components, $_3k_{ij}(Z)$ and $_4k_{ij}(X)$, reflect the dependency of coefficients on relative prices. Depending on the case, prices of inputs can be considered to be determined by exogenous variables, Z, or endogenous variables to the system, X. The changes in relative prices of inputs over time can be very substantial—and lead to major substitutions as between resources. Finally, errors in observations $_5k_{ij}(O)$ have been shown to introduce spurious variability between the a_{ij}'s and the $\bar{a}_{ij}$'s.

In the above discussion the impact of changes in the investment part of final demand on the a_{ij}'s was not specifically analyzed. In a mature economy, where the changes in the capital stock over time are fairly gradual and where the planning horizon is short, it seems unnecessary to study the impact of capital accumulation on the a_{ij}'s. If, however, the intent was to build a development-planning model—as opposed to a stabilization model—this last study would be essential.

In the case of a policy model used to generate quantitative recom-

---

[8] For an interesting theoretical discussion of this argument and for empirical evidence see W. E. G. Salter, *Productivity and Technical Change* (Cambridge University Press, 1960).

mendations for stabilization purposes, any empirical test of the variability of the coefficients and of their causes should provide a series of annual observed a_{ij}'s, if it is to be valuable as a determinant of the loss of welfare resulting from the use of noncurrent coefficients. Given the computational costs and the data problems of deriving annual input-output tables, this type of empirical evidence is quite limited. The results of two studies—one for Norway and one for The Netherlands—will be briefly summarized.[9] The conclusions of these studies appear to be fairly consistent with, and support the findings of, a number of specific industry studies in the United States and the United Kingdom.

The Norwegian study is based on the cork and the woodpulp industries and makes use of annual data for the period 1949-56 from which various coefficients are derived. The main findings are that volume coefficients for raw materials were quite stable over time, with observation errors mainly responsible for these variations. In addition, the average coefficient for the group of firms in the cork industry was more stable than the individual firm's coefficients and technological change as well as the level of output had a strong influence on some coefficients (i.e., labor).

The Dutch study is much more comprehensive than the above, involving annual observed data for twenty-seven industries covering the period 1949-58. The predictive qualities of the input-output matrix were tested by using the a_{ij} matrix for year t, expressed in current value terms, and applying it to the observed set of final demands at time $t + \tau$, to find a conditional forecast of the X_i at $t + \tau$. Since a_{ij} matrices were available for each t from 1949 to 1958, conditional forecasts could be worked out for one, two, three, etc. years ahead ($\tau = 1, 2, 3, \ldots$) and these forecasts could be compared with the observed values of the interindustry deliveries. The prediction error, $e_{it\tau}$, was defined as the forecast error, that is, the difference between (1) the conditional forecast at time t of the interindustry deliveries at some future time $t + \tau$ on the basis of the a_{ij} matrix for t and the observed final demand values at $t + \tau$ and (2) the observed values of input-output figures at time $t + \tau$, divided by the observed values. In other words, the prediction error is expressed relative to the values to be predicted.

Given the large number of forecasts, a mean-square prediction error for Industry i of all forecasts τ years ahead, $m_{i\tau}$, was used to evaluate

[9] See Sevaldson, *op. cit.;* also Guido Rey and C. B. Tilanus, "Input-Output Forecasts for the Netherlands, 1949-1958," *Econometrica*, Vol. 31 (July 1963), pp. 454-463.

the quality of the forecasts where $m_{i\tau} = 1/11$-τ $\sum_t e^2_{it\tau}$. It can be noted that for all predictions ten years ahead ($\tau = 10$) only one observation can be used, since only ten a_{ij} matrices are available.

The results of the study are most revealing. First, for all industries combined, the root-mean-square prediction error is about 7¾ percent if the underlying input-output table is that of the preceding year;[10] second, for longer time differences ($\tau > 1$), the above error increases about proportionately to the square root of τ; third, there is some evidence that the quality of forecasts is better for industries whose inter-industry deliveries are relatively large; and fourth, some evidence that forecasts are superior to naive extrapolations as long as the input-output matrix used to generate them is not more than two or three years older than the ratios of final demand to total production on which the extrapolations are based.[11]

The above evidence (admittedly limited) illustrates in a suggestive way some of the welfare implications following from the quality of the structural parameters. More specifically it would appear that, at least in the case of The Netherlands, input-output coefficients used in connection with a macroeconomic stabilization model might presumably lead to substantial welfare losses if they are not re-estimated every three years.

A more precise quantitative determination of the optimum time lag between a set of estimates of parameters appearing in the relationships of the macroeconomic stabilization model and a set of estimates of input-output coefficients—or alternatively, the optimum period over which a given set of estimates should be used for short-run stabilization purposes—would entail the following comparison. It would depend, as was pointed out above, on the marginal welfare benefits resulting from the use of a current set of estimates as opposed to past (outdated estimates) and the

[10] The mean over i (27 industries) of the $m_{i\tau}$ is shown to increase almost proportionally with τ. (Least squares applied to the 10 means of $m_{i\tau}$, where $\tau = 1, 2, \cdots$ 10, gives the following regression $\frac{1}{27}\sum_i m_{i\tau} = .066\tau$ which holds with very small residuals.) The corresponding root-mean-square prediction error is $(.006\tau)^{\frac{1}{2}}$, thus increasing with the square root of time. Forecasts one year ahead give a root-mean-square prediction error of 7¾ percent, and 11 percent for predictions two years ahead.

The standard deviation of $m_{i\tau}$ on τ came out at $.0072\tau$. Industries for which the prediction error was particularly high include coal mining, footwear, other wearing apparel, and basic metal industries. The first of these industries was a declining industry and the last one an expanding industry, thus suggesting that in such cases the quality of forecasts may be substantially improved by taking technological factors into consideration.

[11] If the same procedure is followed with input-output matrices expressed in constant value (volume) terms—instead of in current value terms—it appears that the time lag over which forecasts are superior to extrapolations is further reduced.

marginal costs of preparing a current set of estimates. Operational rules could be formulated on the basis of past experience which could be used to reach decisions about the optimum timing of a new set of structural and behavioral estimates for a given model and even concerning a new specification of the model.

RECURSIVENESS AND INTERDEPENDENCY
IN ECONOMIC STABILIZATION MODELS

The discussion so far has emphasized the technological basis for an important class of structural economic relationships. These relationships (processes, activities, and interindustry flows) are defined and estimated for particular points in time. Yet it is clear that the input-output mechanism is also involved in transmitting impacts from one industrial sector to another over time. A decline in the demand for automobiles from one quarter to the next leads in general to decreases in steel, coal, and iron production; leads and lags are an important characteristic of these changes.

Behavioral relations are also of great importance in defining the structure of an economic system and the manner in which changes originating in one sector are propagated into other economic sectors, both immediately and over time. Stabilization policy is concerned not only with the levels of economic variables at a given time, but also with the sequence and amplitudes of their fluctuations over successive periods.

A fundamental question in the construction of any econometric model is whether the set of economic relationships to be incorporated is of a recursive or an interdependent (simultaneous) type. The difference between these two types of models may be illustrated by the examples on the next page, where Y stands for national income, C consumption, and I investment, all variables being dated $(t-1, t, t+1$, etc.$)$.[12]

These two models are dynamic and explain, for any set of initial values, a development over time. The arrow diagrams show clearly the difference between the two systems. In the recursive case all arrows within a period are one-way-directed, indicating unilateral relations between variables. In the interdependent model C and Y are interrelated for any given t. Another way of distinguishing between the two systems is to determine whether it is possible, by proper rearrangement of the relationships in the

[12] These examples are based on Ragnar Bentzel and B. Hansen, "On Recursiveness and Interdependency in Economic Models," *Review of Economic Studies*, Vol. 22 (No. 3, 1954-1955), pp. 153-168.

Case 1. A recursive system:

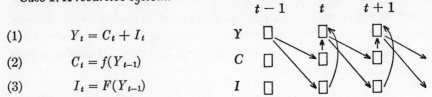

(1) $Y_t = C_t + I_t$

(2) $C_t = f(Y_{t-1})$

(3) $I_t = F(Y_{t-1})$

Case 2. An interdependent system:

(4) $Y_t = C_t + I_t$

(5) $C_t = f(Y_t)$

(6) $I_t = F(Y_{t-1})$

model, to obtain a triangular matrix of coefficients relating current values of the endogenous variables to one another, so that only zero elements appear above the main diagonal. (To isolate this matrix involving only current endogenous variables, we may assume that all terms involving exogenous and lagged endogenous variables have been placed on the other side of the equations from the endogenous variables.) If it proves possible to obtain a triangular matrix with zero coefficients above the main diagonal for the coefficients relating the current endogenous variables to one another, the system is recursive (or consecutive). If some nonzero elements appeared above the main diagonal, the system would be interdependent. It can easily be verified that the first model satisfies the triangularity condition, whereas the second one does not.[13]

Up to this point the distinction between recursiveness and interdependency has been stated with respect to exact models, free from any stochastic disturbances. If the equations of a model contain random variables, the estimation requires further specification of these variables. Different estimation procedures may be indicated depending on whether the system is recursive (least squares) or simultaneous (i.e., limited information maximum likelihood). In the construction of a stabilization model it is essential to concentrate both on the properties of the exact model, which, as will be seen, have important causality implications from the standpoint of economic theory and the theory of economic policy, and on the stochastic part, which has implications for the estimation procedure. The econometric specification of a stabilization model will, of course, have to be concerned with both aspects of this question.

[13] A detailed example of a recursive stabilization model, where the triangularity condition is explicitly shown, is given subsequently (Figure 3-3).

A discussion of estimation procedures is undertaken in the paper by Professor Sengupta. Thus, our analysis here concentrates on the specification of the exact part of a policy model as distinct from the stochastic or statistical part.

Basic vs. Derived Models

The debate between advocates of the mutual and simultaneous interdependency approach and the recursive (causal chain) approach is far from being settled. In many instances the choice of the model depends on what the model purports to explain and on the use to which it will be put. In the present context the model is to explain: first, the impact of uncontrolled exogenous forces (the u_k's in Figure 3-1 above) on the system (for example, what will be the impact of changes in income abroad on domestic exports, output, and employment); second, the impact on the system of those exogenous variables under the control of the policymaker—more specifically, the effect of changes in policy instruments, the z_i's, on the stabilization goal appearing in the welfare function, W, and reflected by such endogenous (target) variables as the level of employment, the price level, and the state of the balance of payments.

A strong case has been made in support of recursive models by a number of writers.[14] The arguments presented are of a general nature, not necessarily limited to policy models. It will be argued, however, that the justifications given for the use of recursive models in explaining economic phenomena seem particularly strong with respect to policy models.

There are two main arguments in favor of recursive models. First, models to be explanatory (as opposed to just descriptive) must be causal, which means that they must express something about the direction of influence between variables.[15] The (nonunit) coefficients in a recursive system have the property of "causal interpretability" in the sense that they

[14] See, for instance, Bentzel and Hansen, *op. cit.*; J. Tinbergen, *On the Theory of Economic Policy* (North-Holland, 1952), and *Economic Policy: Principles and Design* (North-Holland, 1956); R. H. Strotz and H. O. A. Wold, "Recursive versus Nonrecursive Systems: An Attempt at Synthesis," *Econometrica*, Vol. 28 (April 1960), pp. 412-427; H. O. A. Wold, "On the Definition of Causation and Related Concepts," (draft, multilith; Uppsala, 1957).

[15] Strotz and Wold, *op. cit.*, p. 418, define causality as "z is a cause of y if, by hypothesis, it is or 'would be' possible by *controlling* z indirectly to control y, at least stochastically. But it may or may not be possible by controlling y indirectly to control z. A causal relation is therefore in essence asymmetric, in that in any instance of its realization it is asymmetric." Notice also Wold, *op. cit.*, p. 17, "Perhaps what we mean here by 'cause' (independent variable) and effect (dependent variable) simply hinges upon which of the variables are open to active control, accessible to intervention." We shall come back later to this last aspect of causality.

describe the influence of both dependent (endogenous) and independent (exogenous) variables on the resultant endogenous variables. Second, we may conceive of a complete model incorporating explicitly all the actions of each and every individual economic agent—thus a model pushing the disaggregation process over subjects and goods to its ultimate micro-limit—and in which time is introduced so that periods are sufficiently short to correspond to the actions of the subjects; let us call this a "basic model." It has been convincingly argued that this type of model, which is very realistic (but unmanageable) is always recursive if it follows the *ex ante-ex post* approach of the Stockholm school.[16]

A derived model, in contrast to a basic model, is an aggregated and gross approximation of reality. The availability of data often determines the unit of time selected as well as the degree of aggregation, introducing essentially arbitrary elements into the econometric model. These elements themselves may be responsible for the interdependent nature of many derived models.

Two examples may suffice to clarify this last point. First, many time series are only available by quarters or, sometimes, even only on an annual basis. To the extent that the time lags between the plans and the actions of economic subjects and between the actions and their effects on other variables in the system do not correspond to the temporal breakdown of time series (in most cases because the former lags are of a shorter duration than the minimum time span between successive observations in a statistical time series), interdependency may appear in the derived model, simply as a consequence of data limitations. The longer the unit of time in the specified derived (dynamic) model, the more "simultaneous" relationships will be found which, in fact, were not simultaneously determined, as they took place at different points in time within the unit specified by the model. The same phenomenon often holds true for production lags (the speed of response of output to changes in demand) and also, in an even more general and relevant sense, to the various lags which a policy-maker may face; i.e., the lag in observing that an adjustment is necessary, another in deciding what adjustment to make (determining the values of the set of instruments z_j in Figure 3-1), and finally, the lag between changes in the instruments and their impact on the set of targets, the y_i's. It is only in rare instances that the

---

[16] See Bentzel and Hansen, *op. cit.*, pp. 159-160. It should be noted, however, that this last condition may not be necessary. General equilibrium models of the Walras type are static equilibrium systems, specifying the equilibrium conditions. These are derived models in which the interdependency between undated variables should not be interpreted as implying that these variables are determined simultaneously in time.

statistical inputs will coincide with the "true" lags discussed above.

A second example of interdependency in the derived model, when none existed in the basic model, follows from some types of aggregation procedures. If four variables are causally related (so that A causes B which in turn is the cause of C which causes D), grouping together, respectively, A and C in Variable I, and B and D in Variable II introduces interdependency between I and II where the original (basic) system was recursive.

The above examples illustrate the fact that interdependence can be caused by specification errors. As was pointed out by Strotz, the "postulated interdependent model is often only an approximation to a 'latent' recursive model which is thought to provide a better theoretical explanation of the facts."[17] (Still another way in which specification errors of the above type can be made is through substituting stock variables for flow variables.)

In a policy model it is highly desirable to introduce causality explicitly in the sense defined above (see footnote 15). The policy-maker is interested in influencing the target variables, y_i, by way of the policy instruments, z_j, subject to the noncontrollable factors, u_k. In a completely recursive model, where the relations between variables for any given time period are unilateral, it is possible to follow through in a stimulus-response fashion the impact on targets of changes in instruments. Such models are sometimes referred to as pure causal chain systems. In the 1930's, Tinbergen made a pioneer contribution to the specification and estimation of pure causal chain systems. He depicted the whole chain of unidirectional "cause" and "effect" relations in an equation system by means of an arrow diagram.[18]

Causal Ordering and the Operational Use of Stabilization Models

Simon has developed the concept of causal ordering in a purely axiomatic sense.[19] Even in a completely static system, it can be shown that, once the equations have been rearranged so that the coefficient matrix is triangular, different orders of causality can be defined in the sense that

[17] R. H. Strotz, "Interdependence as a Specification Error," *Econometrica*, Vol. 28 (April 1960), p. 428.

[18] Jan Tinbergen, *Statistical Testing of Business-Cycle Theories* (League of Nations, 1939), and "An Economic Policy for 1936" in L. H. Klaassen, L. M. Koyck, and H. J. Witteveen, eds., *Selected Papers* (North-Holland, 1959).

[19] H. A. Simon, "Causal Ordering and Identifiability," in W. C. Hood and T. C. Koopmans, eds., *Studies in Econometric Method* (Cowles Commission Monograph, No. 14; Wiley, 1953), pp. 49-74.

values of first-order endogenous variables can be computed exclusively as a function of the exogenous variables; values of second-order variables, in turn, can be computed as a function of first-order endogenous variables and the set of exogenous variables, and so on for higher causal orders. (Exogenous and predetermined variables are of causal order zero.)[20] A point of interest here is that causal ordering in its present sense is independent of time. In an operational use of the above concept, causal ordering can be interpreted as indicating the direction of influence among variables and defining the stimulus-response chains.

It should be apparent by now that models which are recursive in their exact parts are of great value from a policy standpoint, since they permit a complete unidirectional interpretation of the effects of changes in any given variable (endogenous or exogenous) on the whole system. The impacts of changes in the set of instrument variables can be followed through in a causal way and their effects on the targets, y_i, determined.

To illustrate the properties of recursiveness and interdependence in stabilization models at an operational level, we shall use the 1961 version of the Dutch Central Planning Bureau model of the Dutch economy. This model (which is discussed in more detail in a later section) includes thirty-six endogenous variables.[21] The equations of the model express

[20] It should be noted in this connection that the ordering scheme in Simon's article is in terms of subsets of equations. An equation expressing an endogenous variable exclusively in terms of an exogenous variable and a parameter is called a subset of zero-order in one example (Simon, *op. cit.*, p. 58), while in the next example (p. 59) exogenous variables themselves (expressed formally as functions of known parameters) are defined as zero-order subsets, and relationships giving endogenous variables as a function of only exogenous variables as first-order subsets. Tinbergen in his treatment of this question (*Economic Policy: Principles and Design*, pp. 121-122) adopts the former usage.

The convention adopted in this paper is the latter, namely, to treat the set of exogenous variables as zero-order subsets so that the first causal order is used for those endogenous variables which are determined exclusively by exogenous variables.

[21] The complete model is given in Netherlands Central Planning Bureau, *Central Economic Plan, 1961* (The Hague, August 1961), pp. 124-127. The 36 symbols representing endogenous variables are defined as follows:

Symbols with $\sim$ refer to absolute figures. Unless otherwise stated, symbols without $\sim$ represent changes. In the expenditure categories, incomes, etc., capital letters refer to values in current prices, lower-case letters to volume figures and prices.

a	number of persons employed in enterprises (man years)
L	wage bill of enterprises
Z	nonwage income
T_k	indirect taxes minus subsidies
m	imports of commodities
M	imports of commodities
c	total private consumption
C	total private consumption
P_c	consumption price

endogenous variables in terms of other endogenous variables, lagged endogenous variables, and exogenous variables. Two types of equations appear—the behavioral or reaction equations and the definition equations. The latter do not impose equilibrium conditions, but simply define a new set of endogenous variables.

The system as a whole is interdependent, though the coefficients determining this interdependence are only eight in number. These coefficients appear above the diagonal in Figure 3-3. (See footnote 21 for definition of symbols in Figure 3-3.)

There are two main reasons for the interdependence. First, capacity is explicitly introduced in the model through a generalized capacity-impact curve, $\tilde{w}_1$, which is expressed as a function of the percentage of unemployed, $\tilde{w}$. Second, a number of lagged endogenous variables have lags shorter than a calendar year. For instance, total private consumption, C,

---

P_x	prices of autonomous expenditure
X	autonomous expenditure (government expenditure, investment of government enterprises and residential construction)
i	gross investments of enterprises (excluding government enterprises and residential construction)
I	gross investments of enterprises (excluding government enterprises and residential construction)
P_i	investment price
N	stock formation (expressed as a percentage of total output less stock changes and net invisibles)
b	exports of commodities
B	exports of commodities
P_b	export price
v'	total output less stock changes and net invisibles
V'	total output less stock changes and net invisibles
$P_{v'}$	price of total output (less stock changes and net invisibles)
V	total output
$\tilde{w}$	registered unemployment as a percentage of dependent working population
L^B	disposable wage income
Z^B	disposable nonwage income
T_z''	variation in the incidence of direct taxes on nonwage income
v_a	total output less stock changes and net invisibles (reweighted with intensity of labor demand)
v_m	total output less stock changes and net invisibles (reweighted with import quota)
H	labor costs per unit of total output
$P_{m-v'}$	margin between import price adjusted for the incidence of indirect taxes and the price of total output (with a lag of half a year)
K	gross profits per unit of output
$\tilde{w}_1$	curvilinear indicator of available capacity
π_w Ψ_i Ψ_a Λ	lagged (endogenous) influences

The equations of the 1962 version of the CPB model are shown at the end of the paper by C. A. van den Beld in the present volume.

is expressed as a function of disposable wage income lagged four months, $L^B_{-1/3}$, and disposable nonwage income lagged eight months, $Z^B_{-2/3}$. Since the model is estimated exclusively on the basis of annual observations, the lagged endogenous variables with lags of less than a year are approximated on the basis of the (known) value of the variable in the previous year and the current (unknown) value. Thus, in the above example, $Z^B_{-2/3}$ is arrived at as follows:

$$Z^B_{-2/3} = \frac{2Z^B_{-1} + Z^B}{3}.$$

If time series were available on a quarterly or perhaps, monthly basis, all of these lagged endogenous variables would be truly predetermined instead of a combination of predetermined and current endogenous variables as is the case here. This appears to be a good illustration of one type of specification error discussed in the preceding part of the paper. It is responsible for a major part of the interdependence in the CPB model.

If the percentage unemployed were assumed to be predetermined and if the lagged endogenous variables with lags of less than a year were truly predetermined, the model would become wholly recursive. It can clearly be seen from Figure 3-3 that a triangular (recursive) coefficients matrix results if one abstracts from capacity considerations (i.e., by taking the percentage of unemployment as given) and if the endogenous variables with lags of less than a year were predetermined. All of the nonzero coefficients above the diagonal in Figure 3-3 fall in these two categories.

As an exercise, and on the basis of the triangular matrix only—which abstracts from changes in capacity and presumes the fractionally-lagged endogenous variables to be predetermined (i.e., the eight coefficients above the diagonal are assigned zero values)—the complete causal ordering of the endogenous variables was worked out and is shown in Figure 3-4.

As Figure 3-4 indicates, all endogenous variables can be expressed in terms of an arrow diagram containing ten causal orders (from the first to the tenth causal order). In order not to clutter the arrow diagram too much, only the relationships connecting one order to the next are shown explicitly, i.e., all causal relations between first-order and second-order variables (and generally between order n and order $n + 1$, where $n = 1$, 2, . . . 9). At the same time, the causal relations between sets of variables separated by more than one causal order are indicated in Figure 3-4 by listing under the "effect" variables those "cause" (variable(s)) which are more than one causal order removed. For instance, the volume of exports

FIGURE 3-4. *Causal Ordering Among Endogenous Variables (Dutch Central Planning Bureau Model 1961)*[a]

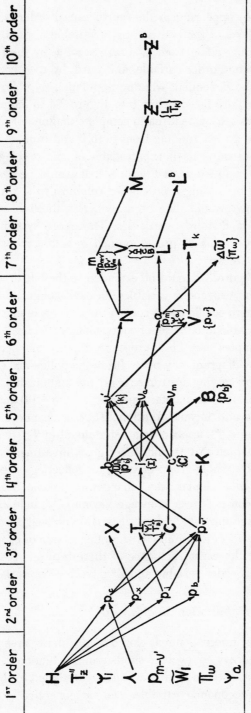

[a] The arrow-scheme was worked out on the assumption that the percentage of unemployment ($\tilde{w}_l$) was given and that lagged endogenous variables with lags of less than a year were predetermined. The Dutch CPB model is in fact interdependent because the above two assumptions are not met.

(denoted by b) appearing in the fourth causal order is influenced, first, by the price level of total output, p_v', a variable in the third causal order (hence the arrow going from p_v' to b); second, by the price level of exports, p_b, a second-order variable; and third, by the percentage of unemployment in the dependent working population, $\bar{w}_1$, a first-order variable. Both P_b and $\bar{w}_1$ are listed below b in Figure 3-4 to indicate that they influence b, (It is self-evident that a complete diagram of the causal scheme would include arrows running from p_b to b and from $\bar{w}_1$ to b).

The policy instruments, noncontrollable factors, and lagged endogenous variables are excluded from Figure 3-4. It would be a simple matter to include them by adding a 0-th order column at the extreme left of the diagram. Arrows would then be drawn from the 0-th order variables to the appropriate first-order variables. The entire system would then be "activated" by means of predetermined or autonomous changes in the 0-th order variables.

Similarly, Figure 3-3 could be extended to the left to include a column for each of the exogenous variables. In each column there would be at least one nonzero coefficient to convey the impacts of changes in the given exogenous variable into the set of endogenous variables.

A few examples may be appropriate, in this connection, to illustrate how the arrow diagram may be useful to the policy-maker in determining the impacts of varying instruments on the stabilization targets. Among the more typical instruments appearing in the CPB model are various types of taxes and income transfers. Thus, a change in direct taxes on nonwage income, $\bar{T}_z$, appears as a determinant of T_z'' (equation 33 of the CPB model) which in turn influences gross investment of enterprises, I, and through I a whole group of variables reflecting output, employment, and income. In a similar way, changes in income transfers associated with wage income, O_L', or nonwage income, O_z', influence, respectively, disposable wage income, L^B, and disposable nonwage income, Z^B. In this last case arrows would go directly from the column of exogenous variables to L^b and Z^b; the causal influence of these transfers is very direct since L^B is an eighth-order variable and Z^B a tenth-order variable.

Closed Loop Stabilization Models

A number of interdependent closed loop systems have been devised by economic theorists to explain short-term fluctuations in the economy. Although most of these models are mainly designed to show how fluctuations in macroeconomic variables can be generated, some at least are

FIGURE 3-5. *Phillips' Closed Loop Stabilization Model*[a]

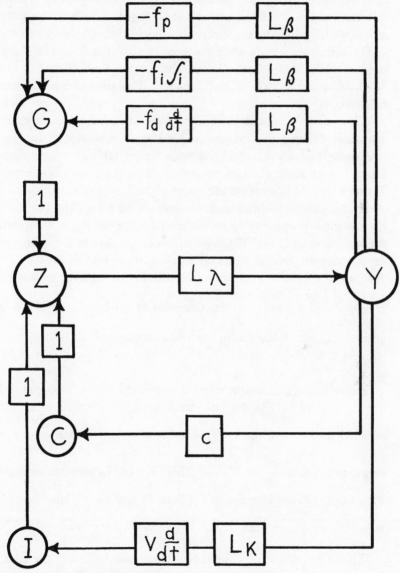

[a] For definitions of symbols, see text.

focused on stabilization policy as such. Probably the best example among the latter group is the model formulated by Phillips.[22]

The model is developed for a closed economy. It consists essentially of a multiplier-accelerator interaction combined with three types of stabilization policies with adjustment lags. Figure 3-5 illustrates the model schematically, showing the various feedbacks through the closed system.[23]

The economic variables are enclosed in circles and include Y (national income, national product), C (consumption), I (investment), Z (unregulated demand), and G (official demand). The arrows show directions of influence.

The symbols enclosed in square boxes are coefficients, lags, or other operators defining the manner and extent of influence of the variables from which an arrow originates upon the variable to which that arrow leads. For example, the two coefficients 1 on the arrows connecting C to Z and I to Z indicate that the effect of each of the variables (C and I) upon Z is simply additive and involves no time lag. The coefficient c is the marginal propensity to consume and L_λ is the lag in the production process between Z and Y. Given an initial increase in Y of one unit, successive circuits around the loop running from Y to C to Z to Y would generate the familiar consumption multiplier as a power series: $k = c + c^2 + c^3 + \ldots + c^n = \dfrac{1}{1-k}$. Specification of the lag L_λ implies a "period analysis" in which the multiplier effect would amount to $c + c^2$ after an elapsed time of $2L_\lambda$, and $c + c^2 + c^3$ after an elapsed time of $3L_\lambda$ and so on.

Similarly, the accelerator effect is expressed by the loop running from Y to I to Z to Y. The marginal response of investment to a change in national income is given by V; if Y increases at the rate $\dfrac{dY}{dt}$, I will increase at the rate $\dfrac{dI}{dt} = V \dfrac{dY}{dt}$. There is a lag L_k between an increase in Y and the induced increase in I. (Both L_k and L_λ are single exponential lags with time constantly equal, respectively, to $\dfrac{1}{k}$ and $\dfrac{1}{\lambda}$).

The system defined by these two loops and including the four variables Y, C, I, and Z, may or may not be stable. This system may be

[22] A. W. Phillips, "Stabilization Policy in a Closed Economy," *Economic Journal*, Vol. 64 (June 1954), pp. 290-323.
[23] This diagram is borrowed from R. G. D. Allen, *Mathematical Economics* (St. Martin's Press, 1957), p. 309. Allen's representation of Phillips' model was used—rather than Phillips' own diagram—because of its simplicity.

written as a set of four equations (constant terms could be added to one or more of the equations without affecting our interpretation of Figure 3-5):

(1) $$Y = Z_{-\lambda}$$

(2) $$C = cY$$

(3) $$I = I_{-k} + \left(V \frac{dY}{dt} \right)_{-k}$$

(4) $$Z = C + I$$

The point of Phillips' model consists in the addition of "official demand" (G, presumably an autonomous component of government expenditures) as a stabilization device to help offset undesired oscillations in the original four-variable system. The object of stabilization policy is to correct a discrepancy between actual and desired production.

Three types of stabilization policies are distinguished by Phillips: proportional, integral, and derivative. These terms refer to the ways in which the discrepancy between actual and desired production (the error in production) can be corrected. More specifically, the amount by which aggregate demand would be changed as a direct result of the stabilization policy if the latter operated without time lag is defined by Phillips as the potential policy demand; the amount by which demand is actually changed at any time as a result of the policy is called the actual policy demand.

Proportional stabilization policy makes the corrective action proportional and of opposite sign to the production error itself. Integral stabilization makes the corrective measure proportional and of opposite sign to the cumulated production error over time, and derivative stabilization makes the correction proportional and of opposite sign to the rate of change of production. The three upper loops in Figure 3-5 illustrate the three types of stabilization policies, where it is assumed that the observation, decision-making, and adjustment lag (L_β) is the same for all three policies.

Depending on the magnitude of the coefficients and the length of the lags specified in the model, various types of fluctuations can be generated by the unregulated part of the system. Official demand, G, is varied according to some combination of the three types of stabilization policies, (1) to attain the desired production level in the shortest possible period and (2) to minimize the dynamic fluctuations around the target level in the process of attaining this desired level. The optimum stabilization policy will be that combination which minimizes some function of both (1) and (2).

Some additional features of Phillips' model deserve comment. First, if all time lags are eliminated, the model becomes completely interdependent and static. When lags are incorporated, the system does not have to be interdependent. Second, the closed loop system provides a suggestive framework within which the impact of built-in stabilizers can be traced. Once automatic stabilizers have been built into the economic system, their dynamic operation can be incorporated in the model through a permanent feedback process, which in this sense will be analogous to the accelerator or multiplier loops. One suggestion for further research would be to determine the extent to which automatic policy buffers can be substituted for discrete quantitative changes in the set of instruments in operational stabilization models.

Third, it is clear that only certain combinations of stabilization targets are attainable at any point in time. To the extent that given sets of targets (i.e., 97 percent of labor force employed, less than a 1 percent increase in the price level, zero balance of payments deficit) are mutually incompatible with the specified model, the policy-maker is faced with the task of selecting from among the sets of attainable values of the stabilization targets the one which will maximize the welfare function, W.

A final observation about closed loop models is that *ex ante* time lags between endogenous variables—as well as policy adjustment lags reflecting the time necessary to observe that a change in policy is desirable, decide on the change, and have the impact of the change be felt on the targets—are, in general, not explicitly incorporated in present operational stabilization models. It would appear highly desirable to explore the degree to which these *ex ante* lags could be made an integral part of models of the Dutch Central Planning Bureau type.

WELFARE CONSEQUENCES OF ERRORS IN DATA AND IMPERFECTIONS IN DATA ADJUSTMENTS

The more important features of this topic as they affect economic policy models have been extensively treated by Professor Theil.[24] A few brief comments seem called for, however, in some cases with particular reference to the United States.

[24] H. Theil, *Economic Forecasts and Policy* (2d rev. ed.; North-Holland, 1961).

Components of Observed Variation in a Single Variable

Errors of concept or coverage in a statistical series can be a major source of inaccuracy in the estimation and use of economic policy models. Until recently, our economic data network in the United States was not designed for tasks as heavy and demanding as the estimation of an economic policy model of 100 to 300 equations. Our series on ownership of real property and value of capital stocks—and indirectly, our estimates of capacity output in different industries—are very weak.

Some commodity flows are relatively well estimated in years when a census of manufactures is taken, but thereafter some very sketchy current data may be used to "move" the census base. Thus, from 1948 to 1957 the U. S. Department of Commerce estimates of consumer expenditures for food drifted upward by nearly $10 billion (about 15 percent) relative to the level implied in Department of Agriculture estimates of quantity of food consumed and Bureau of Labor Statistics estimates of retail food prices. Subsequently, the Department of Commerce adjusted its series downward to the level indicated by the USDA series. The major cause of the upward "drift" was said to be the rapidly widening line of nonfood products sold by supermarkets; the 1947 or 1948 census-based figure on food sales was apparently sound, but the current data from then until 1957 were based on *total* sales of a sample of food supermarkets rather than on sales of food products only.

Errors of measurement, errors of concept, and other systematic biases have been extremely troublesome in the past. Presumably the error of several billion dollars in estimating consumer expenditures for food led to an opposite error of the same order of magnitude in some other category or categories of consumer expenditures.

Some economic time series are estimated on the basis of probability samples—for example, the United States series on labor force, employment, and unemployment. Probability samples are not a panacea and are not always the best devices for estimating change. Under favorable administrative and institutional circumstances, a complete count may be more accurate than a probability sample.

Our best method for estimating changes in the population of the United States is to take an adjusted base figure for a census year, add births and gross in-migration, and subtract deaths and gross out-migration. The statistics on all components of population change are relatively complete and accurate. A probability sample to estimate the total population of the United States at monthly intervals would very likely show a decline of 200,000 or 300,000 people on occasion from one month to the next. Yet everyone knows that the actual population does not change in this fashion; the decrease would be a property of the sample and not of the population itself.

More or less random errors of measurement in an economic time series may be thought of as statistical noise. In addition, an economic time series may contain disturbances or "economic noise." A series on total employment, for example, may change from one month to the next because of a strike in the lumber industry or the cessation of a strike in a large automobile manufacturing concern. These short-term changes in total employment may run counter to the basic trend of demand for labor in the economy at that time. It may be necessary to cumulate changes in employment over a period of three or four months before the desired *information* emerges clearly above this kind of economic noise to indicate that the demand for labor is definitely on a cyclical upswing.

Many of our economic time series are seasonally adjusted. In cases where the seasonal swings in the raw data are quite large, seasonal adjustments are no doubt helpful. However, seasonal adjustment factors are based on averages of a limited number of observations and are subject to errors analogous to the standard error of the mean or median. Thus, seasonal adjustment does not eliminate errors; it redistributes them over time.

Effects of Errors in Several or Many Variables

In terms of Figure 3-1, the sources of error in predicting values of the endogenous variables include: errors of forecast in future values of the noncontrollable (data) variables; *ex post* errors of measurement in the noncontrollable variables; errors in the coefficients connecting the noncontrollable variables to the target variables; errors in the coefficients connecting the instrument variables to the target variables; and *ex post* errors of measurement in the target variables.

The cumulative effect of errors in a multi-equation policy model might at least be visualized as follows:

Chart the historical values of each variable which we invest with welfare connotations—that is, each variable which appears in the relevant welfare or objective function, *W;*

over the planning horizon specified by the policy-maker, draw a preferred time path for each variable with lines above and below it at a distance equal to the estimated standard error of measurement in the target variable *ex post;* and

draw a wider zone about the preferred time path for each such variable representing the combined effect of *ex post* errors of measurement in the noncontrollable variables, errors in the coefficients connecting noncontrollable variables with the variable appearing in the welfare function, and *ex post* errors of measurement in the latter variable.

Logically, a policy-maker using an econometric model could not hope to predict future values of the target variables with greater precision than is suggested by the wider zone. The zone is widened still further if we consider that errors in the coefficients relating instruments to target variables also give rise to uncertainty concerning the future values of the target variables which will emerge as the policy-maker attempts to steer the economy.

In appraising the success of the policy-maker as steersman, we might apply weights to deviations of each target variable from the preferred time path. The weight function would not necessarily be linear; for example, if unemployment rose 2 percent above the preferred time path, the weight assigned to this deviation might be four times as large as that assigned to a deviation of 1 percent. Errors in most price and quantity variables could be translated approximately into billions of dollars (or fractions of a billion dollars) of the resulting error in GNP.

A first-rate steersman might be able to keep each target variable within the widest of the error zones indicated about two thirds of the time. In estimating the total loss of welfare from imperfect steersmanship, percentage deviations from the preferred time path of each variable would be given specific weights, and given percentage deviations in the more important target variables would result in greater losses of welfare than would similar percentage deviations in less important variables.

The joint *(a priori)* probability distribution of all noncontrollable variables in the model would summarize the threat to economic welfare inherent in the noncontrollable factors. It should be possible to estimate the prospective variance of the actual (vector) path of the economy about the preferred (vector) path over a specified time horizon on the assumption that the present settings of instrument variables are not changed.

Then it would be important to determine the sufficiency and efficiency of the instruments available to the policy-maker for correcting possible aberrations and reducing the total welfare loss below a specified level. We might also find that legal limitations on interest rates, debt ceilings, and other factors would limit the usefulness of an instrument and inhibit or prevent the policy-maker from steering the economy back onto a preferred time path if it deviated in a specified direction.

If the effects of all errors in variables and coefficients in the model were converted into equivalent billions of dollars of GNP, we would have a common denominator for appraising the expected welfare gain from reducing any specific source of error.

If certain instruments available to the policy-maker were powerful and flexible, and acted quickly upon the most important targets, the ultimate limiting factors might be measurement errors in the target variables themselves.

SPECIFICATION AND ESTIMATION OF
OPERATIONAL POLICY MODELS

The number of operational models developed so far for macroeconomic stabilization purposes is still quite small. Any attempt at discussing some of the specification and estimation characteristics of these models is therefore almost bound to be based on an extremely limited sample.

The Klein-Goldberger Model of the United States (1955)

Fashions in statistical estimation have changed considerably since 1955, and leading econometricians no longer regard the limited-information, maximum-likelihood method as a panacea. Theil, Basmann, Nagar, and Zellner have explored the properties of two-stage and three-stage least-squares and other k-class estimators. The reasoned skepticism of Wold, Stone, and others has had its effect, and Klein and Nakamura have demonstrated that the limited-information method is more vulnerable than competing methods are to the effects of multicollinearity. However, Table 3-1 is still suggestive as to the relative importance of improvements in economic knowledge and differences in statistical techniques.

Until recently, the best-known published model of the United States

TABLE 3-1. *Klein-Goldberger Model: Comparison of Differences Between (1) Limited-Information Coefficients, 1929-50 and 1929-52, and (2) Limited-Information and Least-Squares Coefficients, Both 1929-52.*[a]

Ratio of differences to standard error of 1929–52 limited-information coefficients[b]	Number of differences between limited-information coefficients, 1929–50 and 1929–52	Number of differences between limited-information and least-squares coefficients, 1929–52
A. *Constant terms:*		
0 −0.49.............	4	7
0.50–0.99.............	4	5
1.00–1.49.............	3	2
1.50–1.99.............	1	1
2.00–2.99.............	0	0
3.00 and over.........	2	0
Total..............	14[b]	15
Average ratio[c]........	1.28	0.57
B. *Net regression coefficients:*		
0 −0.49.............	13	14
0.50–0.99.............	5	6
1.00–1.49.............	5	8
1.50–1.99.............	6	2
2.00–2.99.............	3	4
3.00 and over.........	2	2
Total..............	34[d]	36
Average ratio[c]........	1.13	0.96

[a] From Karl A. Fox, "Econometric Models of the United States," *Journal of Political Economy*, Vol. 64 (April 1956), pp. 128–142; the table is from p. 131.

[b] Equation (11) is omitted from the 1929–50 model on pp. 52–53 (Klein-Goldberger).

[c] Without regard to sign.

[d] The limited-information model for 1929–52 includes 36 net regression coefficients. The 1929–50 model contained 1 less variable in equation (5), and equation (11), containing a single predetermined variable, was omitted entirely; hence the 1929–50 model included only 34 net regression coefficients.

economy was that of Klein and Goldberger (1955).[25] It consisted of fifteen statistically estimated equations and five identities, making a total of twenty equations and twenty endogenous variables.

Klein and Goldberger first fitted their model to annual observations from 1929 through 1950 (omitting the war years 1942-45); subsequently they fitted it to the same observations plus those for the years 1951 and 1952. As a check upon the importance of the statistical methods used, the senior author of this present paper also had each of the fifteen equations (other than identities) fitted to the 1929-52 data by the method of least squares.

Table 3-1 compares the effects upon the model of differences in time periods and of differences in methods of estimation. Differences among the three sets of coefficients are expressed in multiples of the standard errors of the respective 1929-52 limited-information coefficients. If the 1929-50 and 1929-52 limited-information models were based on independent samples from the same universe, we should expect about two thirds of the differences to be less than 1.4 standard errors.[26] Actually, about four fifths of the differences between constant terms and two thirds of those between net regression coefficients fall within this range.

Differences between the least-squares and limited-information coefficients for the same time period (1929-52) are even smaller; all but one of those for constant terms and three fourths of those for net regression coefficients are less than 1.4 standard errors. The average differences between the 1929-52 coefficients derived by alternative methods are also smaller than those between the limited-information coefficients for alternative time periods.

It appears that Klein and Goldberger gained little or nothing of economic importance by using the limited-information method rather than least-squares. The similarity between the results of the two methods also extended to measures of autocorrelation. Seven of the limited-information equations for 1929-52 showed significant autocorrelation; the least-squares versions of six of these seven also showed significant autocorrelation.

---

[25] L. R. Klein and A. S. Goldberger, *An Econometric Model of the United States, 1929-1952* (North-Holland, 1955).

[26] A narrower range should be applicable here, as the two models differ only by the addition of two observations (plus changes in the specifications of two equations). There is no theoretical merit in contrasting differences between time periods and differences between methods; the comparison was stimulated by the authors' comment that differences between the 1929-50 and 1929-52 limited-information coefficients "are not large and can be accounted for by the presence of sampling error" (Klein and Goldberger, *op. cit.*, p. 93).

The Dutch Central Planning Bureau Model (1961)

Typically, the existing stabilization models have a time horizon of one year or less. The endogenous variables are usually expressed in terms of deviations from the initial values (first differences) or in elasticity equivalents (ratio of first differences to initial values).

Two general types of relationships appear: reaction equations and definition equations. In the 1961 model of The Netherlands Central Planning Bureau, for example, the former are subdivided into clusters determining, respectively, expenditure categories (such as aggregate consumption and investment); demand for factors of production and capacity; and prices.[27] The definition equations are subdivided into relations between value and volume variables; expenditure totals; costs and margins; unemployment; incomes; taxes; and finally, lagged influences. The exogenous variables consist essentially of three types: lagged endogenous variables, with lags varying between four months and two years; data outside of the control of the policy-maker (i.e., prices of imports) which have to be predicted; and instrument variables over which the policy-maker has some degree of control, such as income transfers and tax rates. The model contains thirty-six endogenous variables and thirty-six equations. Most of the parameters were estimated by the two-stage least-squares method.

In our Figure 3-3, above, the coefficients matrix of the endogenous variables was worked out for the CPB model. The causal ordering among endogenous variables, shown explicitly in Figure 3-4, is useful in illustrating the impact of changes in instrument variables or other exogenous variables on the stabilization targets. The Dutch CPB models are discussed by C. A. van den Beld later in this volume, so we do not examine them in detail here. Nevertheless, a few important features about the specification and estimation of the 1961 model will be brought out because of their relevance for and potential applicability to stabilization models in general.

First, the base periods for the estimates of the 1961 model covered the years 1923-38 and 1949-57. Since years of high economic activity were more frequent and the quality of the statistical data substantially better in the postwar period, observations for that period were counted twice as heavily as for the prewar years in calculating the coefficients. The theory of this procedure is that the use of periods characterized

[27] See footnote 21, above, and Figure 3-3.

by very different levels of economic activity in estimating the parameters increases the range of situations with which the model can cope. Moreover, weighting observations according to the quality of the underlying statistical time series inputs will, in principle, improve the estimates of the structural parameters.

Second, it is relatively simple in stabilization models to incorporate additional information both in estimating single equations and in specifying the overall model. The estimates can be revised at regular (often annual) intervals in the light of new data. Likewise, the specification of the equations in the system undergoes changes to improve the explanatory properties of the system.

The CPB model was first published for general distribution in 1955. At that time it contained twenty-seven endogenous variables expressed as first differences. It was completely static: no lags appeared anywhere in the system and it was linear throughout. Most of the structural coefficients had been fixed a priori. In the revised (1961) version, the number of endogenous variables (and equations) was increased to thirty-six.

A very significant change was the introduction of lagged endogenous and lagged exogenous variables. For instance, current aggregate consumption was expressed as a function of disposable wage income four months earlier and of disposable nonwage income eight months earlier. Furthermore, monetary variables were incorporated and allowances made for the effects of changes in capacity—on key endogenous variables such as investment and exports—through the introduction of a curvilinear capacity equation.[28]

Relationship Between Stabilization and Development (Growth) Planning Models

It appears instructive to examine at this point the main differences between long- or medium-range growth (development-planning) and stabilization models. The former are only concerned with trends and the specification of the future macroeconomic equilibrium conditions, usually in terms of balance between the availability of and the requirements for resources. Most long-term models assume complementarity in the production function (the possibility of limited substitutability is sometimes introduced). If these models are to be used for policy—as

---

[28] See P. J. Verdoorn and J. J. Post, "Capacity and the Short-Term Multipliers" (paper presented to the 25th European meeting of the Econometric Society, Copenhagen, July 1963).

opposed to pure forecasting—purposes, quantitative recommendations with respect to the policy instruments will depend in large measure on the length of the planning horizon. Substantial differences in the values of instruments will result as the time horizon is varied. This comes out clearly, for instance, when national income is maximized as a function of the proportion of total investment to be devoted to investment goods in a simple Mahalanobis model.[29] It turns out that this proportion will vary substantially depending on the time horizon, i.e., whether national income is to be maximized five, ten, or fifteen years hence.

In addition, uncertainty is compounded as the time horizon is moved farther into the future. More specifically, the assumptions concerning the exogenous conditions as well as the invariances in the structural equations are more likely to be invalidated as the planning horizon increases; therefore the sensitivity of the optimum economic policy to structural and exogenous changes is likely to be a positive function of time.

On the other hand, stabilization models operate typically with short-time horizons. The impact of fluctuations in variables is introduced through lags and the impact of monetary factors can be included. Changes in the external conditions can be incorporated in the model by plugging in new values (i.e., forecasts) of the exogenous variables. The model can be almost continuously readapted to changing external stimuli. The welfare losses resulting from imperfectly specified models, as well as the previously discussed losses from the use of out-dated parameters, can be approximated quantitatively and rules formulated about the optimum timing of new estimates, the best use of additional information, and a revision (or a new specification) of the model.

The introduction of a capacity equation in the Dutch CPB model provides the system with an element of built-in flexibility, since the responses of key endogenous variables, such as aggregate investment and exports, will be greatly influenced by the level of capacity at which the economy operates. Capacity is measured in terms of the percentage of workers unemployed, $\bar{w}$, on the basis that labor, and not capital, is the limiting factor. (Capital goods and raw material shortages can be re-

[29] This model (developed by P. C. Mahalanobis) considers a closed economy and distinguishes two sectors—sector 1 producing investment goods and sector 2 producing consumption goods. The increase in national income, defined as the sum of (1) investment goods and (2) consumption goods produced, is dependent on the allocation of total investment goods output between sector 1 and sector 2. See Mahalanobis, "Some Observations on the Process of Growth of National Income," *Sankhya*, Vol. 12 (1953) p. 307; and "The Approach of Operational Research to Planning in India" *ibid.*, Vol. 16 (1955), p. 3.

moved in The Netherlands through additional imports.) A generalized capacity-impact-curve, $\tilde{w}_1$, which is highly curvilinear is postulated as a function of the percentage of unemployed.[30] Regression coefficients are next computed for a number of endogenous variables (i.e., exports, price level of exports, investment, imports) as a function of the impact curve, Since $\tilde{w}_1$ is a function of $\tilde{w}$ of the form $\tilde{w}_1 = ln\ (\tilde{w} + \eta) - \alpha\tilde{w}$, where η and α are parameters and ln stands for natural logarithm, it follows that different levels of unemployment will affect $\tilde{w}_1$ in a nonlinear way, the impact of which in turn will be transmitted to a number of endogenous variables through the regression coefficients linking $\tilde{w}_1$ or $\Delta\tilde{w}_1$ to them. The annual changes in $\tilde{w}$ and $\tilde{w}_1$, namely $\Delta\tilde{w}$ and $\Delta\tilde{w}_1$, are both treated as endogenous variables. It should be noted that the inclusion of the capacity-impact-curve introduces some difficulties in the solution of the model. A linearized form giving $\tilde{w}_1$ as a function of $\tilde{w}_{-1}$ (last year's percentage of unemployed) can be used.

Where the changes in $\Delta\tilde{w}$ are small or where only one value of $\tilde{w}_{-1}$ is used, as in the preparation of annual plans, simple adjustments can be worked out. Alternatively, when considering different initial levels of employment or larger changes in $\Delta\tilde{w}$, the coefficients of the inverse and the reduced form will be altered. Methods have been worked out to cope with this situation by deleting $\Delta\tilde{w}_1$ from the class of endogenous variables and including it among the predetermined variables.[31]

In a sense, the explicit introduction of capacity provides a bridge between the long-term planning and the stabilization models. In the former, the growth of output is usually made a function of such invariances as the elasticity of capital stock with regard to GNP and the supply elasticity of labor. As pointed out previously, complementarity among resources is customarily assumed. The long-term growth path becomes a balanced full-employment type path. Similarly, stabilization models which do not allow for capacity changes do not permit one to follow through the differential impact of relative input shortages or ceilings on investment and other endogenous variables. On the other hand, where capacity is explicitly included as a variable it implies the possibility of examining the impact of different ratios of inputs on the system. An increase in the percentage of unemployed, $\tilde{\omega}$, in the above model, *ceteris paribus*, amounts to a decline in the labor/capital ratio.

It might be noted in this connection that the selection of labor as the

[30] For a technical discussion of this concept see Verdoorn and Post, *op. cit.*, and CPB (1961), *op. cit.*

[31] See Verdoorn and Post, *op. cit.*, pp. 17-18.

limiting factor is strictly based on the special circumstances prevailing in The Netherlands. In many lesser-developed countries the limiting factors—in both the short and long run—tend to be capital and the availability of foreign exchange to purchase development goods and necessary inputs. (One interesting sideline is that the supply of labor could be very elastic in the long run, but a limiting factor in the short run, requiring substantially different supply elasticities in the development-planning model than in the stabilization model.) In contrast, in countries where the population density is low (Australia, Canada) a labor scarcity could be overcome—at least partially—through a proper immigration policy.

By estimating the parameters of the stabilization model on the basis of observations spanning a relatively long period of time that embraces periods of low-level and high-level economic activity, the range of situations which can be covered by the model is increased. For instance, a stabilization model estimated on the basis of time series covering both the 1930's and the 1950's, and in which an index of capacity is included either endogenously or exogenously, will provide a framework within which the impact on the system of substantial changes in capacity can be measured. It is mainly in this sense that the incorporation of a capacity relationship provides an important link between stabilization and long-term planning models.

The Brookings-SSRC Model of the United States

The most elaborate operational policy model with a short-run stabilization focus is the Brookings-SSRC econometric model of the United States. Its initial development was sponsored by the Social Science Research Council during 1961-63 under a grant from the National Science Foundation. Beginning in September 1963, responsibility for completing the model and for testing and improving it over a period of years was transferred to the Brookings Institution.

Only a few of the model's features will be mentioned here, since a major volume on it is being published in 1965.[32] The model is based on quarterly data and is larger than other models so far developed. In its initial form, it will include more than 200 equations; an expanded version, in terms of 32 producing sectors rather than the 7 sectors provided for in the basic model, will involve 300 to 400 equations.

The large size of even the basic model is the outcome of a deliberate

[32] See footnote to Figure 3-6.

FIGURE 3-6. *Flow Diagram of Brookings-SSRC Econometric Model*[a]

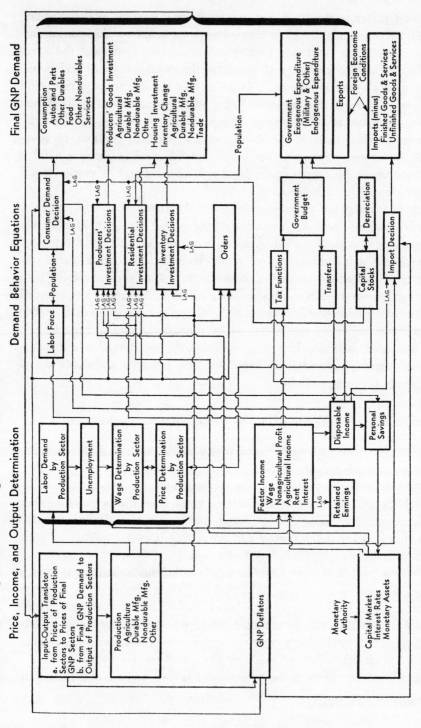

[a] This is a preliminary diagram prepared in 1963. A revised version appears in J. S. Duesenberry, G. Fromm, L. R. Klein, and E. Kuh, eds., *The Brookings-SSRC Quarterly Econometric Model of the United States*, to be published by Rand McNally (Chicago) and North-Holland (Amsterdam) in early 1965.

research strategy. Previous models of the United States economy had been carried out by one or two principal investigators. Treatment of individual sectors of the economy was highly aggregative. Much empirical knowledge and many sources of data available to experts in particular sectors were overlooked.

During 1961-63, the SSRC group sought to overcome these limitations by dividing the exploratory and developmental work on the model among approximately twenty economists. Each major block of equations in the model was made the responsibility of an economist with special knowledge and previous research experience in that area. The various tasks or sectors included the following: (1) consumption; (2) inventories; (3) residential construction; (4) business investment realization; (5) business investment anticipation; (6) foreign trade; (7) production and final demand; (8) price conversion; (9) price mark-up; (10) wage rates; (11) production and hours; (12) dividends and other factor shares; (13) labor force; (14) interest and money; (15) agricultural submodel; and (16) government. Functional tasks cutting across sectors included consistent statistical estimation of all equations and simulation tests of various subsystems and of the model as a whole. The work of the sector specialists was coordinated by means of a three-week workshop in August 1961 and a two-week workshop in August 1962. In addition to facilitating standardization on technical points, the workshop discussions generated a number of insights which could scarcely have emerged from a one- or two-man project.

Figure 3-6 presents a simplified, preliminary flow diagram of the model as it was conceived in 1963. Further changes and improvements will be reflected in the published version of the model which will appear in 1965. Figure 3-6 includes the various components of final GNP demand and behavior equations—reflecting the purchasing decisions of consumers, the investment decisions of producers, and the investment decisions of home-builders. These decisions express themselves as purchases by consumers and as new orders by business firms. The demands for finished goods are transmitted by means of an input-output "translator" into the producing sectors of the economy. The producing sectors respond to changes in the demands for their outputs by changing their levels of employment and capacity utilization, which in turn lead to changes in the levels and distribution of payments to labor and other factors of production. Tax functions and transfer payments further influence the disposable personal income available for consumption expenditures and the after-tax profits available to business firms. These income streams, of course, influence the final demand decisions of consumers and firms in the next time period. The impacts of changes in production upon income payments, changes in income payments upon expenditures, and changes in expenditures upon production constitute the core of this model, as well as of other econometric models.

Further study of the flow diagram will disclose other features. Each arrow, in general, represents several equations. Many of the relationships in the model operate with time lags.

The use of quarterly data should throw more light than annual data do on the mechanisms of inventory cycles and of monetary and fiscal policy. Several sectors of the economy, including agriculture, foreign trade, housing, money and finance, government, and the labor force are treated in greater detail than in previous econometric models. This permits a definition of policy instruments that is clearer and more operational than in previous models of the United States. For example, the equations for the government sector use tax *rates* rather than the amount of tax receipts as the true policy variables; they show that some government expenditures (e.g., transfer payments) are endogenously determined; and they clearly separate federal expenditures from those of state and local governments.

An interesting by-product of the workshop discussions in 1961 and 1962 was the participants' greatly increased awareness of the logical and operational differences between a policy model and a forecasting model. The previous emphasis of most of the individual participants had been either upon forecasting or upon analyzing the effects of policies in particular sectors of the economy. Only gradually did a consensus develop that the model as a whole should be, to the fullest extent possible, structural and policy-oriented. By the end of the 1962 workshop there appeared to be general agreement that appropriate equations in the model should express the mechanisms by which specific policy instruments did in fact influence other variables, including those which were the targets of stipulated policies. The model should, of course, forecast adequately, but this was by no means its sole or even its primary objective.

The Brookings Institution research program during 1964-66 will include a good many applications of the model to simulating the probable economic effects of alternative policy measures. The simulation experiments would elucidate what the model implies as to the consequences of (1) various combinations of initial conditions, (2) specified sequences of policy actions or specified decision rules for manipulating policy instruments, and (3) specified sequences of values of the data or noncontrollable variables. Simulation tests of this type offer almost endless opportunities for exploring the compatibility and joint effectiveness of combinations of economic policies; over the coming decade, they should greatly improve the level of understanding of both academic economists and public officials concerning short-run economic policies.

The Brookings-SSRC model is so designed that it is susceptible of further disaggregation by sectors of the economy and/or by regions and local areas. It has also raised many interesting problems of statistical estimation. For example, the principles of causal ordering and recursiveness that have been mentioned in this paper (and that are mentioned in Professor Sengupta's paper to follow) as applying to individual equations were applied to "blocks" or sets of equations in designing consistent estimation techniques for the equations of the Brookings-SSRC model.

Each of the participating economists in his exploratory work used ordinary least-squares estimates for virtually all of his equations. All variables which were determined outside of a particular sector were taken as exogenous or predetermined in the exploratory work on that sector, even though they might prove to be endogenous from the standpoint of the model as a whole. The later versions of the basic model will eliminate inconsistencies of this kind. It appears that two-stage least-squares and/or limited-information methods will be used to make consistent estimates of the individual equations within each of the major blocks.

CONCLUDING REMARKS

In 1955, toward the end of a year of service on the staff of the Council of Economic Advisers, the senior author wrote a critique of the Klein-Goldberger econometric model of the United States and suggested the development of less aggregative, partly synthetic models, which could take advantage of the detailed knowledge of sector specialists:

. . . Presumably, the model for each sector could be developed in such a way as to leave "handles" or points of entry for each type of policy intervention that might be regarded as worthy of appraisal. The major channels of communication between sectors would also be represented. The logical outcome of this approach would be a model which would permit the advance appraisal of any set of economic policies and programs in relation to any initial positions and trends of the various sectors of the economy. Technical coefficients, which are the mainstay of the interindustry model, would also appear in the model conceived here, but would represent only one of several channels of economic interaction. It would be foolish to attempt to derive this model by a process of simultaneous statistical estimation; it would, of course, be desirable to use as homogeneous a body of statistics as possible for establishing the various restrictions and intersector coefficients.

If we think in terms of the coordination of economic policies and the appraisal of economic developments by the federal establishment as a whole, it is obviously desirable to use the detailed knowledge and skills of specialists on particular economic sectors.

. . . In doing this, we cannot afford to be tied down to a single type of statistical estimation or confined to time series observations drawn from a single limited period. We should not be afraid of the statistical implications of a partly synthetic model if we know the reliability of its basic components. The latter will continue to be useful for intrasector analysis. . . . The major new achievement would lie in the synthesis of these basic components into a model adequately reflecting the interactions between sectors.[33]

These suggestions were "far out" and nonoperational under conditions existing in the federal establishment at that time; besides, exhortation was much cheaper than implementation. That the suggestions seem very moderate today is a tribute to the success with which participants in this conference—and their colleagues—have confronted the difficult tasks of organizing data, specifying causal structures, and estimating relationships in economic policy models.

[33] Fox, *op. cit.;* see footnote a in Table 3-1 above.

4

Specification and Estimation of Structural Relations in Policy Models

JATI K. SENGUPTA[1]

AN ECONOMIC MODEL need not be policy oriented, but, once it is, it becomes subject to constraints that are frequently outside the conventional corpus of traditional economic theory. What are some of these constraints, and why is an economic analysis not sufficient to describe the physique of a policy model? The questions can be answered in part by pointing to the requirements such a model must satisfy, and to the implications thereof.

A basic requirement is that the model must be operational—that is, it must admit of quantification. The degree of quantification may differ, however. At one extreme we may have a completely deterministic model with a set of quantifiable solutions specifying the time paths of the target variables, and, at the other extreme, a quantitative model where the set of target variables, which depend partly on the set of instrument variables, may be subject to evolutionary stochastic processes of a certain type.

Second, a policy model must be capable of helping the "best" decisions to be made, where a choice is involved that is optimal, in some sense, among a number of alternative combinations of the instrument variables. And this requirement that a model must have some degree of freedom— i.e., some open ends to optimize—has two very fundamental consequences.

The first is that the statistical procedure, which may be used to estimate the empirical behavior relations in a part of the total policy model, is no longer independent of the decision-making process implied by the model as a whole. Thus the very purpose of estimation—the objective

[1] Associate Professor of Economics, Iowa State University.

for which it is intended—assumes a critical role. To rely purely on formalistic grounds and define the purpose of estimation as condensation of data may no longer be sufficient or even efficient.[2] To the extent that the optimizing considerations and, hence, the adaptive controls are basic to the specification of an economic policy model, estimation must be viewed as a part of decision theory which generally requires the specification of the loss function for a given difference between the estimate and the true value of the unknown parameter. The unknown parameters may themselves be subject to a set of prior distributions, but for any fixed realization of them the best estimate could be defined only in relation to the specific loss function and the weights involved therein.

In other words, how robust is the estimate when we consider the sensitivity of the posterior distribution to changes in the prior distribution of the parameters of our problem?[3] To see that this context of estimation, although different from the usual large-sample techniques, is directly related to the specification of a policy model, we might consider a macrodynamic economic policy model and ask how robust is the choice of the instrument vector in relation to the optimizing objective function specified in the policy model.

The second consequence is that the objective of optimization in a policy model—implicit in the selection of an appropriate set of instruments—requires in practice a set of boundary conditions or constraints on the range of use of the instrument variables. There may also be certain *a priori* restrictions on the parametric coefficients of the model. Viewed in this array of inequality constraints and restrictions, the estimation procedure for a model clearly turns out to be a special case of statistical programming, where the specification of the statistical distribution of the optimal objective function becomes a very difficult problem even in the asymptotic case of a large sample.

THE ABOVE PARAGRAPHS provide a brief motivation for our specific discussion of some new types of estimation problems and situations; first, estimation objectives in policy models and the extent to which the choice

---

[2] E. J. Pitman, "Statistics and Science," *Journal of American Statistical Association*, Vol. 52 (September 1957), pp. 322-330; J. Berkson, "Estimation by Least Squares and Maximum Likelihood," *Proceedings of Third Berkeley Symposium on Statistics and Probability*, Vol. 1 (1955), pp. 1-11.

[3] D. V. Lindley, "The Robustness of Interval Estimates," *Bulletin of International Statistical Institute*, Vol. 38 (1960), pp. 209-220; H. Robbins, "An Empirical Bayes' Approach to Statistics," *Proceedings of Third Berkeley Symposium on Statistics and Probability*, Vol. 1 (1955), pp. 157-164.

of the model specification is conditioned by them; second, methods of nonlinear estimation with reference to an analysis of economic stability; third, the statistical aspects of what is known as the "problem of steering the economy"—and the implications of adaptive control. Finally, we shall analyze the potential usefulness and implications of estimates which are not statistically pure but mixed in various ways, and then discuss their practical relevance in relation to a statistically specified policy model.

ESTIMATION OBJECTIVES IN POLICY MODELS

Why is estimation necessary at all in a policy model? The basic reason is, of course, that in macrodynamic policy formulation the observational statistical data must be organized in a suitable, summarized form so that we can discriminate between alternative possible situations on the basis of given data. We may also want to identify some basic relations as "structural," among the various alternative relations possible between the four types of variables—targets, instruments, data, and irrelevant variables. These structural equations seek to express relationships among a limited number of variables which would prevail more or less exactly under certain idealized or reasonable conditions.

Another reason for estimation may be that we are interested in prediction. In certain situations of policy-making, prediction may be one among several steps that can help in the process of making best decisions. Thus, for example, in a macrodynamic policy model for analyzing the phases of economic instability (say, recession or recovery), it may not be essential to accept a particular kind of hypothesis or model to predict inventory holdings or other components of aggregate investment; yet when the predictions have some chance of not being exactly correct, certain types of social loss are likely to result. To minimize such losses, we need to select some control variables (i.e., the instruments) and to know how they influence the other variables and the loss function. In other words, we need a theoretical model, where estimation—not necessarily pure statistical estimation—has to be carefully applied at different stages of the policy model.

To identify these different stages we may conceive that, in general, a policy model subsumes three different types of structural systems: (1) a conventional open-static or open-dynamic input-output type of transactions flow where we have observational data for only one year or two; (2) a behavioral equation system purporting to be an approximation to the economic behavior of consumption, investment, inventory holdings, etc., where we have some observational data, but perhaps not enough to fulfill the requirements of a large-sample theory; and (3) a set of inequality restraints and boundary conditions either on the target and the instrument variables or on the individual coefficients and the relations between them. These inequality restraints appear to play a double role in relation to the econometric estimation of the type 2 behavioral equation system: on one hand they minimize the apparent unreality of the catch-all term "residual equational error" in the statistical estimation of behavior equations by explicitly allowing extraneous estimates and/or *a priori* information; on the other hand, by emphasizing the optimization objective of a policy model, they allow estimation to be viewed as a part of decision function theory.

One very important consequence of the latter effect is that, if one drops the requirement of unbiasedness and insists only on the smallness of the mean-square error in statistical estimation, estimators may be found that are better than those computable from the existing "sufficient statistics."[4] A second consequence is that the ordinary regression methods of estimation procedure may require extensive modifications in estimating the response or incidence of the optimal set of instrument variables. Assume, for example, that we must estimate one structural equation specified by the simple consumption function, $C = a + bY$, where C is consumption and Y is national income. Now suppose there exists a critical outside variable—say, the rate of interest, i—such that it alters the parameters of the consumption function in the following manner:

$$C = a_1 + b_1 Y, \qquad if\ i > i_0$$
$$C = a_2 + b_2 Y, \qquad if\ i \leq i_0,$$

where i_0 is the critical level of the outside variable, which may not have been included in the original specification of the consumption function. We note that the critical outside variable, i, may not necessarily be identifiable; hence, if our instrument variables, which are controlled by the policy-maker, affect it directly or indirectly, we must estimate the threshold value i_0 separately to specify more accurately the change in the parameters.

This problem (often referred to as the "threshold effects for parameters obeying different regimes") is perfectly general, although here we used a

[4] J. Neyman, "Two Breakthroughs in the Theory of Statistical Decision-Making," *Review of International Statistical Institute*, Vol. 30 (1962), pp. 11-27.

two-variable model as an illustration.[5] For example, in the Hicksian non-linear model of the trade cycle using a flexible accelerator, there are kinks in the investment demand function, depending on whether there is excess capital or not. An important implication of the problem is that we must have some sort of sensitivity analysis, either through simulation methods or through a more disaggregative analysis of the macroeconomic policy model. The econometrics of model-building has now reached a stage that calls for deeper study both of the sensitivity of models to deformation or excision and of the stability of the estimated coefficients in the face of changing inequality restraints and a change in economic policy.

Let us now consider some basic aspects of estimability of the three types of structural systems mentioned above. Regarding type 1, the input-output system, the difficulty of applying the conventional concept of statistical estimability to the structural coefficients is well known. Thus, research workers have developed indirect criteria for testing the workability of an input-output model and its performance, relative to other methods that use GNP projection or final demand projection by sectors over time-series data.[6] These criteria involve in some way or other a comparison of the actual data of (sectoral) real outputs, with the real outputs predicted from the input-output model or other alternative time series methods. The extent of divergence in predictability by input-output and other methods can be an indirect test of the workability of the input-output model, provided a critical level of the error of prediction to be tolerated is preassigned beforehand.

An application by Barnett, Arrow, Evans, and Hoffenberg of these indirect tests, based on the 1939 U.S. input-output tables, did not show up the workability of the input-output model compared to other projection methods, possibly because the studies made an assumption of constancy of input-output coefficients that was incompatible with the length of the time interval (usually a decade or so) for which predictions were compared. When Hatanaka based the same type of tests on a 1947 U.S. input-output table, the marked superiority of input-output analysis to

[5] See R. E. Quandt, "The Estimation of the Parameters of a Linear Regression System Obeying Two Separate Regimes," *Journal of American Statistical Association*, Vol. 53 (December 1958), pp. 873-880; J. K. Sengupta and G. Tintner, "An Approach to a Stochastic Theory of Economic Development with Applications" (to be published in essays in honor of Professor M. Kalecki); J. R. Hicks, *Contribution to the Theory of the Trade Cycle* (Oxford University Press, 1950).

[6] M. Hatanaka, *The Workability of Input-Output Analysis* (Fachverlag für Wirtschaftstheorie und Ökonometric, 1960); H. B. Chenery and P. G. Clark, *Interindustry Economics* (Wiley, 1959); and K. Arrow and M. Hoffenberg, *A Time Series Analysis of Interindustry Demand* (North-Holland, 1959).

both the time series projection of sectoral output on GNP and the final demand projection in the short range was demonstrated, largely because the 1947 data were more accurate than the 1939, and the prediction interval was shorter. Moreover, the trade and transportation margin rows were deleted from the interacting part of the input-output matrix before the indirect test criteria were applied. These results suggest the need for further study of how the exogenous variables, outside the interacting network of the input-output matrix, effect changes in the input-coefficients even in the short run.

Two basic questions can be posed at this point. First, to what extent could an input-output type system be combined with a set of behavioral relations to form the basic structure of a policy model in its short-run framework? Second, what role can standard statistical methods play in improving the workability of an input-output system as a part of a general policy model?

The first question can be answered only when we have some empirical idea about the sensitivity of the coefficient structure to levels of aggregation of industries—hence, some idea as to what we mean by a structural change of relationships within an input-output model compared to that of a behavioral model. The second question can be partly answered by saying that intercountry, cross-section data based on a uniform classification of industries may provide us at least a small sample in the statistical sense, although the data collection problem would seem to be tremendous and complicated. On the other hand, we might suggest exploring the "inner background" of the aggregative input-output coefficients in terms of transaction flows of an area economy, structured according to the residentiary and nonresidentiary segments approach. The potentiality of a regional programming type approach and the available ancillary information for particular industries or surveys need to be exploited further to improve the efficiency of the input-output mechanism.

Now we come to estimation problems for type 2 of our structural systems—a set of behavioral equations forming a part of a general policy model. (For a review of the technical statistical approaches in this area, the reader is referred to one of the standard econometric texts.[7]) Since we will concern ourselves here with some of the basic questions of statistical estimation, we can well begin with a quotation from Kendall, the theoretical statistician who has made a considerable contribution to applied time-series analysis (which provides the basic ingredients of most econometric models):

[7] See especially J. Johnston, *Econometric Methods* (McGraw-Hill, 1963), and A. S. Goldberger, *Econometric Theory* (Wiley, 1964).

Apart from the two kinds of errors in statistics, we forget sometimes that there are many more egregious errors open to us—asking the wrong question, failing to bring the right hypothesis to test, and specifying a model with so many degrees of freedom that it will fit almost anything. We find this latter effect in time series of economic data, where the series are so short that the information in them, even when wrung out to the last drop, is insufficient to discriminate between different models or wide parametric ranges within the same model.

This is no occasion to depress our spirits by a long catalogue of all the difficulties we have to face. It is something, I hope, that we are beginning to realize their nature and extent. And we can derive much encouragement from the reflection that in recent years there have been several important advances in the direction of subsuming some types of behavior under common laws. The greatest step forward, I think, has been the realization that an apparently constant pattern may be only the steady state of a stochastic process.[8]

The problem of specification of an econometric model is so essential to model-building for policy purposes that it transcends even the need for applying a complicated statistical technique of estimation. Too often the econometric model-builder has to start with a few fairly simple ingredients, plug in some error terms to allow for anything left out, and then assume forthwith that such error terms behave like random variables with some known distributional structure. This may suffice for a first step, but if the alternative specifications of the model with a given number of variables and the sensitivity of the outcome to these alternatives are not analyzed more deeply, our conclusion can never be logically complete or sufficient.

What do we mean by alternative specifications, and how do we perform a sensitivity analysis? An example of the former would be the specification of an interdependent model versus a recursive (causal chain) model, a static versus a structurally dynamic model, or even a linear versus a nonlinear model—each of the three pairs having the same set of variables, but related in different fashion. It is well known that a recursive (causal chain) model (which may also be dynamic and nonlinear) has several flexible features that are very convenient for economic policy models.[9] The system permits, for example, an explicit causal interpretation of the economic behavior relations—in the sense of a stimulus-response relationship that allows an easy change-over when some de-

[8] M. G. Kendall, "Natural Law in the Social Sciences," *Journal of Royal Statistical Society*, Series A (General), Vol. 124 (1961), pp. 1-19.

[9] H. Wold, "Causal Inference from Observational Data: A Review of Ends and Means," *Ibid.*, Vol. 119 (1956), pp. 28-61; and H. Wold, "Construction Principles of Simultaneous Equation Models in Econometrics," *Bulletin of International Statistical Institute*, Vol. 38 (1960), pp. 111-138.

pendent variables (i.e., targets) turn out to be amenable to direct control by the policy-maker through other outside predetermined variables. In other words, the relations of a purely recursive (pure causal chain) system are designed as behavior relations for as many decision-making units as there are independent equations; hence, the behavior of the i-th decision-making unit can be given a stimulus-response or cause-effect interpretation in terms of the i-th equation of the system.

A second advantage of such a system is that predictive inference is always possible, in terms of the parameters of the original system or of those of the reduced form, since the structural relations take the form of conditional expectations when we assume that residuals in each equation, whether lagged or nonlagged, are uncorrelated with the regressor variables and also mutually uncorrelated. Under such circumstances, the estimation procedures turn out to be very simple and the ordinary least-squares regression of the effect variable on the causal variables retains some of its nicer properties: such estimates, for example, are asymptotically unbiased and identically equivalent to maximum likelihood estimates when the joint distributions of error term are normal and the underlying stochastic process is ergodic.

By comparison, an interdependent model of simultaneous equations system in its original form ordinarily permits no causal interpretation of its relations, unless this is viewed as an approximation to the corresponding recursive system. Moreover, there is always a dichotomy between the estimation of parameters in the reduced form and in the original model, except in the just-identified case. Although we are interested in deriving causal and predictive inference from the behavior equations of the original model, to avoid bias and lack of consistency we must apply the statistical estimation techniques to the reduced form of the model. It is only in the special case of a just-identified simultaneous system of linear relations that there is a one-to-one correspondence between the estimates of parameters in the reduced form and the original model, and in this case the estimates of the reduced form by straightforward least squares are equivalent to full information methods of maximum likelihood, the method of instrumental variables, the limited information method, and the methods of two- and three-stage least squares. In the overidentified case when the one-to-one correspondence is lacking, we have available now a number of estimation methods—e.g., maximum likelihood, limited information, two- and three-stage least squares, etc.—which, very broadly speaking, attempt to set up such a correspondence by indirectly using the information contained in other equations of the system and still retain at least the property of statistical consistency of estimated coefficients. But, since consistency as a large-sample criterion tells us nothing about the small-sample properties of these alternative estimators, we do not yet know to what extent such methods would be practically useful for a simultaneous equations system. Monte Carlo methods of investigation have not yet shown a definite prospect or a promising result.[10] However, by the criterion of the smallness of the mean-square error, it appears that the least-squares method may still prove to be superior in small samples to the other alternative estimators.[11]

This view of statistical estimation, which seems to favor a purely causal or recursive type dynamic economic model, may be contrasted with the belief commonly held by economists that the coefficient structure of a recursive model (as distinct from an interdependent model) looks unduly rigid when we abstract from the statistical aspects of estimability. By analogy we might say that, in an input-output model, a recursive coefficient structure reduces the two-way interdependence of an input-output table to unilateral dependence. This asymmetry of the economic and statistical viewpoints concerning the workability of a model type could lead to new lines of approach, which may have far-reaching implications.

One basic approach could be an attempt to specify the operational meaning of "affinity" between two models, each of which purports to be an approximation to one and the same economic reality. An example (although a rather special one) of this approach is the "implicit (or conditional) causal chain model" recently proposed by Wold, which attempts to combine the statistical advantages of a purely recursive (pure causal chain) system with those of the interdependent simultaneous equations model.[12] Like the purely causal chain system, the *conditional* causal chain model is estimated in its original form rather than in the reduced form, and here the least-squares method would, under very general conditions, provide asymptotically unbiased estimates for the parameters.

[10] H. M. Wagner, "A Monte Carlo Study of Estimates of Simultaneous Linear Structural Equations," *Econometrica*, Vol. 26 (January 1958), pp. 117-133.

[11] J. Berkson, *op. cit* (see footnote 2 above); E. Mosbeck, "Experimental Investigation of Studentized Estimates of Coefficients in Structural Equations," *Temp. SP-158*, General Electric Company (California).

[12] H. Wold, "A Generalization of Causal Chain Models," *Econometrica*, Vol. 28 (April 1960), pp. 443-463; R. L. Basmann, "The Causal Interpretation of Non-Triangular Systems of Economic Relations" (with a reply by H. Wold and R. H. Strotz), *ibid.*, Vol. 31 (July 1963), pp. 439-453.

Similarly, the conditional causal chain system shares the two basic features of an interdependent model: (1) introduction of equilibrium relations and other approximations that break the triangularity of the coefficient matrix of the current endogenous variables; (2) the fact that an appropriate assumption about the joint distribution of disturbances defines one and the same stochastic process (e.g., linear and stationary Gauss-Markov process) underlying both the simultaneous equations and the conditional causal chain models. The latter fact points to the startling result that two seemingly different models can be equivalent in terms of the stochastic process they generate, without any discrimination between the models being provided by either the observed nonexperimental data or the underlying economic theory behind the behavior equations.

We might note, however, that there can be other types of "equivalence" between models, and, so long as sample observations are too limited to be discriminatory, we must make some approach toward a sensitivity analysis of the model performance.[13] As an example of the latter we can refer to the very simple method used in the 1960 model for the U.S. economy in recession by Duesenberry and others.[14] To study the average dispersion of income in response to various sequences of the autonomous (instrument) variables, the standard error of estimate for each behavior equation was computed first; then an estimate was made about the dispersion of possible outcomes resulting from a given policy, by assuming that each variable in each quarter is equal to its expected value plus a random term. The random term in each case was experimentally drawn from a universe having a mean zero and a standard deviation equal to the standard error of estimate for the particular equation in question. We note, however, that this model is the completely recursive or causal chain type; thus simple least-squares method with a stimulus-response type interpretation is directly applicable, without the bias which would be caused by simultaneous equations.

Is it possible to construct a quasi-recursive system, not by following Wold's method of deriving an implicit (or conditional) causal chain model through changes in assumptions about the distribution of error terms, but by introducing simultaneity in some but not all of the economic relationships and then performing a sensitivity analysis?

As an example, consider a model with a triangular coefficients matrix,

[13] A. Kshirsagar, "Prediction from Simultaneous Equation Systems and Wold's Implicit Causal Chain Model," *Econometrica*, Vol. 30 (October 1962), pp. 801-811.
[14] J. S. Duesenberry and others, "A Simulation of the U.S. Economy in Recession," *Econometrica*, Vol. 28 (October 1960), pp. 749-809.

except for a few coefficients that lie outside the block-triangular form. If the latter can be assumed to be zero, we get a complete recursive model with all its estimational advantages. In a quasi-recursive model we start out with the initial approximation that these extra coefficients are identically zero; on that basis we obtain an estimate of the recursive coefficients and, hence, an estimate of the error of each equation. If, however, we assume that these extra coefficients are not zero, but subject to a known range determined *a priori,* and that the error structure is normally independent, we now must compute maximum likelihood equations for possible *a priori* values of each set of the extra coefficients and then accept the maximum of the maximum likelihood criterion to define the inclusion of the nonzero extra coefficients. In other words, a quasi-recursive model attempts to generalize a recursive coefficient structure by incorporating extra coefficients with *a priori* bounds and by analyzing the impact of the limiting process when the *a priori* bounds tend to a single point—zero.

An obverse of this procedure is to consider what happens in a recursive model when we replace some or all of the lagged endogenous variables by the nonlagged ones, so that the coefficient structure is no longer triangular.[15] Here we observe the sensitivity of the parametric estimates when we consider the limiting process that all time lags tend to zero.

The above suggestions call for further investigation and research into the basic problem of model specification, which is at least approximately causal in the sense of stimulus-response relationship. But even when we accept that the form of a model is correctly specified, we still need to analyze some special and important problems arising from simultaneity of economic relationships.

One such problem, which is very frequently encountered for econometric models based on time series data, is multicollinearity among the explanatory variables. In single-equation regression models, this leads to singularity in the variance-covariance matrix, so that the estimates of individual coefficients of the intercorrelated variables are either undefined or indeterminate. It is possible, however, to analyze the sensitivity and the existence of a limiting value of an estimated coefficient when the intercorrelation among the set of explanatory variables tends to be perfect (i.e., maximum) multicollinearity. Empirical as well as theoretical investigations have shown that, even in those cases where the limit-

[15] R. H. Strotz, "Interdependence as a Specification Error," *Econometrica,* Vol. 28 (April 1960), pp. 428-442.

ing value of the estimated coefficients exist as the intercorrelation tends to its maximum, there is a marked difference in sensitivity of alternative estimation methods to the presence of multicollinearity.[16] The model which is recursive (or very nearly so) is the least sensitive, because least-squares method is appropriately applicable to each equation separately of the model in its original, rather than reduced form.

The two-stage least-squares methods and, even more so, the limited-information methods of estimation have greater sensitivity, primarily because the parameters in the reduced form must be estimated first and then transformed back to the coefficients of the original model. It may be reasonable to conjecture that economic models having nonlinear structural relations are likely to be more sensitive to this problem of singularity and the lack of any meaningful estimate of some coefficients because the estimating equations are in most cases nonlinear so that there may be some difference between a local and a global solution (e.g., minima in least squares or maxima in maximum likelihood).

Theoretically speaking, there is as yet no completely satisfactory solution to this problem. One technically very interesting suggestion is that the intercorrelated explanatory variables might be replaced by a set of mutually orthogonal index numbers known as the principal components.[17] This is of very little practical use, however, if we are interested in the coefficients associated with the intercorrelated explanatory variables, because there is no unique transformation from the coefficients of the principal component variables back to the original coefficients. Another theoretical possibility is that the extraneous information and the *a priori* restrictions over the coefficients to be estimated can be made use of. For example, suppose that a_1 and a_2 are the two coefficients which are not identifiable due to multicollinearity, although we know *a priori* that they both lie between zero and one. Then, assuming the maximum likelihood method to be applicable in this model, we compute maximum likelihood equations for a_2, supposing a_1 to be fixed consecutively at different discrete points within the interval zero to one. As

[16] For an empirical investigation, see Karl A. Fox and J. F. Cooney, *Effects of Intercorrelation upon Multiple Correlation and Regression Measures* (Agricultural Marketing Service, USDA Bulletin, April 1954; reissued October 1959). And see the theoretical study by L. R. Klein and M. Nakamura, "Singularity in the Equation Systems of Econometrics: Some Aspects of the Problem of Multicollinearity," *International Economic Review*, Vol. 3 (September 1962), pp. 274-299.

[17] T. Kloek and L. Mennes, "Simultaneous Equations Estimation Based on Principal Components of Predetermined Variables," *Econometrica*, Vol. 28 (January 1960), pp. 45-61; H. S. Konijn, "Models Used in Statistical Studies of Relations Between the Uncontrolled Variables," *Australian Journal of Statistics*, Vol. 1 (No. 3, 1959), pp. 82-93.

final estimates for a_2 we consider only the maximum of the maximum-likelihood estimates. It is apparent, however, that this procedure is not unique, since we would ordinarily get two different estimates for a_1 and a_2, depending on whether we keep a_1 fixed first or a_2 fixed first.

Apart from such theoretical suggestions, however, multicollinearity can be considerably reduced by improving data precision and collection to minimize the errors in the explanatory variables. Experiments in running regressions with alternative combinations or decompositions of the observed multicollinear variables may also be helpful.

METHODS OF NONLINEAR ESTIMATION AND
MODELS OF ECONOMIC STABILITY

So far we have discussed methods of estimation on the tacit assumption that the parameters to be estimated enter linearly into the structure of the original form of the model. For most dynamic economic models that are nonlinear in parameters, however, an approximation by a corresponding linear model can be made either by an appropriate choice of the time interval or by an appropriate linearizing of the nonlinear relationship; it has been shown that such linearizing treatment may not only prove to be a very good approximation for short-run purposes, but may also yield quasi-maximum likelihood estimates that are statistically consistent under suitable hypotheses.[18]

However, a model involving nonlinear equations has two basic advantages. First, it offers a wider range of choice of possible paths for a given linear economic relationship. This is particularly helpful for analyzing economic instability in the form of cyclical fluctuations or of an intermixture of trends and cycles; for instance, a linear difference (differential) equation must have at least two lags (second-order terms) to allow the possibility of cyclical behavior, whereas an appropriate nonlinear difference (differential) equation or equations with only one lag (first-order term) can do the job. Similarly, it is well known that the knife-edge stability of the income-path in a Harrod-Domar type growth model can be generalized in two different ways—either by admitting production functions (preferably nonlinear) that are more general than the linear and complementary type, or by introducing capacity constraints, such that certain parameters (or relations) of the structural equations change their regimes when the capacity constraint is violated.

[18] W. C. Hood and T. C. Koopmans, eds. *Studies in Econometric Method* (Cowles Commission Monograph No. 14; Wiley, 1953), pp. 200-212.

The second advantage of a nonlinear model (when it is appropriate) is its capacity to throw considerable light on the sensitivity of solutions of the corresponding linearized model (or models), in respect to the stochastic process underlying the model. Just as the correspondence principle[19] has been used in seeking to establish the stability properties of equilibrium in a static model by analyzing deviations from equilibrium by means of a corresponding dynamic model, the different types of stability of a linear stochastic process model might be analyzed by considering its corresponding nonlinear generalizations.[20]

As a simple example, consider a stochastic process $X(t)$, with its expected value $M(t)$ and its standard deviation $V(t)$, each of which is a function of time in an evolutionary (i.e., nonstationary) sense. Then the relative fluctuation of the stochastic process is measured by the ratio of $V(t)$ to $M(t)$—i.e., the coefficient of variation; the interesting point to study is how the ratio changes over time when $M(t)$ rises at a higher and higher level. The nonlinear processes allow a most generalized study of the time-behavior of this relative fluctuation. Economic models of cyclical growth which emphasize the inseparable intermixture of the phenomenon of growth and cyclical fluctuations would belong to this category.

A nonlinear model, however, presents problems of statistical estimation. If its structure is either completely or very nearly recursive, the least-squares method may be applicable in most situations to each single equation of the model. Hence, for any given equation with m nonlinear parameters b_i to be estimated, we end up with m nonlinear normal equations whose solutions would minimize the sum of squares of the error residuals, which may be assumed to be independently and normally distributed as usual. But, although there are some iterative methods of solving the nonlinear least squares, it is not generally known whether the solution so obtained is a local minimum or an absolute minimum, and it is only for the absolute minimum values that the asymptotic optimality properties apply in a least-squares model which does not contain lagged endogenous variables.

In such cases, some methods of improving the efficiency of iterative

[19] See P. A. Samuelson, *Foundations of Economic Analysis* (Harvard University Press, 1953).

[20] As a simple case of the Markov process (known as the logistic process), it is well known that the expected value of the process is less than the deterministic solution of the corresponding logistic model. For *linear* birth-and-death-process models, however, the expected value solution of the evolutionary stochastic process model generally coincides with the solution of the corresponding deterministic model. See M. S. Bartlett, "Some Evolutionary Stochastic Processes," *Journal of Royal Statistical Society*, Series B, Vol. 11 (1949), pp. 211 ff.

calculation may have to be applied.[21] One method that has some practical virtue is to divide the entire observation into m equal (preferably disjoint and exclusive) groups and then, by averaging for each group, obtain a total of m exact nonlinear equations, which must be solved to obtain a trial estimator of b_i. Under general conditions, a set of trial estimates constructed in such a way is consistent, and with this as the starting value, the standard Gauss-Newton method of iteration can be applied to obtain the minimization of the error residuals. If the first-stage trial estimates are consistent, then the second stage requires only a very few iterations to improve the efficiency of the estimates very considerably.

However, to obtain a set of consistent trial estimates is not always easy; further, the convergence of the Gauss-Newton method of iteration is by no means assured unless certain conditions are fulfilled at each stage of iteration. When it is known that the normality assumption for the error residuals is too restrictive (e.g., a certain type of demand may never be negative), one may have to define a particular type of non-normal process (e.g., the Poisson process) and then apply the maximum-likelihood methods to derive a set of equations which can again be iteratively solved by the standard Gauss-Newton method to obtain a set of estimates for the nonlinear parameters which are statistically consistent. The small-sample behavior of such estimators is not much known.

It might be supposed that things are more complicated when a given nonlinear equation in a recursive model contains either lagged endogenous variables as explanatory variables or error terms which do not have the same variance (heteroscedastic errors). In the former case, it is not known whether the ordinary least-squares estimates, if they are obtainable, have the property of a best estimating function, although there is nothing sacrosanct about any best unbiased type of optimality criterion.[22] In the latter case, some methods are available which provide a correction, so to speak, for the original least-squares estimates by incorporating the additional knowledge about the temporal dependence of the residual errors. It is interesting, however, to note that, under certain reasonable conditions of a linear equation model, the asymptotic results on the efficiency of the ordinary least-squares estimate are fairly reasonably satisfied for even small-sample sizes, and that the difference between

[21] H. O. Hartley, "The Modified Gauss-Newton Method for the Fitting of Nonlinear Regression Functions by Least Squares," *Technometrics*, Vol. 3 (1948), pp. 269-280; D. W. Jorgenson, "Multiple Regression Analysis of a Poisson Process," *Journal of American Statistical Association*, Vol. 56 (June 1961), pp. 235-245.

[22] J. Durbin, "Estimation of Parameters in Time-Series Regression Models," *Journal of Royal Statistical Society*, Series B, Vol. 22 (1960), pp. 139-153.

the ordinary least-squares estimate and the Markov estimate (i.e., the estimate which incorporates the heteroscedastic variance structure) turns out to be very small in the numerical investigations.[23] This may raise our hopes about the operational validity of the straightforward least-squares method even in nonlinear models of a recursive type.

For a nonrecursive simultaneous equations model that is nonlinear, the situation is more complicated, because we have to apply our estimation techniques to the reduced form of our original model, although we are interested in the parameters of the original model. If the model is non-linear in its variables but not in its parameters (or can be taken to be approximately so), we can still apply quasi maximum-likelihood methods of estimation, assuming the residual errors to be mutually independently distributed, approximately like the joint normal distribution. Frequently, however, an explicit solution of these maximum-likelihood (ML) equations would be difficult to derive, because the Jacobian of the transformation would contain unknown values of the variables. It has been suggested that we should replace the unknown values by their observed sample means, to obtain an explicit solution of the ML equations.[24] This of course involves a linearization of the structural equations. An alternative method that seems to be applicable in this case is to minimize the sum of squares of the reduced form disturbances.[25] The quasi-normal equations that would be nonlinear in this case could be solved by an iterative procedure, using the standard Gauss-Newton technique mentioned before. This method, sometimes called simultaneous least-squares, appears to be largely distribution-free and computationally less complicated.

THE NET PURPORT OF THIS DISCUSSION is twofold. First, although it is easy to show that a first-order linear differential (difference) equation with real coefficients can never generate cyclical fluctuations—and that its corresponding mixed difference-differential equation can,[26]—the statistical estimation problem involved in the latter is invariably nonlinear; thus,

[23] M. Rosenblatt and others, "Regression Analysis of Vector-Valued Random Processes," *Journal of Society of Industrial and Applied Mathematics*, Vol. 10 (1962), pp. 89-102.

[24] L. R. Klein, *A Textbook of Econometrics* (Row, 1953), pp. 119-121; E. Williams, "Exact Fiducial Limits in Nonlinear Estimation," *Journal of Royal Statistical Society*, Series B, Vol. 24 (1962), pp. 125-139.

[25] T. M. Brown, "Simultaneous Least Squares," *International Economic Review*, Vol. 1 (September 1960), pp. 173-191.

[26] W. Leontief, "Lags and the Stability of Dynamic Systems" (with a reply by J. D. Sargan), *Econometrica*, Vol. 29 (October 1961), pp. 659-673.

at one stage or another, linearizing approximations must be applied. This holds good more appropriately in the case of a system of dynamic linear equations. The sensitivity of the nonlinear specification of the original model to the linearizing approximations necessitated by the estimation procedure will ultimately determine the econometric usefulness of the many nonlinear models of economic fluctuations available in recent literature.

Second, if it is our objective to devise measures of control over economic instability, it is necessary and useful to analyze the efficiencies of alternative types of control, both linear and nonlinear, by systematically studying the time path of response of the endogenous variables to a unit shock in one single period or to a shock which is sustained over time.[27] Such a study might appear to be theoretical, but we believe it could offer practical dividends of immense significance—for example, in deriving the optimum path of nonlinear control to achieve a certain type of stability, and in calling in question the very concept of economic equilibrium.

ADAPTIVE OPTIMIZATION AND CONTROL IN POLICY MODELS

The preceding papers have made clear that a quantitative policy model has three basic ingredients: (1) a welfare function, W, of the policy-maker, which is a function of the target variables, T, and the instrument variables, I; (2) a statistical model, M, which sets up a statistical relationship essentially between the target variables, T, and the instrument variables, I (this can be written in a shorthand notation as $T = M(I)$); and (3) a set of optimizing constraints that specify the optimization of the welfare function when the target variables and the instrument variables are subject to some boundary conditions. This aspect of optimization involves questions of statistical decision-making which are distinct in many ways from questions of model-building. In dynamic models where time, t, enters essentially into the specification of the equational relationships of the model (including the welfare function), optimization procedure must have some adaptive character. It must show, for example, the sequential aspects of incorporating new information and data, the dynamics of ad-

---

[27] H. Theil and J. C. G. Boot, "The Final Form of Econometric Equation Systems," *Review of International Statistical Institute*, Vol. 30 (1962), pp. 136-152; "The Present Position of Econometrics": A Discussion opened by Joan Robinson, J. Downie, and C. B. Winsten, *Journal of Royal Statistical Society*, Series A, Vol. 123 (1960), pp. 274-296.

justment and change-over to new decision rules, and even the sensitivity of the optimal set of instrument variables under different dynamic situations.

We note, in the simple case when the target variables, T, are a certain function of the instrument variables, I, the statistical error term, u, and time, t, that is, $T = M(I, u, t)$, that we may substitute this into the welfare function, such that it becomes a function of the instrument variables, the error term, and time alone—i.e., $W = W(I, u, t)$. One type of adaptive optimization problem is how best to adjust the instrument variables so that the welfare function is maximized (i.e., the derivatives of W with respect to I are kept close to zero in a statistical sense). And this problem immediately leads to a dynamic statistical (or stochastic) programming problem, because the error term introduces risk and uncertainty in the decision-making process and the additional boundary conditions on the instrument variables impose a programming framework. One approach to this problem is very similar in principle to the approximation method of nonlinear regression described above. We try to obtain a trial solution for the optimal subset of the instrument variables by considering deterministic equivalents of the original stochastic programming problem, and then try to improve the solutions at successive stages by incorporating the information about the statistical distribution of the welfare function.[28]

Alternatively, the optimizing behavior may be of the "satisficing" type, in which case we may be interested in keeping W as close to a desired value W^* as possible (or alternatively, keeping W equal to or above a minimum level W_0).[29] The specification of a loss function is now required, to indicate how far the deviation of W from W^* will be tolerated. Once the loss function is specified, the selection of the optimum subset of the instrument variables must involve minimization of this loss function in some sense. The optimization procedure is now implicit, and depends very essentially on how we specify the desired level of welfare, W^*, and the shape of the loss function. To show the incidence of the sequential aspects, let us consider a simple situation in which statistical data are available at discrete and equal time intervals (say quarterly), each interval being called a phase. We suppose further that the situa-

[28] J. K. Sengupta, G. Tintner, and B. Morrison, "Stochastic Linear Programming with Applications to Economic Models," *Economica*, Vol. 30 (August 1963), pp. 262-276.

[29] A. Charnes and W. Cooper, "Deterministic Equivalents for Optimizing and Satisficing under Chance Constraints," *Operations Research*, Vol. 11 (January-February 1963), pp. 18-39; J. K. Sengupta, G. Tintner, and C. Millham, "On Some Theorems of Stochastic Linear Programming with Applications," *Management Science*, Vol. 10 (October 1963), pp. 143-159.

tion remains constant during a phase, but may change from one phase to another. We denote the instrument (controlled) variables used in the k-th phase by $I(k)$. Now suppose that the desired level of welfare, W^*, is given, as also are the statistical data acquired during the k-th and previous phases; the question then is how best to change the control variables from $I(k)$ to $I(k + 1)$ so that the loss during the $(k + 1)$th phase is minimized. Principles of statistical prediction are now applicable, so that we must estimate from our past data (both actual and predicted) the optimal value of the instrument variables to be expected in the $(k + 1)$th phase and then set $I(k + 1)$ equal to it.

The situation becomes rather different when the desired level of welfare, W^* (say, the desired level of stability in a stabilization policy model) is not a fixed preassigned constant, but is subject, for example, to a prior statistical distribution having a not very small range. Questions of deriving optimum decision rules now have a different complexion. Is it possible, for instance, to derive a decision rule which is optimum for a fixed value of W^*, when this optimum is insensitive to or independent of a rather general class of prior distributions of W^*? This decision rule, when it exists, defines what are usually called Bayesian solutions for a fixed set of observations. The assumption of any particular prior distribution may appear to be very objectionable, although the approaches to an "empirical Bayes problem and the compound decision functions" by Robbins and an "objective Bayesian calculus" by Cornfield may give us some hope that the possibility of utilizing the accumulated experience may be incorporated in an objective manner into the set of optimum decision rules (i.e., the optimum selection of a subset of instrument variables at each subsequent phase).[30]

A third type of basic question to be investigated regarding adaptive optimization and control in policy models is the interaction between the short-run and long-run efficiency and implications of alternative control measures, particularly when some variables—such as investments in inventories and balance of payments—have random components.[31] It is now well known, from Phillips' analysis of alternative stabilization policies for correcting the deficit in output from the full-employment level, how an "integral correction policy" which depends on the cumulated past deficits is more effective, under certain conditions, than the "proportional correction policy" which only raises demand by some fraction of the

[30] J. Neyman, op. cit. (see footnote 4, above).
[31] G. E. P. Box and G. M. Jenkins, "Some Statistical Aspects of Adaptive Optimization and Control: with Discussion," Journal of Royal Statistical Society, Series B, Vol. 24 (1962), pp. 297-343.

deficit.[32] However, Phillips' analysis did not incorporate either the incidence of the random elements in the problem or the derivations of the optimum time paths of control (instrument) variables when both the expected value and the variance of the deficit around the full employment level are taken into account in the objective function itself.[33]

In other words, the control policies in the Phillips' model are not adaptive in character since the model does not optimize any measure of performance of the dynamic system. The recent advance of control-system theory has emphasized, however, that stability characteristics alone, which may be requirements of a good system design and for which the criteria of Routh, Hurwitz, Lyapunov, and Nyquist have been applied in linear and nonlinear servo-design theory, do not necessarily guarantee a suitable and optimum control policy. An admissible control must have an optimizing character in some sense—e.g., minimizing the error of the system under control or satisfying certain specifications of accuracy and speed of performance of the system under control.

An extension of the Phillips' approach, in terms of adaptive control theory, is reported elsewhere.[34] Therefore, we only note that here again it may be very convenient to obtain a deterministic equivalent of the dynamic equations of the model and then derive a set of time paths for optimal control by using the deterministic model which does not involve any random term. This set of first-stage solutions for optimal control could then be improved, as more and more data are available to estimate the nature of the statistical distribution of the random variables of the problem. One might also investigate the usefulness of deriving optimal

[32] A. W. Phillips, "Stabilization Policy and the Time-Form of Lagged Responses," *Economic Journal*, Vol. 67 (June 1957), pp. 265-277.

[33] J. K. Sengupta, "On the Relative Stability and Optimality of Consumption in Aggregative Growth Models," *Economica*, Vol. 31 (February 1964), pp. 33-50.

[34] J. K. Sengupta, "Policy Criteria for Stabilization and Growth" (to be published in *Oxford Economic Papers*, March 1965), and "Economic Policy for Stabilization and Growth under National Economic Planning" (paper presented at the Conference on National Economic Planning, University of Pittsburgh, March 25-26, 1964); J. K. Sengupta and E. Thorbecke, "Some Observations on the Theory of Economic Growth: Balanced and Unbalanced," *Zeitschrift für die gesamte Staatswissenschaft*, April 1964, pp. 243-263.

Some of the literature on control-system theory may be usefully referred to here: W. C. Schultz, "Control System Performance Measures: Past, Present, and Future," *IRE Transactions on Automatic Control*, Vol. AC-6 (February 1961) pp. 22-35; D. S. Adorno, "Optimal Control of Certain Linear Systems with Quadratic Loss," *Information and Control*, Vol. 5 (No. 1-2, 1962), pp. 1-12; R. Bellman, *Adaptive Control Processes* (Princeton University Press, 1961); R. F. Kalman and R. W. Koepcke, "Optimal Synthesis of Linear Sampling Systems Using Generalized Performance Indices," *Transactions of American Society of Mechanical Engineers*, Vol. 80 (November 1958), pp. 1, 820-821, 826.

decision rules, which are truncated in the sense that they incorporate only the first one or two moments of the distribution of the objective function, although in the long-run situation emphasis on other moments may also be necessary.

THE APPROACH OF MIXED ESTIMATION METHODS

Methods of estimation are called mixed when at some stage or other the usual statistical method of estimation has to incorporate extraneous information, which is *a priori* (or subjective) in nature rather than statistical.[35] There are, in our opinion, two basic situations in which such methods can play an important role in the econometric estimation of the statistical part of an economic policy model.

The first arises when the individual coefficients of a single-equation multiple-regression model are not separately identifiable, either due to multicollinearity or to the absence of nonsingularity. This apparent conflict between the economic motivation of the single-equation behavior relation and its nonidentifiability in terms of statistical estimation from observational data can be partly resolved by introducing appropriate inequalities and bounds on the individual coefficients, although in some cases the latter inequality restrictions must be strong enough to remove singularity (i.e., some coefficients may have to be given judgment estimates). When the *a priori* quantitative inequalities on the parameters (coefficients) are such that the parameter vector lies within a convex linearly bounded subspace and the ML method is applied for estimation, it is generally impossible to maximize the likelihood function by differentiation. Assuming a quadratic loss function, however, the likelihood maximization problem becomes a quadratic programming problem, and it has been shown that the point estimates of the parameters under constraints are more efficient statistically than the corresponding unconstrained estimates, although the former are in general not unbiased.[36]

A second situation where the extraneous *a priori* information is useful arises when, in a regression model, it is assumed that not all the regressors are observed without error and that the conditional expected value

[35] H. Theil and A. S. Goldberger, "On Pure and Mixed Statistical Estimation in Economics," *International Economic Review*, Vol. 2 (1961), pp. 65-78.

[36] H. O. Hartley, "Regression Estimates by Nonlinear Programming" (unpublished paper, Statistical Laboratory, Iowa State University, 1962); W. T. Lewish, "Linear Estimation in Convex Parameter Spaces" (unpublished Ph.D. dissertation, Iowa State University, 1963).

of the regressand, given the true values of the regressors, is a linear function of the latter. Just as in the Bayesian estimates, where the parameter is assumed to have an initial prior distribution—unknown but fixed —the *a priori* inequalities help to impose a class of distributions for the observational errors. Hence, ordinary least-squares estimates of a single-equation model can be appropriately adjusted to be made consistent by incorporating the *a priori* knowledge about the variances and covariances of observational errors. The most important question, however, is how to devise or especially deduce some "initial distribution function" as a substitute for the *a priori* distribution of the observational errors.

At this stage one might refer to the fundamental contribution by Herbert Robbins in which he tried to define an empirical Bayes-estimate $\tilde{\theta}$ of a parameter θ (given a fixed number of sample observations) such that $\tilde{\theta}$ will be almost as accurate as the efficient estimate $\hat{\theta}$, where $\hat{\theta}$ is calculable only with complete knowledge of the *a priori* distribution of θ.[37] Robbins also showed that the gain in precision of the empirical Bayes-estimate $\tilde{\theta}$, compared to the non-Bayes estimates of θ, depends on the nature of the prior distribution and may be very considerable (when the gain is measured in the sense of mean-square error).

The existence of such an empirical Bayes-estimate immediately showed that in our estimation procedure we need not ignore the randomness of the parameter θ or seek solutions which in a sense are independent of a large class of prior distributions to which θ may belong. However, as Robbins has emphasized, the question is still open as to how one may select an empirical Bayes-estimate which is in some sense the best in a certain class, if not in all. It appears that the mixed-estimation approach, which for the first time introduced Bayesian reasoning into the estimation of econometric models, could have considerable impact on our outlook, particularly in such special problem areas as multicollinearity, tendency toward nonidentifiability in case of observational errors,[38] and even the cases when the parameters have random components.

CONCLUDING REMARKS

A brief review of some of the broad results of our survey of estimation methods in economic policy models may be useful to the reader.

[37] H. Robbins, *op. cit.* (see footnote 3 above), pp. 131-148.
[38] H. S. Konijn, "Identification and Estimation in a Simultaneous Equations Model with Errors in the Variables," *Econometrica*, Vol. 30 (January 1962), pp. 79-87.

1. The specification of the structure of a policy model subsuming different types of economic relations, some of which may be based on very small and finite samples of observations, must always precede the search for methods and techniques of statistical estimation which are in some sense best. Statistical estimability per se, or the mere convenience of statistical estimation, should not be our only criterion in specifying the economic behavior relations of a macroeconomic policy model, partly because the economic situation is frequently one of a small finite sample and the idea of repetitive observations is often not realized. It is always appropriate, however, to consider the empirical implications of alternative specifications of a model whenever this is possible.

2. From an operational standpoint, one may usefully emphasize that most estimation procedures (e.g., maximum likelihood, k-class estimators, simultaneous least squares) have more or less the same asymptotic properties in typical large-sample ($N \to \infty$) situations. It has been said, for instance, that the ML method is just one out of an infinity of estimation procedures yielding what are known as the best asymptotically normal estimates which have the same optimum asymptotic properties as the ML estimates.[39] Some recent attempts have been made to define a class of superefficient estimates which have asymptotic variances smaller than those of ML estimates, and even the concept of efficiency in estimation has been linked with closeness of approximation to the derivative of log likelihood function so that we can have efficiency of first-order, second-order, and even higher. For economic models, however, the important question is the sampling behavior of these alternative estimation methods in small-sample situations. For such situations one needs to be more careful. One may have to look at the whole likelihood function, rather than any first- or second-order approximations, and with the use of high-speed computers such comparative evaluation of alternative estimators is needed.

3. When the purpose of estimation is not purely a convenient way of summarizing the existing statistical data, it may be worth considering how sensitive a particular type of estimate is to the imposition of a certain class of initial distributions for the unknown parameter. The sequential nature of economic information and the possibility of constructing Bayes-estimates in an empirical manner, even in small-sample situations, may give us reasonable hopes of investigating the application of such distribution-free and nonparametric methods to economic situa-

[39] C. R. Rao, "Efficient Estimates and Optimum Inference Procedures in Large Samples," *Journal Royal Statistical Society*, Series B, Vol. 24 (1962), pp. 46-72.

tions. The methods of mixed estimation which seem to define how best to combine "internal" and "extraneous" estimates of a parameter may then be viewed as operational methods to solve the problems of singularity in statistical estimation.

4. In problems of economic instability and the derivation of optimal stabilization policies it may prove useful to investigate the sensitivity of alternative types of linearization applied to a nonlinear model. The estimational difficulties for nonlinear models are, of course, far greater, yet in some instances the *a priori* information on some crucial parameters can make the estimation procedure rather tractable and this may help considerably in deriving methods of optimal nonlinear control.[40]

5. Considerable insight into the economic problems of stabilization policies could be gained from research knowledge and methods available in other areas—and especially in control-system engineering where the evaluation of alternative types of control measures, e.g., discontinuous, singular, and others, is attempted in very general and specialized situations.[41]

[40] W. L. Stevens, "Asymptotic Regression," *Biometrics*, Vol. 7 (1961), pp. 247-267.

[41] I. Flügge-Lotz, *Discontinuous Automatic Control,* (Princeton University Press, 1953); L. S. Pontryagin, "Optimal Regulation Processes," *American Mathematical Society Translations,* Series 2, Vol. 18 (1961); C. D. Johnson and J. E. Gibson, "Singular Solutions in Problems of Optimal Control," *IEEE* [formerly *IRE*] *Transactions on Automatic Control,* Vol. AC-8 (January 1963), pp. 4-14.

5

The Objectives and Instruments of Economic Policy

ETIENNE S. KIRSCHEN[1] and LUCIEN MORISSENS[2]

TOGETHER WITH SEVEN OTHER ECONOMISTS, we have been engaged in a research project on the economic policies pursued from 1949 to 1961 in nine Western countries: the United States, the United Kingdom, the Common Market countries, and Norway. The study was published in 1964, titled *Economic Policy in Our Time*.[3] It presents a classification of objectives and instruments; examines the extent to which the instruments were used to achieve the objectives; discusses various aspects of the process of decision-making; compares the economic policies followed with respect to inflation, recession, expansion, and income distribution; analyzes the policies pursued in the framework of international cooperation and European integration; and surveys individual economic policies of eight of the countries.

Much of the substance of the present paper is drawn from this study.[4] We use some of its terminology and classifications, and we present its findings with respect to specific interrelations between objectives and the factors influencing the choice of objectives. We have, however, tried

[1] Professor, and Director, Department of Applied Economics, Free University of Brussels.

[2] Assistant, Department of Applied Economics, Free University of Brussels.

[3] E. S. Kirschen (Belgium), J. Benard (France), H. Besters (Germany), F. Blackaby (United Kingdom), O. Eckstein (United States), J. Faaland (Norway), F. Hartog (Netherlands), E. Tosco (Italy), and L. Morissens (Belgium), *Economic Policy in Our Time* (North-Holland, 1964).

The study is in three volumes: I. General Theory; II. Country Studies: Economic Policy in the United States, United Kingdom, and Norway; III. Country Studies: Economic Policy in Belgium, The Netherlands, France, Italy, and Western Germany.

[4] This material is in general paraphrased, and on occasion blended in with additions made for the present paper. In any case, the authors are grateful to North-Holland Publishing Company for permission for use of the excerpts and tabular material.

here to go somewhat more deeply into the discussion of objectives. Our additions especially concern the relationships between objectives and aims; the methods of quantification, the actual importance, and the changes over time for selected objectives; and a few practical cases of interrelations between objectives.

OVERALL TERMINOLOGY

By "policy," we mean action taken by the government in pursuit of certain aims, examples of which are:

raising the population's standard of living;
preserving law and order;
guarding the freedom of expression and choice;
reducing social tensions;
defending the country from outside attack;
making adequate provision for health and education.

It must also be recognized that governments in the eight countries chosen for special study were elected, and that one of their aims was to keep the electorates' support. All these aims have, to a greater or lesser extent, an economic aspect. The standard of living is obviously an economic matter, but the other aims, too, usually require some kind of government intervention in economic affairs. Preparations for defense or expenditure on health, for instance, require that resources are diverted from productive uses.

Economy policy, therefore, is the economic aspect of government policy in general: it is *the deliberate intervention of the government in economic affairs to further its aims.* In pursuit of these aims, governments have tended to set for themselves certain specific *objectives* which can be stated in economic terms, and which (at least in principle) are capable of measurement (either ordinal or cardinal).

To put its economic policies into effect, a government either alters certain economic quantities (such as bank rates or tax rates), or makes changes in the economic structure (such as nationalization). The economic quantities which the government can change, or the types of intervention in the economic structure, we call *instruments*. The government selects, from a wide range of instruments, those that will in its opinion most nearly achieve its objectives. The use of an instrument does not normally bring about changes in objectives directly: it operates on other economic quantities. For instance, a government may have expansion of production as its objective. It may choose to increase private consumption, investment, or exports, and to effect these increases it can select from a large number of possible instruments—such as a guaranteed minimum wage or export subsidies.

Finally, the use of a particular instrument on a particular occasion we call *measure*. A measure is taken to promote one or more objectives. This means that there is no measure without an objective.

THE OBJECTIVES OF ECONOMIC POLICY

For economic analysis as well as for political decision-making a classification of the objectives is necessary. There are many ways of classifying objectives, but none of them is perfect. The reasons for this deficiency are the following:

1. Economic policy was not devised in one day by a brain trust. Objectives appeared in the course of history, one by one, as new problems arose and as policy-makers became more fully conscious of old problems. This process resulted in overlappings and contradictions. Some objectives are complementary—when the achievement of one helps in the achievement of another; other objectives conflict—when the achievement of one is detrimental to the achievement of another.[5]

2. Problems are not considered in the same way by the politician (who makes decisions) and by the economist (who sometimes inspires decisions). The politician may be led to classify objectives according to the preferences expressed by the various policy-makers who influence economic policy; from this point of view, he will distinguish objectives which serve the general welfare of the nation from those which serve particular interests, and, among the latter, he will consider separately the objectives aiming at the promotion of various particular interests. The economist, on the other hand, will tend to rationalize economic policy on the basis of his views about the workings of economic mechanisms. In his classifications, he might thus use such criteria as demand, production, or incomes, which will obviously lead to something very different from the list of objectives stated by politicians.

In *Economic Policy in Our Time* objectives were classified according to the following statement of principles:

In producing our classification of objectives, we tried to find the one which

[5] This point of conflict is discussed in the later section "Conflicts and Choices."

was most useful in showing up the important differences in the policies of our nine countries. The classification has been derived partly from the analysis of actual economic policy in these countries, and it takes into account the objectives which the various governments themselves have stated from time to time. It also uses the various systematizations which have been prepared by other economists.

The criteria applied in our classification are the following:

1. The number of objectives was kept small enough to render the classification easy to handle, but large enough to keep international comparisons meaningful.

2. The objectives were divided into two groups: mainly short-term and mainly long-term. This is because it is of interest to examine separately the various methods used in the different countries to counteract short-term cyclical fluctuations, and the methods used to pursue longer-term economic policies. However, all the short-term objectives have long-term aspects as well. For instance, the objective of maintaining full employment was most commonly a short-term cyclical problem, but governments have also had long-term full employment objectives, e.g., of reducing structural unemployment.

3. The longer-term objectives were divided into major and minor ones. If, in the years we were surveying, most countries had an objective and most countries considered it important, then we classed it as a major objective—otherwise as minor.

4. When an objective appeared to be the result of a regrouping which is meaningful for the economist but not for the policy-maker, we subdivided the objective. This is the case for the improvement in the allocation of factors of production. But when an objective had a composite nature that was not the result of economists' arrangements, the objective was not subdivided. Thus, we kept together the protections given to various industries, the satisfaction of the various collective needs, or the improvement in the pattern (i.e., relative importance of the various items) of private consumption.

5. When an objective could be given two opposite meanings, we did not subdivide it into two objectives. For example, the improvement in the distribution of income can mean a move toward greater or lesser equality; similarly, according to its state, a balance of payments can be improved either by reducing its deficit or by reducing its surplus. Thus, when we use the word "improvement" this implies nothing more than that, in the judgment of the government which took the measures, any change was an improvement.

6. We have not included all the various objectives which may have been in the mind of some particular minister in one or other of the nine countries at some time. At various times, for instance, some people have elevated to the rank of objectives such things as the balanced budget, the reduction of the national debt, or the preservation of a particular exchange rate. We regard these matters as constraints on the use of instruments.

Aims and Objectives

The classification of objectives (as formulated in *Economic Policy in Our Time*) is shown in the left-hand column of Table 5-1. At the head of the columns are listed the main aims which seem to have been expressed by the various objectives. There are of course many overlappings between the aims, mostly because aims incline to be philosophical notions. (The x's in the columns mean that the aim was expressed by the objective.)

DESCRIPTION OF SELECTED OBJECTIVES

In this section the first four objectives in Table 5-1 will be considered. For each objective we give a definition, the methods of quantification, and the actual developments.

Full Employment

1. Definition: Prevention or reduction of unemployment. Governments have been mainly concerned with the objective of preventing and reducing short-term cyclical unemployment, caused, for example, by a decline in exports or by the ending of an investment boom. But some have also had long-term policies which were specifically directed to reduce noncyclical unemployment: for instance, frictional unemployment—unemployment due to the delay in matching vacancies with the unemployed who are capable of filling them; or structural unemployment—for instance, unemployment due to the decline of a particular industry, or to the fact that industry is moving away from a particular region.

2. Methods of quantification: Full employment may be expressed as a given or a maximum ratio between the number of unemployed and the working population; or it may be expressed as an equality between the

TABLE 5-1. *Classification of the Objectives of Economic Policy and Aims Expressed by These Objectives*[a]

Objectives	Internal Aims						External Aims			
	Material welfare	Equity	Reduction of social tensions	Promotion of human values	Ethics and religion	Protection of persons and properties	External security	Political power	International solidarity	Personal aims
Mainly Short-Term 1. Full employment	x	x	x	x					x	
2. Price stability	x	x	x						x	
3. Improvement in the balance of payments	x							x	x	
Mainly Long-Term (*major*) 4. Expansion of production	x							x	x	
5. Improvement in the allocation of factors of production (a) Promotion of internal competition	x	x	x							
(b) Promotion of co-ordination	x									
(c) Increase in the mobility of labor, within countries	x			x						
(d) Increase in the mobility of capital, within countries	x									
(e) Promotion of the international division of labor	x						x	x	x	

TABLE 5-1 (*continued*)

Objectives	Internal Aims						External Aims			Personal aims
	Material welfare	Equity	Reduction of social tensions	Promotion of human values	Ethics and religion	Protection of persons and properties	External security	Political power	International solidarity	
6. Satisfaction of collective needs: (a) General administration	x	x	x		x	x				
(b) Defense							x	x		
(c) International affairs	x						x	x	x	
(d) Education	x	x		x	x			x		
(e) Public health	x	x		x						
7. Improvement in the distribution of income and wealth	x	x	x	x						x
8. Protection and priorities and particular regions or industries	x	x	x	x	x					x
Mainly Long-Term (minor) 9. Improvement in the pattern of private consumption				x	x					
10. Security of supply	x						x	x		
11. Improvement in the size or structure of the population	x		x		x	x	x	x		x
12. Reduction in working hours	x			x						

ᵃ The x's in the columns mean that the aim was expressed by the objective.

number of unemployed and the number of unfilled vacancies.

3. Developments: Leaving aside the objective of structural full employment, the definition of short-term full employment—the level at which further anticyclical action against unemployment is considered unnecessary—has varied considerably, and governments have been content to take no further anticyclical action with unemployment percentages ranging from 1½ to 5 percent of the working population. The concern about full employment does not appear to be closely correlated with the volume of unemployment. Some rough actual quantifications are as follows:

> *Norway:* A yearly average number of registered unemployed of little more than 1.5 percent of the total labor force (as in 1958) was in the view of most people too high to be tolerated.

> *United Kingdom:* Any government would have been seriously worried if unemployment rose above 3 percent; in fact, both labor and conservative governments have taken inflationary steps while the unemployment percentage was well below 3 percent.

> *United States:* The 5 percent unemployment did not lead to immediate action, possibly because many of the unemployed were teen-agers (who do not vote), or colored people (who often do not vote either).

> *Belgium:* A 3 percent figure was stated once, but this was only achieved at the very top of expansion periods.

> *Italy, Germany, and The Netherlands:* Full employment was mainly a long-term objective. In this respect, it was important in all three countries, but especially in Italy.

> *France:* There were few unemployment problems.

> *Luxembourg:* There was no problem at all.

In the field of short-term policy it is difficult to stress changes over time, because the importance attached to objectives and their quantification depends essentially on the economic situation. In two countries, however, the concern about full employment seems to have increased: in Belgium progressively and in the United States from 1961 onward.

In general, during the period under consideration, the business cycle problem was viewed more and more in the context of economic growth. Rather than merely seeking the identification of turning points, policymakers began to consider rates of expansion and to be concerned about any slowing down of these rates, independent of the classic symptoms of the business cycle. This was the case in France from the beginning of the period, onwards, and, later, in the United Kingdom, the United States, Belgium, Italy, and Norway.

Price Stability

1. Definition: Maintaining general stability of prices. Throughout most of our period, most governments tended to regard price stability as a short-term problem: the tendency to rising prices was something to be corrected by "conjunctural" policies. More recently, an increasing number of governments began to regard this tendency as a long-term problem which might require structural changes in the economy.

2. Methods of quantification: The objective may be expressed as a maximum annual increase in the retail price index.

3. Developments: No one of the nine governments considered here has in fact been successful in maintaining stable prices for a period longer than a few years, and it is probably true to say that most governments would consider that they had achieved "price stability" if they kept the average annual rise as low as 1 to 2 percent a year.[6] This is because they considered that this objective conflicted with other objectives, in particular with the expansion of production and with full employment, and governments have tended to consider these other objectives as more important than complete price stability. Price stability being mainly considered as a short-term problem, the concern changed according to the economic situation, but probably became somewhat greater over the period.

Considering the various countries, one can say:

Germany: Very important objective.

Belgium: Very important; almost every rise, even limited to a few products, was combatted.

France: Important; this objective seems to have led to the formation of right-wing governments to correct the effects of policies pursued by left-wing governments.

United States: Important as a long-term problem linked with the increasing worries about the balance of payments.

United Kingdom: An annual rise much above 4 to 5 percent would be considered as a failure to achieve price stability.

Norway, Netherlands, and Italy: Little weight by itself but fairly important in that it is complementary to the improvement in the balance of payments.

[6] Some economists have considered that stable wages and falling prices would be preferable to stable prices and rising wages. But no postwar government has in fact had an objective more ambitious than price stability.

Improvement in the Balance of Payments

1. Definition: Maintaining a "satisfactory" balance of payments and a "satisfactory" stock of gold and foreign exchange. Usually, the objective was the short-term one of maintaining or increasing exchange reserves. Sometimes there was concern about the balance of payments on current and/or capital accounts (when a rise in the reserves results only from the inflow of short-term money). Some countries, in addition to the short-term difficulties with their exchange reserves occasioned by the trade cycle, also had a long-run need to improve the proportion of their output which is exported, notably to meet import developments. A balance of payments surplus was thus needed. Some countries aimed to reduce the rate at which their reserves were rising—partly because they considered that their export surplus was becoming inflationary, and partly because other countries were protesting that their own reserves were being run down too fast. There were other long-term balance of payments problems as well—such as the problem of changing the regional pattern of exports: for instance, by increasing the proportion going to dollar markets.

2. Methods of quantification: The objective could be expressed in one of the following ways: minimum level of exchange reserves; minimum ratio between the reserves and the value of imports; difference between exports and imports (in current and/or capital accounts).

3. Developments: Most countries defined their reserves as the Central Bank's holdings of gold and convertible currencies. In addition to gold, the two currencies which were in fact used as reserve currencies in the postwar period have been the dollar and the pound sterling. Some countries included their credit with the European Payments Union in the period when the Union was functioning, and some did not.

The level which countries regarded as satisfactory varied considerably from country to country.[7] Clearly the position was different for countries such as the United States and the United Kingdom, which, because their currencies are reserve currencies, had large short-term liabilities. Some countries have become accustomed to high levels of reserves in relation to imports; other countries have become accustomed to low levels. In some countries, also, the level of reserves considered desirable has varied,

[7] In some countries, part of the stock of gold had to be held as backing for the internal monetary circulation, and so could not strictly be regarded as part of the stock available for meeting a payments deficit.

according to whether stocks of materials were high or low. But most governments had some level in mind—a level which might change from time to time—below which they did not wish the reserves to fall. Further, many countries tended to take some action if the reserves were falling faster than a certain rate from whatever level.

Here also, changes over time depended on the economic situation. Some countries, however, were confronted with almost chronic balance of payments difficulties. In the various countries, the importance and changes over time were as follows:

> *Netherlands:* The objective was very important throughout, especially in 1950-51 and 1956-67; it was both short- and long-term. There was apparently a norm of 500 million guilders of current surplus.
>
> *United Kingdom:* Very important objective, with interruptions in 1954 and 1958-59 only.
>
> *Norway:* The objective was given high priority, especially in 1950-51, 1954-57, and 1961; it was considered from the short- and long-term points of view.
>
> *France:* Important until 1958, especially under right-wing governments.
>
> *Italy:* Important at the beginning of the period only (1949-55); it was defined as a long-term progressive reduction of the deficit, a short-term reduction of fluctuations, and an adequate composition of reserves.
>
> *United States:* The objective appeared in 1959.
>
> *Germany:* Important in 1950-52; soon afterward, the objective changed into a reduction of the surpluses.
>
> *Belgium:* The objective was minor, except at the time of a surplus on the EPU countries (1951-52).

Expansion of Production

1. Definition: "Satisfactory" rate of growth in the real national product. Generally, the objective is to increase the rate of growth per head of the population, since this is a measure of the increase in the standard of living. In some cases, however, the overall rate of growth also mattered, when expansion was linked to the political power of the nation.

2. Methods of quantification: This objective could be expressed as a minimum rate of increase of the GNP (total or per head).

3. Developments: The emphasis on expansion of production became greater during our period of analysis. The development of national economies has, of course, been the subject of discussion and analysis for at least two hundred years, but to consider it an objective of economic policy, one has to find the confirming evidence of active policy measures. In

this sense—explicit concern plus action—the objective of expansion came into its own in the advanced Western countries during our period of analysis.

It would nevertheless be a mistake to suppose that expansion became the central objective of economic policy in all the countries. Governments are usually happy to point with pride when the economy happens to be growing rapidly, but the extent to which economic policy was explicitly designed to achieve a high rate of expansion differed enormously among the countries and over time.

France: Very important objective; expansion was considered both on a general and on a sectoral basis by industry; in recent years a regional point of view was taken. The Second and Third Plans (1954-57 and 1958-61) stated a 25 percent increase in five years; the Fourth Plan (1962-65) forecast an increase of 5½ percent per year.

Italy: Very important objective, but much of the concern was about the expansion of the southern regions.

Norway: Very important objective, considered from the general, sectoral, and regional points of view. The 1962-65 Plan set a target of 4 percent per year.

Belgium: Expansion became an important objective by the end of the period; general and regional development was emphasized. A 4 percent growth rate was set by the government in 1958, and a 3.9 percent growth rate was set in the first four-year plan (1962-65).

United Kingdom: In the first part of our period, expansion was viewed as an increase of industrial production, restoration of the export position, the breaking of bottlenecks, and the completion of the process of reconstruction from World War II. At the end of the period there was a revival of concern: in 1963 the National Economic Development Council recommended a yearly growth of 4 percent.

Netherlands and United States: Increased importance was given to the objective.

Germany: Expansion was important during the first half of our period only, not so much for itself as because of its links with reconstruction and full employment.

International institutions: The OEEC set an objective of 25 percent over five years for member countries (1952); similarly, OECD set an objective of 50 percent over ten years (1962).

There was also a change of emphasis during the period studied. Particularly in the earlier part, expansion was chiefly associated with an increase in the rate of capital formation, and direct taxes and government lending were the instruments best suited to accelerate capital accumulation. Toward the end of the period, governments began to turn to other aspects of expansion, including investment in education and the acceleration of technological progress. The early emphasis on capital accumulation can be readily understood in the context of the situation: with reconstruction incomplete and a large backlog of technology ready for introduction, the returns from capital accumulation were very high. As reconstruction was completed and European technology came close to the frontier of knowledge, the emphasis inevitably changed.

THE INSTRUMENTS OF ECONOMIC POLICY

The instruments are commonly listed in five categories: public finance, money and credit, the exchange rate, direct controls, and changes in the institutional framework. Instruments included in each category are shown in Table 5-2.

1. The instruments of *Public Finance* cover most income and expenditure items of central governments and local governments, as well as balances between income and expenditure.

2. The instruments of *Money and Credit* include those which serve to make it either more difficult or easier for persons, companies, or governments to borrow money; they include, for instance, measures designed to change the rate of interest or to increase or reduce bank advances.

3. The *Exchange Rate* is the ratio between the national currency and one or more foreign currencies. Changes in the exchange rate include both general revaluations and devaluations, changes for particular transactions, or changes against particular currencies. They also include any change in the type of exchange-rate system.

4. The instruments of *Direct Control* include the powers to fix prices, quantities, or values, generally by fixing maxima or minima.

5. The general categories of *Changes in the Institutional Framework* are identified in Table 5-2: (1) the changes that alter the basic system within which other instruments are used—for instance, a substantial change in the credit system; (2) changes that do not affect the other families of instruments, but have a direct bearing themselves on the process of production—for instance, anticartel legislation; (3) changes that create new international institutions, and which, therefore, limit the freedom of national governments.

THE USES OF INSTRUMENTS

The uses of instruments may take various forms. Usually, they are imperative, backed by the force of the law. This is the case for government revenue instruments and, generally, for direct controls.

A government may at times use persuasion (mainly in the field of money and credit and of direct control) with the threat—expressed or implied—of statutory measures if its wishes are not complied with. In some cases, however, persuasion amounts to little more than mild suggestion, or the government refrains from showing the instruments which it will use if need be. For example, it may be arbitrary to say that a general campaign against price rises is a use of price control, when in fact the government may have recourse to an increase in direct taxes. Such a campaign has nevertheless been considered as a use of price control, for there is no dividing line between the strong and the mild varieties of persuasion.

The dividing line between the various categories of instruments is not always clear, and the classification given in Table 5-2 can thus be criticized. Among the borderline cases of classification are the following:

1. Restrictions exercised in the field of credit were included among the money and credit instruments; this seemed more appropriate than leaving them with price and quantity controls.

2. All government debt operations—both new borrowing or lending and operations in existing debt—have also been considered as money and credit instruments, though there are strong grounds for listing them in public finance.

3. The dividing line between changes sufficiently large to be considered changes in the institutional framework and changes within the existing framework is also necessarily an arbitrary one. For instance, the decision to impose indirect taxes on a new range of goods would not be considered an institutional change big enough to be included here. On the other hand, the creation of a tax on the value added counts as a change in the institutional framework. Similarly, the setting up of any major new machinery or institution for exercising direct control is included among changes in the institutional framework; the operation of the machinery or institution after it is set up is included among direct controls.

Table 5-2 (drawn from *Economic Policy in Our Time*) shows which instruments were used for each objective and which objectives were served by each instrument in the eight countries (synthesized) during the period of our consideration. When the letter I replaces a cross in the table, this indicates that the policy-makers considered an instrument to be particularly important for an objective.

Since such tables indicate the relations between instruments and objectives which the governments used in their economic policies, they provide a basis for beginning the construction of economic policy models. The information must, however, be supplemented by:

1. Relations between instruments and noncontrollable variables (such as private investment and foreign trade) and between such variables and objectives, as the instruments often act on the objectives through such variables.

2. Other possible relations between instruments and objectives which were not used by the governments but could have been used if the governments had so desired.

3. Relations indicating unintended effects of instruments on objectives.

4. Relations between objectives (some information on this subject is given in the section that follows).

CONFLICTS AND CHOICES

So far, objectives have been dealt with independently of each other, and we have only endeavored to find out which instruments were used consciously in order to reach them. In actual fact, of course, matters are much more complicated, since in present-day economies interrelationships are numerous and important. Some of the instruments used for one objective may have effects on other objectives; some instruments interfere with each other; and the total number of available instruments is sometimes smaller than the total number of objectives. The objectives will be found to be either independent, or complementary, or conflicting. These various interactions may reinforce the efficiency of instruments, but may also weaken their effects and lead to conflicts that can only be solved by choices.

One could conceivably construct a table that shows, for a given country and at a given time, all the relationships between objectives, but because of the changing effects of instruments on objectives, we have not attempted to do this. Some material, however, can be drawn from the national studies

TABLE 5-3. *Main Cases of Conflicts Between Objectives in Nine Countries*[a]

	Price stability	Balance of payments (reduction of surplus)	Expansion of production	Coordination	International division of labor	Collective needs (all)	Redistribution of incomes	Protection
Full employment	x	x						
Price stability			x			x	x	
Balance of payments (reduction of deficit)			x		x	x	x	
Expansion of production							x	x
Internal competition				x				x
International division of labor								x

[a] The x's indicate the most important conflicts experienced in one or more of the nine countries studied.

TABLE 5-4. *Intended Complementaries Between Objectives in Belgium*[a]

	Balance of payments (reduction of surplus)	Expansion of production	Mobility of labor	Mobility of capital	International division of labor	Collective needs	Redistribution of incomes	Protection	Pattern of private consumption	Security of supply
Full employment		x	x		x		x	x		
Price stability	x						x			x
Expansion of production				x	x	x	x	x		
Internal competition					x					
International division of labor								x		
Collective needs							x			
Redistribution of incomes								x	x	
Protection										x

[a] The x's indicate that both objectives were pursued by the same measure or set of measures.

of economic policy, 1949 to 1961. As illustrations of practical cases of interrelations, we present: the main conflicts between objectives; all cases of intended complementarity between objectives in Belgium; and the main cases of complementarity in other countries.

Table 5-3 indicates the main conflicts between objectives, with the x's in the columns indicating the most important conflicts experienced in one or more of the nine countries studied. In most cases the conflict is between an objective served by increased government expenditures and/or reduced taxes (full employment, expansion of production, satisfaction of collective needs, improvement in income distribution) and an objective served by reduced expenditure and/or increased taxes (price stability, reduction of the deficit in the balance of payments). Sometimes, however, the conflict is between an objective which requires trade liberalization (international division of labor, internal competition, price stability) and an objective which requires restrictions (reduction of the deficit in the balance of payments, protection).

Table 5-4 presents the intended complementarities between objectives in Belgium. The example of Belgium is used here because the country has been exhaustively investigated in our study. The x's in the columns mean that both given objectives were pursued by the same measures or set of measures. Full employment is complementary to various other objectives, and there is also substantial overlapping between expansion of production and other objectives.

The most common cases of intended complementarities found in the other countries studied were the following:

full employment and expansion;
full employment and protection;
price stability and balance of payments;
price stability and redistribution of incomes;
expansion and collective needs;
expansion and protection;
redistribution of incomes and protection;
redistribution of incomes and pattern of private consumption.

Choices of Objectives

The order of priority of the objectives that are in fact selected depends on: the economic structure of the country; the disequilibriums (economic fluctuations as well as social or political events); the preferences of the various policy-makers; and the influence of the various policy-makers.

Only the last two elements (which comprise the role of the policy-makers) are dealt with here.

In a democracy the powers of the state are exercised by parliament and the administrative government. The latter is, in its turn, the result of coalitions of political parties. However, the party (or parties) in power must come to terms not only with the opposition, but also with other categories of policy-makers, notably the administration and interest groups.

We shall therefore here consider, first, the preferences of the main categories of policy-makers, and, second, their respective influences on economic policy.

Preferences of political parties. Table 5-5 (drawn from *Economic Policy in our Time*) indicates the *a priori* preferences of three political groupings found in eight of the countries. Three objectives not included in the table, since they were considered negligible by almost all of the political groupings in these countries, are improvement in the pattern of private consumption; security of supply; and improvement in the size or structure of the population.

Preferences of administrations. Government administrations play a decisive role in the choice of instruments, for this requires the assistance of experts. And although the administration role is less important for the choice of objectives, it is still not negligible. Administrations are obviously preoccupied with objectives within their own fields of reference. Thus, a Ministry of Finance will be particularly concerned with short-term economic objectives (notably, price stability and improvement in the balance of payments), as also will the Central Bank. A planning commission or bureau, the industrial ministries, or the general directorate for industrialization will be preoccupied with the objective of expansion, while ministries for special sectors (agriculture, industry, commerce, transport) will frequently support the claims of corresponding interest groups for protection, priorities, and distribution of income.

The preferences of an administration are a function, on the one hand, of its recruitment system and of its standing and, on the other hand, of studies that it may undertake concerning the social and economic needs of the community. Thus, an administration which goes in and out of office with the political party in power (as in the United States) has few preferences clearly distinct from those of the party, at least for some time after an election; the most important exceptions are those parts of administrations with the most permanent structures, in particular (as in

TABLE 5-5. *Preference of Political Groupings with Regard to Objectives of Economic Policy: Synthesis for Eight Countries (excluding Luxembourg)*[a]

Objectives	Socialists	Center	Conservative
Dominant	Full employment. Improvement in income distribution.	—	Price stability.
Dominant or Significant	Collective needs (other than defense). Expansion of production.	Price stability. Expansion of production.	Collective needs (defense).
Significant	Reduction in working hours. Allocation (coordination).	Full employment. Collective needs (all). Allocation (international division of labor). Improvement in income distribution.	Improvement in the balance of payments. Allocation (international division of labor). Protection-priorities.
Significant or Minor	Protection-priorities. Price stability. Allocation (international division of labor). Allocation (internal competition).	Protection-priorities. Allocation (internal competition). Improvement in the balance of payments.	Expansion of production. Full employment.
Minor	Improvement in the balance of payments. Collective needs (defense).	Allocation (coordination). Allocation (mobility of factors of production). Reduction in working hours.	Allocation (internal competition). Collective needs (other than defense). Allocation (mobility of factors of production).
Negligible	Allocation (mobility) of factors of production).	—	Improvement in income distribution.
Negligible or Hostile to the Objective	—	—	Reduction in working hours. Allocation (coordination).

[a] Source: *Economic Policy in Our Time*, Vol. 1, p. 227, Table IX-2.

the United States) the armed forces, the public works department, the federal reserve system. Similarly, in Norway, where the Socialist party has been in power for twenty-five years, a slow penetration of the administration by the party—or at least its views and preferences—appears to have occurred, and the definitions of the main objectives of economic policy seem to be made in common, notably in the preparation of the four-year program before each electoral campaign for a new parliament.

But in the countries endowed with very stable administrations (United Kingdom, Netherlands) and very centralized ones (France), the administration plays an active role in the choice of objectives, and divergence of views as between administrations and the politicians in power may very well occur when their standpoints diverge, owing, for instance, to different social backgrounds. Thus to define valid and coherent objectives may become more difficult.

Perhaps as important as an administration's recruitment methods are its rejuvenation and the modernization of its intellectual training. A relatively young administration will be more receptive to objectives for expanding production than to those for price stability or the maintenance, at any cost, of the exchange reserves. Above all, it will be more acutely conscious of interdependence between objectives and instruments, of the essential unity of economic policy, and consequently of the need to test (as far as possible) its internal consistency *ex ante*. On the other hand, there is danger that a young administration will overlook the preoccupations of the people, and steep itself in technocracy.

Finally, it is the job of an administration to undertake studies, as objectively as possible, of existing or potential public needs. In this respect, an administration's tasks have been very greatly enlarged in the last ten years in most of the countries under examination. Admittedly, with the disappearance of the wartime economies, its powers of direct economic management have been reduced, but its responsibilities for study and forecasting have grown. Not only has the apparatus of official statistics been generally extended, but a number of objectives in political economy are no longer decided on without detailed study in advance, conducted by trained administrators. This is the case with housing, town-planning, education, and public health.

Apart from these "public needs," the intellectual activity of administrations has developed differently according to country and subject. In countries politically attached to economic liberalism (Germany, Belgium, and the United States) or principally preoccupied with financial equilibrium (England), the role of the administration is especially important for

TABLE 5-6. *Influence of the Policy-Makers in the Pursuit of Selected Objectives: The Eight Countries Taken Together, as of the End of 1960*[a]

Influence	Mainly Short-term Objectives	Expansion of Production	Improvement in Income Distribution	Protection or Priorities
Dominant	Government. Central Bank.	——	——	Interest groups (farmers).
Dominant or Significant	——	Government. Ministries.	Government. Interest groups (farmers; trade unions).	——
Significant	Ministries. Political parties.[b]	Interest groups (employers). Political parties.[c]	Interest groups (employers). Ministries.	Government. Interest groups (employers).
Significant or Minor	Interest groups (employers).	Central Bank.	Political parties.	Political parties. Parliament. Ministries.
Minor	Interest groups (trade unions). Foreign or international organs.	Interest groups (trade unions).	Parliament.	Foreign or international organs.
Minor or Negligible	Parliament.	Parliament. Political parties.[d]	——	Interest groups (trade unions).
Negligible	Political parties.[e] Interest groups (farmers).	Interest groups (farmers). Foreign or international organs.	Central Bank. Foreign or international organs.	Central Bank.

[a] Source: *Economic Policy in Our Time*, Vol. 1, p. 234, Table IX-3.
[b] Belgium, Germany, Norway.
[c] Belgium, Italy, Norway.
[d] Countries not listed in (c).
[e] Countries not listed in (b).

definition and the measurement of objectives concerned with the trade cycle. In other countries, the role extends more and more to objectives concerned with structure—notably economic expansion, improvement in the allocation of factors of production, and the priorities and forms of protection for industries or regions.

This extension of the field of administration into matters of economic policy is not, however, caused only by the pressure of indisputable necessity. In part it is the effect of "Parkinson's Law," whereby all established administrations tend to develop and perpetuate themselves, whatever their utility at any given moment.

Preferences of interest groups. The preferences of interest groups are concerned with partial objectives inspired by the particular interests which they defend. The efforts of these groups are therefore directed fundamentally toward the following objectives: protection and priorities to particular regions or industries; improvement in income distribution; improvement in the allocation of factors of production through internal competition. The criteria for their choices are simple: the defense of acquired positions and the conquest of new positions favorable for the economic or social group which they represent.

Respective influence of the policy-makers. The influence of various policy-makers in the choice of objectives has been studied for some objectives. The findings appear in Table 5-6 (again drawn from *Economic Policy in Our Time*).

The table suggests that, wherever the influence of pressure groups is great and that of political parties and parliament is moderate, the influence of the administration is moderate also; such is the case with redistribution of income, with protection, and with priorities. Wherever the influence of pressure groups is moderate and that of political parties and parliament is weak, the role of the administration is dominant or significant; this is true of short-term objectives and of expansion. It would appear, therefore, that the influence of an administration is an inverse function of the influence of interest groups and political parties.

6

Short-Term Planning Experience in The Netherlands

C. A. VAN DEN BELD[1]

THE NETHERLANDS CENTRAL PLANNING BUREAU was established in 1945, at a time when the need for detailed economic controls was urgently felt. In 1947 it was given definitive statutory basis by the Central Economic Plan Act, which also defined the government's responsibility for regularly presenting a Central Economic Plan. The Act made it clear that the Bureau's functions concerning the plan were advisory and preparatory only, and included no executive power. The plan was described as "a set of consistent estimates and policy directives for the Dutch economy," which should contain "information on the future development of production and prices, on future national income and expenditure and their components—in short, on all those variables considered relevant for the co-ordination of economic, social, and financial policy."

Short-term annual planning had actually been initiated in 1945, and the plans for the next few years depended rather heavily on detailed government controls. As economic conditions improved, however, stress was increasingly laid on forecasting and the realization of targets via macroeconomic policy instruments. It was this change in emphasis that gave the system of short-term planning its definitive form.

Long-term projections were not neglected, however. Those made some ten years ago have recently been revised, and techniques for obtaining such projections are now much improved. Nevertheless, a long-term planning system, whereby policies would be systematically coordinated to realize long-run national development goals, does not yet exist. This

---

[1] Staff member of The Netherlands Central Planning Bureau, and former head of the Short-Term Planning Division of the Bureau.

paper, therefore, mainly concentrates on experiences in the field of short-term macroeconomic forecasting and planning. Certain aspects of medium-term planning that were introduced in 1963 will, however, be discussed briefly, since the experience, recent though it is, is of some interest.

SHORT-TERM PLANNING ACTIVITIES

The relationship of the Central Planning Bureau to government officials and agencies and to citizen groups, as it goes about its preparatory and advisory duties pursuant to the Central Economic Plan, is intricate. As Figure 6-1 indicates, the Bureau both gives and receives information and advice relevant to the plan. Certain aspects of these relationships and activities leading up to the final version of the plan have become institu-

FIGURE 6-1. *Informative and Advisory Contacts in Short-Term Planning*

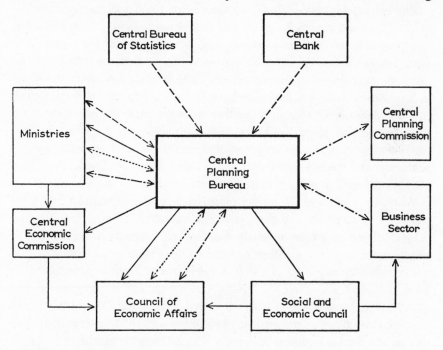

LEGENDA :

- – – ➤   *information*
———➤   *advice*
·······➤   *first version Central Economic Plan*
—·—·➤   *final version Central Economic Plan*

tionalized.[2] In the next few paragraphs these aspects are briefly described —using 1963 as our example of the base year for the next year's plan.

On the third Tuesday in September 1963 the central government presented its budget proposals for the calendar year 1964 to Parliament. At the same time the so-called Macroeconomic Estimates for 1964 were published (a custom that began in 1961). These estimates, which can be considered a preliminary version of the plan, are essentially global forecasts on the basis of policies outlined by the government prior to that time. Their content is the responsibility of the CPB, and work on them had been progressing since May 1963, initially on the assumption of unchanged policies. Bureau personnel had also discussed the forecasts with the relevant ministries. Later, a final discussion on the policy assumptions took place in the Council of Economic Affairs, a Cabinet subcommittee whose meetings are attended by the president of the Netherlands Central Bank and the director of the CPB. To facilitate discussion and evaluation, alternative forecasts, derived from alternative policy assumptions, are often presented.

The calculations were closed at the end of 1963, and the final version of the plan was due to be published in February 1964. The forecasts of this version may differ from those of the Macroeconomic Estimates for a number of reasons—the most obvious of which is that statistical data on developments since September usually have become available. Revisions in the original forecasts may also have become necessary because, before the calculations are closed, a number of large firms are interviewed on their investment plans, sales expectations, and so on; further, the final estimates are specific to branches of industry, as well as being macroeconomic, and the industry forecasts provide a check on the macro figures. Finally, the policy assumptions themselves may have to be revised.

When the final version of the plan is ready, it is discussed first with the ministries and then in the Council of Economic Affairs. It is also the subject of a conference held by the Central Planning Commission, at which industrialists and other experts are asked for comments.

The advisory activities of the Central Planning Bureau over the years have included, for example, giving advice on the revaluation of the guilder (1961) and working with the interdepartmental Central Economic Commission on measures against unemployment (1952). Activities in behalf of the Social Economic Council, which the government calls on for

[2] The institutional aspects are fully discussed in *Scope and Methods of the Central Planning Bureau* (The Hague, 1956). This publication also contains the earlier models, short- and long-term.

certain kinds of advice, deserve special mention. The Council is a non-governmental body made up of representatives of worker and employer organizations and of independent experts who represent the general public interest, among them the president of the Netherlands Bank and the director of the CPB. Its advice to the government—sometimes on general economic problems, more often on social problems—has greatly influenced social policies. Many of the reports it makes to the government are largely based on quantitative information provided by the CPB.

THE TECHNIQUES

Forecasting Method

Short-term forecasts in The Netherlands are for the most part based on econometric models. The precedent for building such models was set in 1936, when Tinbergen constructed a system of simultaneous equations to predict the macro effects of the devaluation of the guilder in that year. After the end of World War II, the Central Planning Bureau carried on the Tinbergen tradition.

Up until 1958 the models were rather static. Recent models have been much more dynamic, as can be seen if the model published in the Central Economic Plan for 1955 is compared with the one published in 1961.[3] Nonlinearities have also been introduced in recent models and use has been made of more refined methods of parameter estimation. But both older and newer models are macroeconomic, describing short-term (i.e., annual) movements of the economy, and constructed for purposes of prediction as well as the calculation of policy alternatives.

The 1962 model (shown here, together with a list of symbols, at the end of this paper) consists of thirty-six equations, including definition equations.[4] The reaction equations refer to the categories of expenditure: private consumption, private investment in fixed assets, stock formation, and merchandise exports; the price levels of the expenditure categories, including the price of autonomous expenditure on goods and services;

[3] See the Central Economic Plans for 1955 and for 1961. When models or other subjects of general interest are discussed in (an appendix to) a Central Economic Plan, the Plan is published both in Dutch and in English.
[4] The model is taken from a paper by P. J. Verdoorn and J. J. Post, "Capacity and Short-Term Multipliers," presented to the 25th European meeting of the Econometric Society, Copenhagen, July 1963. See also P. J. Verdoorn and C. J. van Eijk, "Experimental Short-Term Forecasting Models for the Netherlands" (Central Planning Bureau, 1958; mimeographed), where a number of models are presented and extensively discussed.

the level of wages in industry; the volume of merchandise imports; labor demand and supply; and finally the supply of liquidities.

This is not a pure demand model. Only in case of high unemployment is the level of production fully determined by factors on the demand side. However, when capacity limits tend to be reached, the effect thereof on production is increasingly felt; this explains the nonlinearities, referred to above, in the recent models.

A number of variables in the model are predetermined, others are jointly dependent. The latter are predicted on the basis of the model. The values of the predetermined variables, the most important of which are the volume of world trade, the price levels on world markets, and the instrument variables, are obtained from outside the model. The prediction of world trade and prices is based on econometric models for a few other countries, on the information provided by international organizations, and so on. Predetermined, too, are the values of the lagged endogenous variables, or, more generally, the situation in the base period. As noted earlier, the situation in the base year for the Central Economic Plan must in part be estimated, since the prediction period is always longer than one year. This is particularly true of the first published version of the plan, the so-called Macroeconomic Estimates.

The model approach of predicting the values of the remaining variables suggests a purely mechanical procedure, but in practice this is not so. The model outcomes are always checked on the basis of any additional information. The results of the investment survey, for example, may be preferred to the model outcomes. Adjustments may also be made for existing capacity shortages or, in a trivial case, for assumed changes in weather conditions.

Policy Actions and Outcomes

The relation between policy actions and outcomes can be easily obtained from the solution of the model. An example of this relation is shown in Table 6-1, which indicates the short-run effects of a 100 million guilder increase in government expenditure.[5]

The short-run effects of policy actions vary with the initial situation. In this connection, the initial level of unemployment—used as a measure of capacity utilization in general—is of crucial importance: the capacity factor plays a nonlinear role in no less than six reaction equations.

The relation between policy actions and those outcomes which repre-

[5] From Verdoorn and Post, *op. cit.*

TABLE 6-1. *Short-Term Effects of 100 Million Guilder Increase in Government Expenditure (in the first year)*

Impact on	Initial Unemployment Level			
	1%	3%	5%	15%
(in millions of guilders)				
Volume of Private Consumption	+ 2	+ 5	+ 6	+ 9
Volume of Private Investment	+ 11	+ 6	+ 4	+ 1
Volume of Merchandise Exports	− 81	− 43	− 26	− 2
Current Account of the Balance of Payments	− 131	− 104	− 93	− 76
(in percent)				
Unemployment	−0.04	−0.04	−0.04	−0.04
Wage Level	+0.12	+0.07	+0.05	+0.02
Price Level of Consumption	+0.15	+0.10	+0.08	+0.05

sent policy targets deserves special notice, the policy problem being which values should be assigned to the instrument variables in order to realize the targets. A fairly large number of actions can be introduced into the model. Autonomous components can be inserted

into the equation(s) for:	to study the short-run effects of:
direct taxes[6]	changes in tax rates on wage and non-wage income respectively
indirect taxes[6]	changes in tax rates on consumption etc.
wages in industry	changes in wage policy and introduction of social security measures
prices	price stabilization policies, rent control, and changes in the rate of exchange
supply of liquidities	changes in monetary policy
imports and exports of commodities	trade liberalization measures
labor supply	shorter working hours
investments in industry	changes in license policy

[6] The model presented on p. 159 does not contain separate tax equations. Autonomous changes in tax rates then have to be inserted into those equations in which tax revenues appear as explanatory variables.

Policy actions in the field of government expenditure on goods and services, government transfer payments, and government-controlled residential construction have to be added to the above listing of instruments.

The calculation of the effects of policy actions is not always confined to the first-year-effects of Table 6-1. The occurrence of important lags in the system makes it often desirable to cover a somewhat longer period to see the implications of a certain policy measure more fully.

Policy Decisions

The instruments discussed above have been for the past ten to fifteen years the most important ones in the government's short-term policy. The short-term policy targets, on the other hand, have referred mainly to the level of unemployment, the balance of payments current account, the price level of consumption, the distribution of income, and, in connection with the long-term growth potential of the economy, the level of investment.

Given these instruments and targets and the information provided by the model, there remains the problem of policy formulation. In the theory of quantitative economic policy this problem is solved by introducing a social welfare function, that is, a weighted average of flexible targets. To complete the analysis that results in the formulation of an optimum policy, the policy-makers must also take into account boundary or limiting conditions and the inherent uncertainties in predictions.

The theory of quantitative economic policy has found much practical application in The Netherlands, insofar as models make it possible to arrive at alternative predictions under alternative policy assumptions. However, the mathematical approach to the optimum solution of the decision problem has never been applied in practice.[7] Indeed, this would be an unrealistic approach under present circumstances, since not much can be said as yet about the weighting coefficients appearing in the welfare function. One practical way out of the difficulty has been found in the interweaving of informative and advisory contacts (see Figure 6-1) when the plan is being prepared, which implies that a maximum regard is being given to existing preferences.

Given the circumstances, it is impossible to generalize on the practical

---

[7] A social welfare function derived by "imaginary interviewing of the policymakers" is given by C. J. van Eijk and J. Sandee, "Quantitative Determination of an Optimum Economic Policy," *Econometrica*, Vol. 27 (January 1959), pp. 1-13.

solution of the decision problem. Illustrative examples must suffice, and a few of them are provided in our later discussion of policy experience.

THE ACCURACY OF THE FORECASTS[8]

The predictive qualities of the Central Economic Plans can be tested by comparing their final versions with the actual outcomes of the years concerned. However, in a number of cases the forecasts, as they stand, and the observed data of the relevant year are not directly comparable, because of unforeseen policy changes. The revaluation of the guilder in March 1961 is a good example of a change that was not envisaged in the Central Economic Plan for 1961. If the forecasts are to be comparable to the actual course of events in 1961, the revaluation effects must be included in the forecasts. It is of course necessary to estimate these effects; this can be done by means of the econometric model now in use.

After being corrected for unforeseen policy changes, the predictions can be compared with realizations. It should be noted that this process tests more than the predictive power of the model, since prediction errors may also result from errors in the forecasts of the predetermined variables.

The measure of predictive accuracy used is

$$U'_{i,t} = \frac{U_{i,t}}{S_{R_i}},$$

where $U_{i,t} = F_{i,t} - R_{i,t}$, that is, the forecast minus the realized percentage change in variable i at time t. S_{R_i} denotes the root-mean-square of the observed percentage changes in variable i, taken from zero. This statistic is meant to represent the normal intensity of change of variable i during the period of observation.

The inequality coefficient used to measure the quality of m forecasts in a given period of time is

$$U_t' = \sqrt{\frac{1}{m} \sum_i U'^2_{i,t}}.$$

[8] This section is taken from "Ten Years of Forecasts and Realizations," an inquiry into the quality of the predictions by the Central Planning Bureau, 1953-1962, by P. de Wolff and C. A. van den Beld (paper presented at the Ottawa meeting of the International Statistical Institute, August 1963).

A measure of the predictive accuracy of the forecasts for one variable over a number of periods can be obtained in a similar way.[9]

Obviously, $U_t' = 0$ in the case of perfect forecasts. The coefficient has no finite upper bound. When its value approaches unity, however, the forecasting results have to be considered as bad—in the case of predictions for one variable over time, as bad as no-change extrapolation.

The accuracy of some of the predetermined forecasts is indicated in Table 6-2. A distinction is made between noncontrolled and controlled (instrument) variables. Some of the latter were not corrected for unforeseen policy changes, to avoid possibly senseless comparisons. Government expenditures, for example, were not corrected, since during the period of observation supplementary budgets were of minor or even negligible importance; import prices, however, were adjusted for the revaluation effect in 1961.

TABLE 6-2. *Inequality Coefficients for Predetermined Variables*

Predetermined Variables	1953–1962	1958–1962
Controlled		
Wage Level in Industries	0.29	0.20
Government Wage Bill	0.29	0.12
Other Public Consumption Expenditure	0.69	0.47
Public Investment Expenditure	0.92	0.22
Total Impulse Government Budget[a]	0.40	0.27
Volume of Residential Construction	0.70	0.54
Noncontrolled		
Price Level of Commodity Imports	0.56	0.56
Volume of World Trade	0.63	0.54
Competitive Price Level on Foreign Markets	0.74	0.68

[a] Change in total government expenditure plus autonomous change in tax revenue.

The inequality coefficients in Table 6-2 vary between rather wide limits. Changes in wages were relatively well predicted. (Wages are frequently considered as a completely predetermined variable; this means that the wage equation is deleted from the model.) The errors in estimating government expenditure, however, appear to have been large. In this context it is noteworthy that the central government budget is an

[9] R. Ferber and P. J. Verdoorn, *Research Methods in Economics and Business* (Macmillan, 1962), pp. 476 ff. This inequality coefficient is also given by Verdoorn and van Eijk, *op. cit.* (see footnote 4, above), where a comparison is made with Theil's inequality coefficient in his *Economic Forecasts and Policy* (North-Holland, 1958).

authorization rather than a performance budget; forecasting errors then easily occur. The external variables are especially difficult to predict. The volume of world trade is considerably underestimated in periods of rapid expansion, and foreign prices are subject to small erratic fluctuations which cannot be foreseen.

Table 6-2 shows that predictive accuracy improved considerably in recent years. This is especially true of government expenditure estimates, probably because of a more stringent budgetary policy. But the inequality coefficients of the external variables have remained high. Some exogenous forecasts are illustrated in Figure 6-2 (page 144), where they are plotted against observed values. The 45° line is the line of perfect forecasts. Points below it in the first quadrant, or above it in the third, mean underestimation of changes. Underestimation is relatively frequent, but has become less so in recent years.

The inequality coefficients of the main jointly dependent or endogenous variables are shown in Table 6-3. Again, there was considerable improvement in recent years, partly because of improved predetermined forecasts, but largely because of the more dynamic models that have been used since 1958.

The prediction of those endogenous variables which represent targets of economic policy has to be considered separately because of the possible impact on policy decisions. Four such variables are shown in Figure 6-3: unemployment, the balance of payments current account, the price level of consumption, and the volume of investment in fixed

TABLE 6-3. *Inequality Coefficients for Jointly Dependent Variables*

Variables	1953–1962	1958–1962
Employment in Industries	0.30	0.18
Price Level of Consumption	0.42	0.46
Volume of Private Consumption	0.42	0.16
Volume of Commodity Imports	0.42	0.20
Volume of Production in Industries	0.48	0.38
Price Level of Exports	0.54	0.59
Unemployment	0.56	0.48
Volume of Commodity Exports	0.58	0.57
Balance on Current Account of the Balance of Payments	0.75	0.44
Volume of Gross Investment in Industry[a]	0.77	0.50
Price Level of Gross Investment	0.80	0.53
Non-Wage Income	0.82	0.64
Formation of Stocks	1.04	0.44

[a] Residential construction not included.

FIGURE 6-2. *Forecast (F) vs. Realization (R): Predetermined Variables*

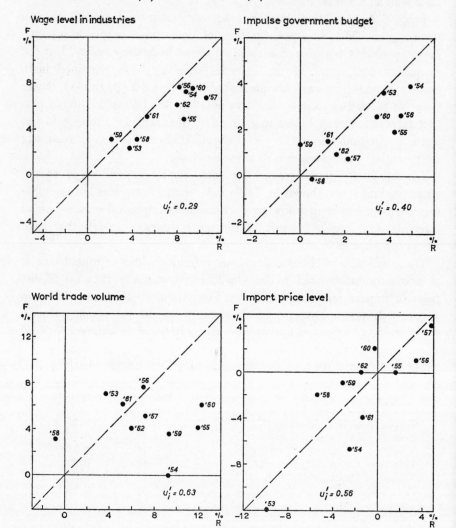

144

FIGURE 6-3. *Forecast (F) vs. Realization (R): Endogenous Variables (Targets)*

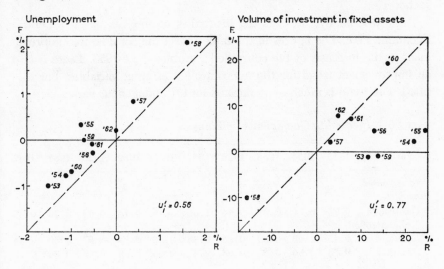

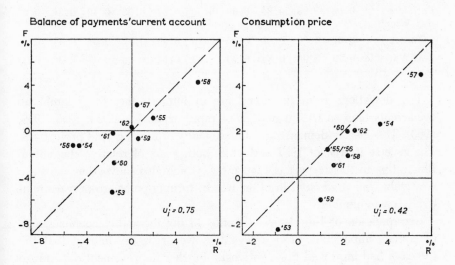

assets. The central tendency error in forecasting changes in unemployment is very systematic. Since increases in unemployment were overestimated and decreases underestimated, the *level* of unemployment was systematically overestimated. (The possible effects of these and certain other prediction errors on policy actions are discussed in the following section.)

Table 6-4, finally, presents the inequality coefficients of each Central Economic Plan. The figures in the table reflect the considerable improvement in the forecasts of the controlled variables since 1958. There is also an improvement trend for the noncontrolled external variables, but it is small. The trend is much more marked for the endogenous variables.

TABLE 6-4. *Inequality Coefficients by Plans*

Variables	1953	1954	1955	1956	1957	1958	1959	1960	1961	1962
Predetermined Variables										
Controlled	0.71	0.74	0.91	0.54	1.06	0.46	0.18	0.38	0.23	0.42
Noncontrolled (external)	0.43	1.06	0.69	0.76	0.38	0.68	0.78	0.57	0.50	0.34
Subtotal	0.63	0.85	0.83	0.63	0.87	0.55	0.50	0.46	0.36	0.39
Endogenous Variables of Which:	0.86	0.93	0.84	0.66	0.50	0.53	0.58	0.48	0.36	0.22
Targets	0.67	0.90	0.89	0.66	0.39	0.50	0.77	0.28	0.37	0.18
All Variables	0.79	0.90	0.84	0.65	0.67	0.54	0.55	0.47	0.36	0.28

The deviations from the trend are of interest, too. In general, the coefficients tend to rise in periods of rapid expansion (1954, 1955, 1959, 1960). This clearly demonstrates the difficulty of making bold projections. The reverse is true of 1957 and 1958, both years of relative stagnation. Illustrative in this respect is Figure 6-4, which also shows that signs are relatively well predicted; in other words, turning-point errors were relatively few in number.

Extrapolation of the observed trends in the inequality coefficients is, of course, impossible. More relevant, however, is the finding that the forecasts had improved in recent years. Further improvement depends to a large extent on better predictions of external data.

FIGURE 6-4. *Forecast (F) vs. Realization (R): Central Economic Plans*

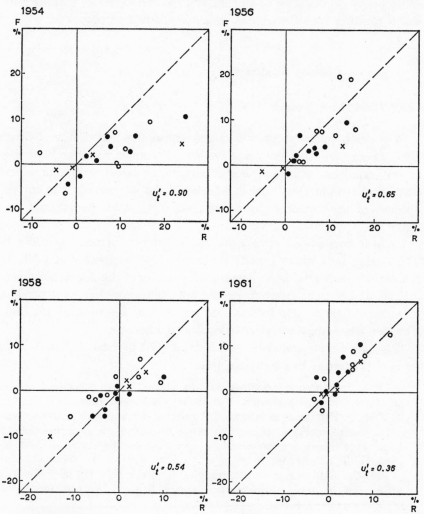

o exogenous variables
● endogenous variables
x target variables

147

The results that have been shown here apply not only to the final versions of the Central Economic Plans, but also to the first versions, since experience thus far has indicated that the later versions are only slightly superior in accuracy to the earlier ones. This is important, because policy actions tend to be based on the early versions that are published together with the central government's budget proposals.

SHORT-TERM POLICY EXPERIENCES[10]

Short-Term Developments, 1950-62

In general, economic growth characterized the period from 1950 to 1962. There were, however, some cyclical movements, resulting in periods of very rapid expansion and shorter periods of relative stagnation in production. Unemployment varied between 1 and 4.5 percent; the current account of the balance of payments showed violent fluctuations (see Table 6-5, page 150).

Cyclical fluctuations often arise from external factors, especially in The Netherlands where exports are a very high percentage of GNP. In the period considered here, however, the causes of the fluctuations were internal rather than external. Export possibilities, insofar as dependent on external demand and internal cost levels, were favorable all the time. The fluctuations must therefore be explained otherwise.

This may be illustrated by events from 1953 to 1959, a period of six years characterized by a complete cycle.

1953: Favorable competitive position abroad, some capacity surpluses at home. Increase in exports. Upturn in private investment.

1954-55: Expansion in internal and external demand gathers momentum.

1956: Bottlenecks in production result in balance of payments deficits. High wage increases because of low unemployment. Fall in profits and depletion of liquid reserves.

1957-58: Fall in investments, resulting from the 1956 fall in profits, etc. Sharp rise in prices restricts consumption demand. Rise in unemployment. No wage increases.

1959: See 1953.

This very short sketch (which is also a description of some of the lines of thought underlying the econometric model) shows how the internal

[10] Short-term policy experiences are discussed at some length in C. A. van den Beld, *Conjunctuurpolitiek in en om de jaren vijftig (Short-Term Policy in the Fifties)*, Monograph No. 8 (Central Planning Bureau, 1963). Publication of an English translation of this monograph is planned.

fluctuations did take place. Prior to 1953, developments were similar, subject also to the shocks caused by the Korean war. And developments after 1959 had at first many points in common with those in 1954-55; when capacity limits were reached, however, at the end of 1960, instabilities—in particular in the balance of payments—could be avoided. Changes in policy, to be discussed below, explain this to a large extent.

Government Budgetary and Monetary Policy

Since 1958 the central government's budgetary policy has been based, more explicitly than before, on two principles: (1) that a certain level of the budgetary impulse corresponds with the trend of economic development, the impulse being defined as the sum total of changes in government expenditure and autonomous tax reductions (which may be negative); (2) that the budgetary impulse may be larger or smaller than "normal" depending on the cyclical situation.

The longer-term analysis of the trend of economic development was introduced to arrive at a more careful establishing of priorities for longer-run development. The short-run budget analysis is, as will be clear, an impulse rather than a surplus analysis, which is in conformity with the econometric model line of thought where impulses are exogenous, surpluses endogenous. Budget surpluses or deficits are, however, not completely ignored, for this would ignore the liquidity effect of the budget. Here again, a distinction is made between short- and long-term policy. A constant short-term government debt, that is, zero creation of liquidities, seems to have been the long-term rule.[11]

The budgetary and monetary policy actually followed by the government is indicated in Table 6-6, which should be compared with Table 6-5. The budgetary policy up to 1958 appears to have been procyclical rather than anticyclical, the impulse being large at low unemployment levels and vice versa. In this sense government monetary policy up to 1956 was procyclical too. The explanation of these procyclical actions is that some increase in unemployment was accepted to restore balance of payments equilibrium (in 1951-52 and 1957-58). However, the automatic tendencies toward balance of payments equilibrium were underestimated.

In 1954-55, budgetary policy contributed considerably to the expan-

---

[11] The monetary analysis in its various aspects is discussed by Th. A. Stevers, *Monetary Statement and Monetary Analysis*, Monograph No. 7 (Central Planning Bureau, 1959).

TABLE 6-5. *Economic Indicators, 1950-1962*

	'50	'51	'52	'53	'54	'55	'56	'57	'58	'59	'60	'61	'62
Percentage Increase in Industrial Production	5	3	2	8	7	7	5	3	0	5	10	2	3
Unemployment Percentage	2.8	3.2	4.6	3.3	2.3	1.6	1.2	1.5	2.9	2.2	1.4	1.0	0.9
Surplus on the Balance of Payments Current Account (as percentage of GNP)	−6	−1	8	6	1	3	−2	−2	4	5	3	1	1

TABLE 6-6. *Budgetary and Monetary Impulses (as percentage of GNP in preceding year)*

	'50	'51	'52	'53	'54	'55	'56	'57	'58	'59	'60	'61	'62
Budgetary Impulse[a]	3.2	2.4	−0.3	4.4	3.7	5.8	4.4	1.8	1.2	−0.2	3.0	1.4	0.9
Creation of Liquidities by the Government[b]	−0.8	1.1	−3.9	−3.9	−1.1	−0.5	0.4	2.2	0.6	−2.8	−3.0	−1.1	0.4

[a] Changes in government expenditure plus autonomous tax reductions.
[b] Changes in short-term debt.

sion of internal demand, which caused balance of payments deficits in 1956-57. This is to be explained partly by the too-optimistic balance of payments forecasts, and partly by political considerations resulting in higher wages and lower taxes.

Lowering of tax tariffs could be avoided in the over-full-employment period 1960-61, and it proved even possible to raise the tariffs to reduce the expansion of investments. Monetary policy, too, was restrictive at that time. Balanced growth at very low levels of unemployment was the remarkable result. Obviously, the effect of the existing planning procedures on budgetary and monetary policy cannot be fully ascertained. As far as stabilization is concerned, however, the policies have been more successful in recent years than earlier, and without doubt this has some connection with the improvements of the forecasts. On the other hand, the experience in the earlier years shows the possibly destabilizing effects of political considerations, as well as the acceptance of some unemployment in order to restore balance of payments equilibrium.

Wage Policy

In the period from 1945 to 1959 wage increases in The Netherlands had two components, namely uniform increases and so-called incidental adjustments in wage levels by industry and profession. The uniform increases, reflecting most clearly government controls on wages, were based on different criteria: (1) prior to 1953 they were connected with the cost of living index; (2) after 1954 the share of wages in national income was used as a criterion, but the connection with the cost of living index was partially maintained, since uniform wage compensations were given, for example, when rents were raised.

A new wage system was introduced in 1959, to make government controls less rigid and to realize more differentiation in wages by branches of industry. Labor productivity increases were used as a provisional basis for differentiation. In 1962, however, this criterion was abandoned, and it was then decided that the Social Economic Council should report twice a year on the desirable development of the national wage level, using as a criterion the general economic situation in the near future. The reports would indicate the policy line for wage negotiations between employers and employees, who might use various criteria for wage differentiation. It was agreed that rigid controls by the government would be introduced only in very exceptional circumstances.

Again, the relation between planning procedures and actual wage developments is difficult to ascertain. Some insight is gained, however, when postwar wage movements are explained in terms of the criteria mentioned earlier. For this purpose, annual prewar and postwar data were used to establish the curvilinear relation between the percentage increase in wages and the level of unemployment (Figure 6-5a), and this result was inserted into postwar quarterly data. Using moving averages of quarterly figures and leaving aside autonomous wage compensations (say when rents were raised), the following relation is obtained for the period 1950-62 (Figure 6-5b):

$$l = \frac{11.8}{\bar{w}_t + 2.8} + 0.5p_{c-1} - 1.0\Delta\left(\frac{\tilde{L}}{\tilde{Y}}\right)_{-3} - 1.0h - 1.0 \qquad (R = 0.76)$$

where l = percentage increase in the level of wages in industry, p_c = percentage increase in the price level of consumption (1951–53 only), $\Delta(\tilde{L}/\tilde{Y})$ = change in the share of wages in national income (1954–58 only), $\bar{w}$ = level of unemployment (%), and h = percentage change in the standard number of working hours.

The important influence of the labor market situation on the movement of wages, which makes wages an extremely difficult instrument to handle, is revealed in Figure 6-5a. Nevertheless, price movements and the share of wages in national income have to be inserted as additional explanatory variables. This reflects the policy impact on wages, via the criteria used for uniform wage increases. Another conclusion from the above relation is that the reduction in working hours (in 1961 and 1962) resulted in a correspondingly lower rise in wages.[12]

The change in the wage policy criterion in 1954 was perfectly understandable after the long period of wage restraints. The resulting wage increases, however, contributed to the instabilities in 1955-56, an effect similar to the procyclical effect of the budgetary policy discussed in the preceding section. They contributed also—via reductions in profits and liquid reserves—to the stagnation in investments during 1957-58. But, considered over the period as a whole, wage levels remained rather low. This is evident from the situation on the labor market in these years.

Not much can be said so far about the most recent system of wage policy. Following the first report of the Social Economic Council in 1962, some wage restraint was realized in 1963.

In practice, the Social Economic Council has based its wage reports partly on the Macroeconomic Estimates, which are also among the data

---

[12] The wage equation presented here differs from the 1962 model's more general one, which is derived from prewar and postwar data on unemployment, prices, etc., but which does not take fully into account the institutional factors of the period 1950-62.

FIGURE 6-5a. *Percentage Change in Wages (l) vs. Unemployment Level* ($\bar{w}$), *1923-62 (annual)*

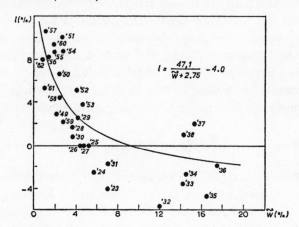

$$l = \frac{47.1}{\bar{w} + 2.75} - 4.0$$

FIGURE 6-5b. *Percentage Changes in Wages (l) Explained, 1950-62 (3 quarters moving averages)*

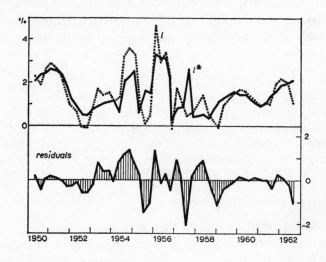

153

used by the Minister of Finance for his budget proposals. This system works satisfactorily when there are no large differences between the wage levels in the Estimates and those advised by the Council. When the differences are substantial, however, the government must either reject the agreement reached in the Council or adapt its own budgetary policy and/or monetary policy to the advice. The latter course was chosen at the end of 1963, when extreme structural tensions on the labor market had led to very considerable wage demands, on which agreement could be reached, first between employers and workers, later between the groups in the Social Economic Council. Instabilities similar to those of 1956-57 probably cannot be avoided in 1964-65. Balanced growth at low levels of unemployment appears, again, a difficult goal to attain.

The 1957 Program of Expenditure Restriction

The instabilities, noted earlier, that developed in the second half of 1956 had not been foreseen in the 1956 Central Economic Plan. The problems were numerous: the balance of payments account and the government account showed deficits, which were also expected to continue into 1957, and prices were rising sharply. The government felt obliged to intervene, and sought advice from the SEC.

The Central Planning Bureau provided the Council with information on the 1957 forecast (assuming policies unchanged) and on the relation between policy actions and outcomes. Discussion in the Council was ample, but agreement was reached fairly quickly on a program of action, which, with some modification, was accepted by the government. The program called for:

	Millions of Guilders (on annual basis)
Reduction in real wage income	125
Reduction in real profit income (via price policy)	100
Increase in indirect taxes (including tariffs of public enterprises)	375
Reduction in government expenditure	235
Reduction in investments by public enterprises	50
Reduction in fiscal investment facilities	50
Increase in taxes on corporations	50

The relation between these actions and the outcomes for 1957 is indicated in Table 6-7. The rather inflexible target of the program was to improve the balance of payments current account, to eliminate the deficit predicted for 1957. Some increase in the low level of unemployment was therefore accepted. Price rises, however, were less acceptable, since a rise of more than 4 percent was already expected. The program's restriction on domestic expenditure, necessary to attain the balance of payments target, was spread nearly equally over private consumption, private investment, and government expenditure. The reductions in disposable wage and nonwage income were also about equal in magnitude.

TABLE 6-7. *Consequences of the 1957 Program*[a]

	Initial Situation		Effects of the Program on 1957 Outcomes
	1956	1957 Forecast[b]	
National Income at Factor Cost (billions of guilders)	25.52	27.63	−0.23
Wage Income (billions of guilders)	14.30	15.66	−0.17
Volume of Industrial Production (1956 = 100)	100	102.2	−1.1
Unemployment (percent)	1.2	1.5	+0.4
Volume of Private Consumption (billions of guilders)	18.62	19.20	−0.26
Volume of Investments in Fixed Assets (billions of guilders)	6.66	7.11	−0.21
Surplus on the Current Account of the Balance of Payments (billions of guilders)	−0.59	−0.21	+0.30
Price Level of Consumption (1956 = 100)	100	104.4	+0.1

[a] See *Netherlands Central Economic Plan 1957*, Chap. 7.
[b] Assuming policies unchanged.

The relative merit of the program is not relevant to the present discussion. The important point is that agreement on a program of action *could* be reached on the basis of planning methods and techniques now traditional in the Netherlands.

Experience with this program (and others) also shows the large number of boundary and other conditions introduced in such circumstances. It is true that high priority is given to the central target—in the 1957 program to the restoration of balance of payments equilibrium. Many boundary conditions, however, arise from the actual state of affairs. Action is limited, for example, because reductions of any size in incomes and expenditure are strongly resisted or technically impossible, and still further limited because income distribution effects must be taken into account, which makes the formulation of a balanced program still more difficult.

The Revaluation of the Guilder in 1961

After the 5 percent revaluation of the German mark in March 1961, The Netherlands guilder was revalued by the same percentage. The decision had to be made very quickly, and the government asked advice from the director of the Central Planning Bureau and the president of the Netherlands Bank.

TABLE 6-8. *Some Short-Term Effects of the 5 Percent Revaluation of the Guilder*[a]

	Initial Situation: 1961 Forecast[b]	Effects on 1961 Outcomes
Surplus Current Account Balance of Payments (billions of guilders)	1.00	−0.14
Price Level of Consumption (1960 = 100)	101.5	−1.2
Volume of Investments (billions of guilders)	9.40	−0.02
Unemployment (percent)	1.0	+0.1

[a] From *Netherlands Central Economic Plan* (1960 and 1961).
[b] Assuming policies unchanged.

An excerpt from the Central Planning Bureau's advice is presented in Table 6-8, showing the short-run relation between this policy action and a few important policy targets. Rather much weight was assigned by the government to the price effect of the revaluation, in view of existing inflationary tendencies. In general, however, the effects of the revaluation appeared to be small, and actual developments in the course of 1961 and 1962 confirmed this.

THIS VERY SHORT SKETCH and the earlier sketch of the 1957 Program illustrate the advisory work of the Central Planning Bureau in specific circumstances. The examples also show how policy decisions—though of course not exclusively dependent on the quantitative information given by the CPB—are rationalized.

MEDIUM-TERM PLANNING

In connection with the elections held in May 1963 it was thought desirable to collect material that could serve as a basis for a 1963 to 1967 economic program, four years being the normal Cabinet period.

The study by the Central Planning Bureau on this subject stressed the necessity of establishing priorities as to the distribution of national expenditure, since in this relatively short period economic growth could be more or less considered as a datum.[13] On the other hand, a very large amount of (the increase of) the national product was being claimed by political parties and other pressure groups—for such matters as more aid to developing countries, tax reductions, road construction, increased military expenditure, reduced working hours, higher old-age pensions, and more industrial research. In fact, the total amount involved in the claims appeared to be far greater than the expected increase in real GNP over four years. Thus, the problem was (1) to specify all the existing demands, (2) to estimate the future rate of growth, and (3) to calculate the means available to meet the demands.

The last two problems were solved by means of a simple model, in which

> the possible rate of growth and the corresponding volume of investments were considered as data (obtained from longer-termed projections);
> the balance of payments current account was assumed to be in equilibrium all the time;
> the level of wages in industry was estimated as a function of labor productivity and, alternatively, as a function of the labor market situation which implied some rise in prices; and finally
> the volume of government expenditure and tax tariffs were assumed constant.

In this way, a quantitative estimate could be obtained, under alternative wage and price assumptions, about the means available for increased government expenditure, tax reductions, and so on. After the establishment of priorities (which is obviously not the task of the Central Planning Bureau) the four-year program could be put into effect.

A new step toward a more systematic form of medium-term planning was recently taken. The Cabinet announced in 1963 that it would put greater emphasis on growth as a policy target, and, therefore, on medium-term planning. The basic idea is to arrive at four-year forecasts for certain important industrial sectors. Undoubtedly, this system of planning will be of an informative nature only, as far as the private business sector is concerned. It is certainly not intended to introduce measures to enforce the realization of sector targets, foreseen in such forecasts.

[13] *Increase and Spending of National Income in the Next Four Years,* Monograph No. 9 (Central Planning Bureau, 1963; in Dutch only).

SUMMARY

1. A system of short-term macroeconomic planning has been developed in The Netherlands to make the best possible use of the available policy instruments.

2. This system involves short-term forecasting by the Central Planning Bureau on the basis of econometric models. The short-term effects of policy actions are also obtained from these models.

3. The forecasts are published in the Central Economic Plan, which thus contributes to the coordination of economic, social, and financial policies.

4. An early version of the plan is published together with the central government's budget proposals; this reflects a connection between these two instruments.

5. Model revisions have contributed to the higher accuracy of the forecasts in recent years.

6. Stabilization policies have been more successful in recent years than in earlier years.

7. The rationalization of policy decisions that can be obtained along the lines indicated is also apparent in cases like the revaluation of the guilder.

8. The short-term planning methods have also been introduced into the organized business sector, particularly as they play a role in the Social Economic Council's wage reports.

9. Medium-term planning is still in an early stage; but new steps toward giving it a more systematic form have been taken by the present Cabinet.

THE 1962 MODEL[a]

I. Reaction Equations:
i. Expenditure categories

(1) $$C = .58L^B_{-1/4} + .19Z^B_{-3/4} + .40\Delta p_c - .19\Delta C_{-1} + .06c^r_{-1} - .50$$

(2) $$I = .68p_i - 4.54\Delta \bar{w}_l + .75c^r_{-1} + .73(Z_{-1} - T_Z'') + .50$$

(3) $$N = .32v' + .76K - 1.29\tilde{N}_{-1}/\tilde{V}'_{-1} + .15p_m + .38t^* + .08$$

(4) $$b = 5.28\Delta\bar{w}_l - .99(p_b - p_b') - .69\Delta p_{v'} + 1.39b_c - 1.02(p_b - p_b')_{-1} + .18$$

ii. Factors of production and capacity

(5) $$m = .91v_m + .29\Delta v_m + 2.10N - .34p_{m-v'} + .37\Delta p_{v'} - 4.08\Delta\bar{w}_{l-1/2} - .30k + .26k' + 1.00$$

(6) $$a = .26v_a + .24K + .11p_{m-v'} + .04c^r_{-1} - 1.07\Delta\bar{w}_{l-1} + .50$$

(7) $$\Delta\bar{w} = -.50a + .34\frac{\Delta\tilde{P} - \Delta\tilde{a}_0}{\tilde{P}_{B-1}} - .03\Delta\tilde{T}_c + \Pi_w - 9.48$$

iii. Wages and prices

(8) $$l - .68l_{-1} = .44p_c - .99(\Delta\bar{w}_l - .68\Delta\bar{w}_{l-1}) - 2.16(\Delta\bar{w}_{l-1} - .68\Delta\bar{w}_{l-2}) + .33\{(v' - a)_{-1} - .68(v' - a)_{-2}\} + .51$$

(9) $$p_c = .45H_{-1/2} - .55(v - m)_{-4}/10 + .26p_{m-4/10} + .22T_{K'-1/2} - .09c^r_{-1} + .14$$

(10) $$p_i = .24H + .43p_m + .38p_{i-1} + .90$$

(11) $$p_b = .27H + .38p_m - 4.63(\Delta\bar{w}_l - .48\Delta\bar{w}_{l-1}) + .31p_b' - 1.38$$

(12) $$p_x = .40H + .53\Delta H + .25p_m + 44p_{x-1} + .57$$

II. Definition Equations:
i. Relations between value and volume variables

(13) $$C = c + p_c$$

---

[a] From P. J. Verdoorn and J. J. Post, "Capacity and Short-Term Multipliers" (paper presented to the 25th European meeting of the Econometric Society, Copenhagen, July 1963).

$$(14) \qquad X = x + p_x$$

$$(15) \qquad I = i + p_i$$

$$(16) \qquad B = b + p_b$$

$$(17) \qquad M = m + p_m$$

$$(18) \qquad V' = v' + p_{v'}$$

$$(19) \qquad V = v + p_{v'}$$

ii. *Expenditure totals*

$$(20) \qquad v' = .48c + .14x + .11i + .27b$$

$$(21) \qquad v_a = .46c + .20x + .16i + .18b$$

$$(22) \qquad v_m = .45c + .15x + .11i + .29b$$

$$(23) \qquad p_{v'} = .47p_c + .14p_x + .11p_i + .27p_b$$

$$(24) \qquad V = .44C + .14X + .10I + .25B + .92N + .06D$$

iii. *Costs and margins*

$$(25) \qquad H = l - (v' - a)_{-1/2}$$

$$(26) \qquad p_{m-v'} = p_m - p_{v'-1/2} + .06T'_{K-1/3}$$

$$(27) \qquad K = p_{v'} - .27l - .30p_m - .06T'_{K-1/3}$$

iv. *Unemployment*

$$(28) \qquad \Delta\bar{w}_1 = 4.34\Delta\ln(\bar{w} + 2) - .2\Delta\bar{w}$$

$$(29) \qquad \Pi_w = 3.94(\tilde{P}_{-1}/\tilde{P}_{B-1}) \text{ (for period 1923-1938)}$$

$$\Pi_w = 4.55(\tilde{P}_{-1}/\tilde{P}_{B-1}) \text{ (for period 1949-1960 and ff)}$$

v. *Incomes*

$$(30) \qquad L = a + l$$

$$(31) \qquad Z = 3.77V - 1.06L - .24T_K - 1.23M - .24F$$

$$(32) \qquad L^B = .87L + .87O_{L'}$$

$$(33) \qquad Z^B = 1.50Z + 1.50O_{z'}$$

vi. *Taxes*

$$(34) \qquad T_K = V' + T_K'$$

$$(35) \qquad T''_z = \Delta(\tilde{T}_Z/\tilde{Z}_{-1})$$

III. *Monetary Equation* (only needed when forecasting more than one year ahead):

$$(36) \qquad C^R = 3.77E + .83\Delta E - .68C^R_{-1} + 1.04\Delta V'_{-1/4} + .97r_e$$
$$+ .13S_{-1}^* + .20$$

The complete model consists of 35 equations and also has 35 endogenous variables. The endogenous variables of the system fall into five groups, that are related to:

Resources: a, l, L, Z, T_K, m, M
Expenditures: $c, p_c, C, p_x, X, i, p_i, I, N, b, p_b, B, v', p_v', V', v, V$

Unemployment
(capacity): $\tilde{w}$
Secondary
Incomes and
Taxes: L^B, Z^B, T''_z

Composite
Variables: $v_a, v_m, H, p_{m-i}', K, \Delta\tilde{w}_1, \Pi_w$

LIST OF SYMBOLS

Symbols without special indication refer to percentage changes. Levels are indicated by $\sim$. Capital-letter symbols refer to values, lower-case symbols to volumes and prices.

	a	number of persons employed in industry (man years)
	$a_\bullet$	number of persons employed in the government sector (man years)
B	b	exports of commodities
	b_c	competing exports
C	c	private consumption
C^r	c^r	deposits at the end of the year
D		net invisibles
E		balance of payments current account (as percentage of total output less inventory change and net invisibles)
F		depreciation
H		wage costs increase in excess 'of labour productivity increase (equation 25)
I	i	gross investments in fixed assets in industry (excluding investment by public enterprises and residential construction)
	k	quantitative import restrictions (1932–1937)
	k'	rate of liberalization (1949–1955)
K		gross profits per unit of output—equation 27
	l	level of wages per standard year of 300 days
L		wage bill in industry
L^B		disposable wage income (including transfer income)
M	m	imports of commodities

N		inventory change (as percentage of total output less inventory change and net invisibles)
O_L'		income transfers to wage income including government wages and direct taxes on cash basis
O_Z'		income transfers to non-wage income including direct taxes on cash basis
P		population of working ages (14–65 year)
P_B		wage and salary earners
	p_b	price of commodity exports
	p_b'	price of competing exports
	p_c	consumption price
	p_i	investment price
	p_m	import price
	p_{m-v}'	margin between import price adjusted for indirect taxes and the price of total output (less inventory changes and net invisibles)—equation 26
	p_v'	price of total output (less inventory change and net invisibles)
	p_x	price of autonomous expenditure
	r_e	exchange rate
S		excess of GNP at factor costs over consumption
$\tilde{T}_c$		minimum temperature below zero (sum of monthly averages)
$\tilde{T}_K$		indirect taxes minus subsidies (amount)
$\tilde{T}_K'$		incidence of indirect taxes minus subsidies ($\tilde{T}_K' = \tilde{T}_K / \tilde{V}'$)
	t^*	prewar downward trend (1923 = 15, 1938 = 0)
$\tilde{T}_Z$		direct taxes paid by non-wage earners (amount on cash basis)
T_Z''		variation in the incidence of direct taxes on non-wage income—equation 35
V	v	total output
V'	v'	total output less inventory change and net invisibles
	v_a	total output less inventory change and net invisibles (reweighted by labour intensity)—equation 21
	v_m	total output less inventory change and net invisibles (reweighted by import intensity)—equation 22
	$\tilde{w}$	percentage level of unemployment (also used as general measure of capacity utilization)
	$\tilde{w}_1$	curvilinear transformation of $\tilde{w}$—equation 28
X	x	autonomous expenditure (government expenditure, investment by public enterprises and residential construction)
Z	z	non-wage income
Z^B		disposable non-wage income

7

Quantitative Planning Of Economic Policy in The Netherlands

WILLEM HESSEL[1]

THIS PAPER DESCRIBES, AND EXAMINES CRITICALLY, the conduct of quantitative planning of economic policy in The Netherlands, especially in regard to the procedures, the targets, and the instruments. And since wage policy has played a dominant role, special attention will be given to it here.

Dutch planning has been concerned primarily with short-term stabilization goals, with special emphasis on the influence of the distribution of income on aggregate demand. One of the principal stabilization policy instruments has been government control of the wage level, but recently there has been a trend toward a new relation between planning and economic freedom—in the field of wages as well as private investments.

The system is also now tending toward more explicit concern with economic growth. Dutch policy has always been concerned with providing a favorable climate for private investments; now, however, a trend can be seen toward "indicative prospects" (that is, not production targets but production indicators) for individual sectors. In this connection, it should be mentioned that the increasing shortage of building construction capacity constitutes one of the problems that can be a serious threat to economic growth. In this paper, however, investment problems will be dealt with only insofar as they relate to the planning of national expenditures.

[1] Formerly director of the Scientific Bureau of the Netherlands Federation of Trade Unions (NVV) and member of the Dutch Social Economic Council; since September 1964 professor of economics at the University of Enschede.

163

THE PROCEDURE

Aside from the Ministries, a number of institutions—inside and outside the government—are involved in the planning procedure, as C. A. van den Beld has pointed out. Of these, the Central Planning Bureau (CPB), established by statute, and the Social Economic Council (SEC), nongovernmental and made up of independent experts and representatives of worker and employer organizations, play major advisory roles.[2]

The CPB advises both the government and the SEC, mainly on the technical aspects of the plans. It also prepares quantitative material for the advisory reports which the government requests from SEC, and which concern both economic and social problems, especially in regard to choices of policy instruments and targets. When the SEC advice concerns wage policy specifically, another private institution—the Labor Foundation (FL), made up of worker and employer representatives—enters the planning picture. It becomes the duty of the FL to implement wage policy within the limits determined by the government after having received the SEC report. A controversial point is how narrow or wide these limits should be.

The proposal has now and then been made to limit the advisory activity of the SEC by directives from Parliament. This would impair SEC's responsibility as an independent advisory body, since it would then be subject to a body that has decision-making responsibility, as SEC at present does not. In theory, the relationship of Parliament and SEC has always been one of mutual independence; in practice, of course, each body has influenced the other to some degree, and a decision of Parliament or of the government is often a datum for the SEC. But, if the SEC is to be useful, it must have the right to advise the government to deviate from a decision previously made or from a majority opinion of Parliament—and it must make at least moderate use of this right.

A basic problem of the planning procedure is the relative position of the main policy instruments. The SEC recently advised the government to liberalize its wage policy to a degree that would enable private organizations (such as the employer organizations and the trade unions) to take more responsibility. On the basis of past experience, the SEC also argued

[2] Since the general functions of these two groups have been described in Mr. van den Beld's paper, I will note specific functions only as they apply to the present discussion.

that more emphasis should be put on budgetary, monetary, and price policies, including the furthering of competition by eliminating some of the restricting activities in the private sectors.

The model used by the Central Planning Bureau is the skeleton of the annual forecasts for general economic development during the year ahead—the so-called Central Economic Plan. During the years of its existence, the CPB has won the good will and confidence of both employers' organizations and trade unions by its objectivity and capability. To make programming workable in a society, this kind of confidence is needed; otherwise any detail of the plan and any implicit assumption could become disputable (as has often been the case in West Germany).

The preliminary forecasts are discussed in the Central Planning Commission (made up of representatives of various private organizations and of government agencies). These discussions relate less to the bones of the planning skeleton than to its flesh, in that they are based on common sense, special experience, general opinions, and so on. Discussion items have included, for example: the influence of liquidities on investments; cyclical movements; increase of exports; effects of reduction of working hours on production; the relation of price increases to wage increases and vice versa.

The export forecasts take a central position and are therefore the most disputable elements—and sometimes also the Achilles' heel of Dutch planning. More than once they have been criticized by the trade unions. During such discussions the trade unions have put forward technical points not always taken seriously by the technical experts: when the CPB expects that the increase of a certain quantity in year t will be half or less of the increase of the same item in year $t - 1$ it must advance special arguments, because such a retardation is, as a rule, only possible when at the end of the second year the increase is nil. The CPB often neglected or denied this hidden assumption.

There is without doubt a certain tendency to underestimate changes in the various economic items, which can be attributed partly to the fact that it is not possible to predict cyclical movements—whereupon human prudence plays a role. Some experts have argued that underestimations are useful as automatic safety margins, but it is very doubtful if in practice they can be anything but margins of waste. In a growing economy such as that of The Netherlands, characterized by periods of expansion exceeding the periods of retardation, the tendency to underestimate changes has led to underestimation of the tolerable increase of the wage level—with the result that the employers' organizations are more inclined to accept the forecasts of the CPB than the trade unions are. In September 1963 the wage policy came to a crisis. The regular underestimation had led to a structural tension on the labor market, with the result that "black" (not allowed) wages exceeded 6 percent.[3] The real danger was a black wage explosion. And in September 1963 the explosion indeed occurred.

THE TARGETS

During the Phase of Reconstruction

During the reconstruction period after 1945, the targets in the forefront were (1) a reasonable degree of employment, and (2) balance of payments equilibrium. To realize these two targets at least two instruments were (and still are) necessary: wage policy and price policy. Both policies were pursued very stringently, and the tensions between them were high. At the end of 1952, for example, the discussions in the SEC came to the conclusion that the employment target could not be fulfilled simultaneously with balance of payments equilibrium; the SEC therefore advised the government to take inflationary measures. However, in 1953 both targets were fulfilled; the increase of exports had been underestimated. The Dutch economy had reached normal peacetime relationships sooner than was expected.

During the Phase of Normal Development

In accordance with the new situation, in 1953 the SEC formulated five targets as the basis of its advisory activities in the future: (1) a reasonable degree of employment; (2) equilibrium of the balance of payments; (3) a reasonable distribution of income; (4) a stable price level; (5) a reasonable level of investments.

Targets 1 and 2 were already, as far as necessary, quantitatively fixed; targets 4 and 5 were not fully elaborated. Relatively more attention was

---

[3] Wages that exceed the maxima of the approved agreements are termed "black wages" and are illegal.

given to the elaboration of target 3, since the SEC wished to establish it for the near future as a basis for wage policy. The starting point was the wage share of national income during a period with reasonable employment and equilibrium on the balance of payments (so-called basic period). The new situation made this technique possible. Proposals were made to investigate how this share, in the long run, could increase without affecting employment and the balance of payments.

The Netherlands Federation of Trade Unions (NVV) published a study on income distribution as a basis for a quantitative program. The main thesis of the study was that tax policy and subsidies policy should be used as instruments to reach a fair secondary distribution (distribution of available incomes). For the primary distribution, education policy was advocated. The subsidies policy is still controversial.

The Problem of Rising Prices

During the prosperous years after 1953, target 4—a stable price level—attracted more attention. The steady inflation of international prices had made it a difficult problem to combine a more stable national price level and balance of payments equilibrium. As a consequence, problems concerning the groups with low fixed incomes—the so-called forgotten groups—increased.

One of the difficulties was how to combine a stable price level with a flexible price structure (relative prices). Compensating price movements must be fostered. Compensatory decreases have to be given, especially in rapidly expanding industries with high productivity increases, and this does not seem to be natural, particularly when these industries are at the same time exporting industries. The results of many discussions of these problems (in which the SEC was not much involved) were: (1) a combined wage and price policy (which will be discussed below); (2) a revaluation of the guilder after the revalution of the D-mark.

The solution provoked much controversy. A leading view was that the national price level must follow the international price level. The alternative—regular revalutions of the guilder—seems not to be a practical solution; as a policy instrument, changing the rate of exchange should be reserved for exceptional situations.

QUANTITATIVE GUIDELINES

Budget Policy

To reach continuity, Dutch planning has used certain guidelines. (Up until now, the SEC's advice about them has been asked only in regard to wages and prices, on which its advice was that guidelines would not be fruitful.) For the budget policy, a structural guideline is introduced on the following calculation: projecting a structural yearly increase of 4 percent for real national income, the increase of tax revenues will be 5¼ percent, as a consequence of the progressive rates. So the sum of tolerable tax decreases and government expenditure increases is 5¼ percent of real national income.

A scheme of priorities should be the basis for deciding which of the many desiderata, including tax decreases, can be realized. The above calculation leaves the loan policy out of scope; nevertheless, taxes and loans are alternative methods to finance government expenditures. In the near future, related questions will certainly be discussed.

The proposed guideline, accepted by the government, was that government expenditure would increase less than income, leaving room for tax decreases. Experiences with it were not very successful, owing partly to certain political pressures and partly to certain more or less automatic tendencies. The line was constantly surpassed, for it is not only very difficult to forecast changes in government expenditures but also to keep any changes within narrow limits. The budget, for example, gives only the ceilings, yet some items of the actual expenditure can be lower. And during the year, supplementary budgets are processed by Parliament—and this could not be prohibited without impairing the flexibility necessary to democratic procedures. Furthermore, the expenditures are never fully centralized.

Monetary Policy

For monetary policy, the Netherlands Central Bank uses the rule that in general the interior creation of liquidity must be 40 percent of the projected average yearly increase of real national income, which is 4 percent. Thus the guideline of interior liquidity creation is 1.6 percent of national income, which means that a price inflation has to be financed by the surplus on the balance of payments. To the degree that public budget financing does not or cannot compensate for the difference between the guideline and the actual interior liquidity created by private financial intermediaries, the Central Bank has ways and means of filling the positive or negative gap. It stands to reason that a restrictive monetary policy is easier to apply than a stimulating monetary policy. But the question arises whether the surplus on the balance of payments is sufficient to finance the degree of price inflation which is necessary to reach external equilibrium. Thus, in practice, it is difficult to give a final answer to the question: has monetary policy been successful up until now?

Wage Policy

From 1954 until 1956 a fixed relation drawn from a basic period between the average wage income and the national income per head of the active working population was applied to short-run wage policy. In 1959 this guideline was replaced by another, which was also used for price policy. It can be expressed as follows:

$$w = a_1 + 1/2(a_2 - a_1)$$
$$p = w - a_2,$$

where w is the wage increase in a given industry, a_1 the national productivity increase, a_2 the productivity increase of the industry, and p the price increase or decrease in the industry. For the year 1962 the following formula was used:

$$w = 1/4(a_2 + 3a_1).$$

These guidelines have now been dropped, mainly because wage and price policies cannot be pursued by rules of thumb.

SPECIAL ADVISORY ACTIVITY OF THE SEC

Most of the SEC's advice to the government deals with such specific problems as social insurance, reduction of working hours, and so on. In 1957 and 1959, however, it provided the basis for the economic policy as a whole. In 1957, the immediate cause was a deficit in the current account of the 1956 balance of payments and the consequent expectation of inflationary pressures during 1957. In 1959, the immediate cause was the government's wish to decrease the budget's subsidy burdens, in order to safeguard other essential governmental tasks; giving priority to this decrease, the government asked the SEC for advice on its possibility, taking into account the restoration of balance of payments equilibrium.

Before we describe how the SEC handled these two appeals for advice, some comment about the relation between the actual procedure in the SEC and the idea of a preference function will be useful.

SEC and the Preference Function

1. The bargaining procedure in the SEC is not a game isolated from the society as a whole and the actual political situation. The interactions are extremely complex.

2. The preferences of the members influence each other, either in a diverging or a converging way. Compromises are not only calculated but also created. The process is creative, and unanimity is not always the desideratum.

3. Not only the targets but also the instruments and qualitative means are objects of preference.

4. A sharp distinction between preferences and restraints is not always possible. The interpretation of restraints and uncertainties is influenced by the preferences.

5. Basically, the preferences are not only a matter of personal predilection. They are also the result of interpretation, knowledge, intuition, theoretical insight, etc. So, for instance, it cannot be said that a trade unionist always and unrestrictedly gives greater weight to full employment than to price stability. To a high degree, preferences are determined by an objective, overall idea of how the general economic mechanism works.

6. Consistency in the choices is necessary. Inconsistency is a sign of a lack of understanding or of foresight; consistency is furthered by the discussions in the SEC.

7. It would be very difficult to posit a preference function in which the right to take part in decisions (the basis of democratic procedure) has a quantitative place.

8. Not only is the average or total value of an element in a preference function important, but also its distribution over various groups.[4] So, for instance, besides the average wage increase, there are the wage increases in different industries. This problem cannot be solved without

---

[4] See J. Tinbergen, *Economic Policy: Principles and Design* (North-Holland, 1956), p. 12.

accepting a certain freedom of bargaining at industry-level and at plant-level.

9. Every decision has legal aspects, and some members of the SEC are lawyers—whose ways of thinking are not the same as those of econo-mists. In essence, the "languages" are different. It is not surprising that the lawyers do not bow easily to the idea of a quantative preference function. Tinbergen writes that various elements of the "social climate" enter into the welfare function that is in the policy-maker's mind. The difficulty is to formulate this very complicated function explicitly.[5]

Nevertheless, some approach to an explicit formulation, as far as this would be possible, would be instructive to the SEC (and to the policy-maker in general). Tinbergen mentions three ways for constructing a preference function: explicit collection of data through questions to policy-makers; analysis of practical decisions to discover the implicit valuations that played a role in them; a trial construction on the basis of some intuitive knowledge about policy-makers' preferences.[6] Future discussions could perhaps be rationalized somewhat along these lines.

Expenditures Restriction in 1957

The program of expenditure restriction that SEC advised in 1957 was as follows:[7]

	Forecast	Target	Difference
Private Consumption	18.80	18.53	− .27
Government Expenditures (wages excluded)	2.84	2.68	− .16
Gross Private Investments (stocks excluded)	6.65	6.38	− .27
Surplus Current Account	+ .03	+ .38	+ .35

These measures were also proposed: restriction of wage increases; re-striction of government expenditures; tax increases, including abolition of the reduction for investments; reduction of subsidies on consumer goods and, consequently, increases of prices.

The SEC was unanimous on the whole program, which it believed would lead to a balanced distribution of the necessary restrictions on expenditures. And should the combination of measures be altered, the

[5] *Ibid.*, p. 11.
[6] *Ibid.*, pp. 17, 18.
[7] In billions (mld.) of guilders (gld.), at 1955 prices.

SEC believed that cooperation between employers' and workers' organizations would in part be destroyed. In the opinion of some commentators, the program was an intolerable pressure on the government. Yet it seems clear that government control of wage policy cannot be accepted unless private organizations have influence on other parts of economic policy. Programming is the recognition of this essential interdependence and of the necessity for coordination.

The program of restriction demonstrated (1) that it was possible to reach agreements on a national level, and (2) that the balance of payments played a dominant policy role. The advice of SEC, as usual, was not binding. The government made some alterations in the program, but agreement was finally reached with the Labor Foundation on wage policy. At the time of programming, the figures of the current account were (in mld. gld.):

1956	1957		1958
Forecast	*Forecast*	*Target*	*Forecast*
− .10	+ .03	+ .38	+ .20

The realized figures were:

1956	1957	1958
− .69	− .48	+1.50

A comparison of estimations, targets, and realizations shows that the margin of unforeseen changes was broader than the margin of decisions. Development during 1956 and 1957 was less than was expected, but the recovery in 1958 was exceptional, considering that a surplus of + .50 was regarded as being normal. Two points should be especially noted: the cyclical fluctuations were underestimated; the expected increase of private investments in 1957 was too high and in 1958 too low (time-lag and reaction was underestimated).

There is reason for some skepticism about the program's efficiency. One might surmise that private investments were restricted less (or more) by a shortage of liquidity or capital, rather than by the program. A deficit on the balance of payments combined with a sound monetary policy limits investment expenditures by a shortage of liquidity.

Expenditures Increase in 1959

At the end of 1958 the SEC was asked to advise about the reduction of consumer subsidies on milk, subsidies on housebuilding, farmer subsidies, and a further increase of house rents, taking into account the introduction of some new social insurance programs (widow and orphan insurance and a general scheme for children's allowances). The problem was as follows.

The wage policy was based on the annual calculated "room" for wage increases, taking into account the five targets (noted above) proposed in 1953. One of the limits for nominal wage increases is the competitive power with regard to other countries. A decrease of subsidies means a price level increase. So the proposed subsidy-elimination measures would offset part of the nominal wage increases and consequently restrict the real wage increases. In addition, the restriction of wage increases advised in 1957 was still in effect. It was clear that the restoration of balance of payments equilibrium made expansion of expenditures possible; the government, however, claimed a part of the expansion room for its subsidy-elimination measures.

The trade unions were unwilling to accept this disposition of the problem, especially since they considered subsidies to be an instrument for a reasonable distribution of wealth. At the same time, the majority in Parliament resisted the planned continuation of the tax measures adopted in the 1957 restriction program. The result was that the Government resigned. Under these circumstances, SEC had no chance to submit a unanimous advice; nevertheless it went beyond the usual limits of requested advice and widened the policy decision problem.

Among the forecasts of the CPB for 1959 and 1960 were the following:[8]

	1959	1960
Increase in volume of exports	6.0%	7.5%
Increase in gross national product	3.0	4.5
Increase in private consumption	3.0	3.0
Increase in private investments	−1.0	10.0
Surplus current account (in mld. gld.)	1.25	−.83

One of the leading opinions in the SEC was that the excess surplus on the current account was the result of restrictions on investments, and that a restoration of the normal level of investments would result in a normal surplus of + .50 after 1960. The trade unions, however, criticized the CPB's exports forecast as well as the above opinion.

The report of the SEC contained: the unanimous opinion that a certain increase of total expenditure was possible; three alternative combinations of proposed measures; some proposals about the house rents policy, the consumers' subsidies policy, and the wages policy. The three alternative

[8] This was the first time CPB had published forecasts for a two-year period.

combinations were chosen on the basis of a tabulation of the calculated influence of:

1. 100 mln (million) increase in government expenditures;
2. 25 percent rent increase;
3. 100 mln farmers' subsidies decrease;
4. 100 mln consumers' subsidies decrease (controversial);
5. 100 mln decrease direct taxes (controversial);
6. 100 mln decrease indirect taxes (controversial);
7. 1 percent wage increase (controversial);

on:

1. the current account;
2. the consumption price level;
3. the government budget;
4. employment;
5. the private investments level;
6. real available wages;
7. real national income;
8. the level of export prices.

This advice of the SEC shows very clearly how far economic policy can be quantified. The policy problem is reduced to the choice between different quantified alternatives; the decisive responsibility of the policy-maker, however, is *not* restricted to this choice but extends to the acceptance of uncertainties.

It is instructive to compare the above CPB 1959 and 1960 forecasts with a later forecast for 1960 and with the realized figures for 1959 and 1960.

	1959		1960		
Increase in:	*Forecast*	*Realized*	*Forecast I*	*Forecast II*	*Realized*
Volume of exports	6.0%	12.0%	7.5%	8.0%	14.5%
Gross national product	3.0	5.0	4.5	5.5	8.0
Private consumption	3.0	3.5	3.0	5.5	8.0
Private investments	−1.0	8.5	10.0	14.0	15.0
Surplus current account (mld. gld.)	1.25	1.8	−.83	−.7	1.2

The difference between the first and the second forecasts for 1960 was partly due to the decisions made by the government about the increase of expenditures; except for private investment it was much smaller, however, than the difference between both sets of the forecasts and the realizations. In other words, the margin of action was again smaller than the margin of unforeseen changes.

CYCLICAL ASPECTS

So far, forecasts of cyclical movements have been mainly unsuccessful. Generally speaking, in the first phase of the upswing, the increases of exports and productivity were underestimated. These underestimates were the basis of wage policy, so the first phase of the upswing was characterized by rapidly increasing profits and liquidities, which can be called "profit inflation." In the second phase, wage increases, increases of consumption, and increases of private investment went hand in hand, creating a situation of over-full employment. Black wages increased (which means that wage policy becomes less effective in the same degree as it becomes more necessary).

From the viewpoint of stability, the wage increases came *too late* and were *too large*. The policy in practice was, not stabilizing, but to a certain degree pro-cyclical. A comparison with competing countries shows that in The Netherlands the level of wage costs fluctuated more than elsewhere. It stands to reason that this experience did not work in favor of control of wage increases.

Another problem is the policy aimed at stimulating private investments in fixed assets. Private investments are indirectly subsidized by tax reductions, with the consequence that the built-in stabilizer of progressive tax rates is weakened. It seems to be very difficult to create investment incentives which will lead to a high, and at the same time stable, investment level. When, however, it is true—and it could be—that investments cannot be postponed from periods of expansion to periods of retardation, the policy-maker has to choose between a high but fluctuating investment level and a low but rather stable level. Our knowledge about the actual relation between stability and growth has been inadequate, with the consequence that we cannot yet draw final conclusions about the efficacy of wage policy and tax policy applied up until now.

CRUCIAL EXPERIENCES WITH WAGE POLICY

In the evolution of wage policy in The Netherlands four phases can be distinguished:

1. Controlled nationwide wage increases, based on increased costs of living.
2. Controlled nationwide wage increases, based on the increase of national income.
3. Controlled wage increases, based on differences in productivity increases.
4. Controlled wage increases, based on a yearly fixed target for the national average wage increases.

The transition to phase 2 was the result of the improved economic situation after the period of reconstruction, as noted earlier. The transition to phase 3 was the product of pressures to liberalize wage increases and to reduce government control; the result was, however, a more detailed control, and this led to the transition to phase 4. Technically speaking, the method of controlled nationwide wage increases is the most efficient. When different increases are allowed for different branches, satisfactory control is theoretically and practically impossible.

The criterion for wage differentials included in the formula $w = a_1 + \frac{1}{2}(a_2 - a_1)$ is based on the assumption that compensating price movements can be induced. One may question whether it is realistic to expect that growing industries with productivity increases above the national average will decrease their prices—especially when, as in The Netherlands, the expanding industries are mostly exporting industries. A more fundamental criticism is that the wage differentials increase is unlimited when time and growth go on. Transition to a system of nationwide wage increases would finally be unavoidable.

ELEMENTS OF THE PROBLEM

The wage problem in The Netherlands has been determined by the following elements:

1. The control of wages is, in practice, control of collective agreements. The collective agreement contains maxima and minima for basic wages and regulations for different sorts of additional payments, such as piece rates, holiday payments, merit rating, etc.

2. A part of the national wage bill (higher salaries) is not regulated by collective agreements and is therefore not controlled.

3. In different ways, the actual wages can exceed the agreed and approved wages. These "black" (illegal) wages are not controlled by definition but fluctuate between 3 and 7 percent of the total wage bill.

4. The uncontrolled part of the total wage bill, including black wages, fluctuates in relation to the degree of employment. Generally speaking,

about 50 percent of the yearly increases of the wage bill is uncontrolled.

5. The degree of control of the collective agreement cannot be too intensive to maintain a certain margin for freedom of bargaining.

6. Since 1945, The Netherlands has been confronted with the problem of over-full employment, notwithstanding a high birth rate. The increase of exports had regularly been more than was projected. Thus, especially in the export industries, the degree of employment had been extremely high. In addition, labor demand in the building industry has exceeded labor supply. Under these circumstances, the control of wages has been very difficult.

A New Concept

As a result of experience, the three trade union centers recently formulated a new wage policy based on a threefold responsibility:

1. The government's part in wage policy should be restricted to such *ultima remedia* as: marginal control of excessive wage increases that threaten the common interest; a general wage freeze in exceptional situations; regulation of the climate for collective bargaining by an adequate use of other instruments.

2. The Labor Foundation should have the right to reject excessive agreements.

3. The trade union centers should try to set up a system of internal coordination on wage claims in the different branches of industry. (A countervailing internal coordination on the employers' side would be useful.)

The basis of activities would be semiannual reports of the SEC concerning both the economic situation and the efficiency of the various instruments. The practical difficulty was that—to implement the concept— both the government and the FL would have to change their attitudes about the field of wages from *full engagement* to *reserved attention*. The new concept was in general accepted by the SEC, which advised the government to introduce the policy—and it was introduced at the beginning of 1963. Nevertheless, the government's attitude was, in practice, not changed, and this intensified the wage policy crisis of September 1963.

SOME PROPOSALS

In general, it can be said that the recent trend of Dutch planning has been away from detailed controls and toward regulation of a climate that would create incentives leading in the "right" direction. The following items represent my own opinion of what is needed to carry this trend further:

1. The employment and investment targets need further elaboration.

2. Equilibrium between national supply and demand on the labor market is not sufficient; there should also be equilibrium on the different parts of the labor market. A sectoral shortage of labor could be the immediate cause of cost inflation.

3. A systematic policy is necessary to further labor mobility in all relevant directions.[9]

4. Control of investments cannot be the task of the government. But, assuming the freedom of private investments, how can a sufficient structural level and a reasonable stability be obtained? Experience shows that private investments fluctuate very strongly. The target should be a reasonable rate of growth, but the contribution to growth of the same amount of investment is likely to be different in different industries. The problem to be solved is: how can the government stimulate private investments that make a large contribution to the growth of national income?

5. Labor mobility and investment policies need to be based on projections of the development of the various industries and also of the public sector. This could be the task of the Central Planning Bureau; the task of the Social Economic Council would be to advise the government about the possible instruments and the targets.

[9] Recently the government asked the SEC to advise on this.

8

French Planning

BERNARD CAZES[1]

EVERY DISCUSSION of a given country's economic planning ought to start with a definition, because "planning" has been assumed to be inconsistent with the market economy. Reference to history is in this case of little help. Either we are dealing with relatively recent history—in which the role of the Soviet experiment engenders heated debate on what has taken place in the Soviet Union since 1928-29 rather than a technical appreciation of the possibilities and limits of an economic plan —or we are dealing with such ancient history that the notion of planning cannot be found.

What remains then for "plan," historically, is only the connotation of order or method, generally applied to the field of thought or of discourse rather than to the field of action. It is significant that the *Encyclopedie* of Diderot and d'Alembert, so modern in many respects, did not attribute to the word more than its architectural and rhetorical meaning. Further obscuring the word is the abuse it has suffered by being used to describe any project—whether coherent or not—that is offered to the consideration of public opinion.

THE NATURE AND ROLE OF THE FRENCH PLAN

France's first four-year "Plan for Modernization and Equipment" (adopted in 1947 and occasionally called the "Monnet Plan" after Jean Monnet, the first General Commissioner of Planning) provided a statement which those responsible for French planning consider to be a worthy definition:

> For all the essential activities, and those making use of common and limited resources (energy, steel, foreign exchange stocks, the labor force), the

[1] Special Assistant to the General Commissioner of Planning.

179

work of modernization could not be accomplished successfully by isolated cases of initiative ignoring each other: the French, in order to succeed in this field, must undertake the work of modernization with a common point of view, so that each activity is supported by the other and so that the shortcomings of one activity or another do not delay general progress. We must, therefore, act according to a plan, and the entire nation must associate itself with it. Such a plan (and it is in this spirit that the first plan of modernization here proposed has been formulated) is essentially a *method of convergence to action* and the means by which everyone can direct his effort in relation to the general effort.[2]

Subsequently, planning was given an "official" definition, in the text of the law approving the Second Plan (1954-57):

The Second Plan for Modernization and Investment, defined in the document annexed to the present law, is approved as an instrument for orienting the economy and as a framework for investment programs in the metropolitan and overseas territories.

This formula was used almost unchanged in the texts of the decrees approving the four-year plans which followed—the Third (1958-61) and the Fourth (1962-65).

Note, however, that these are not definitions of planning in general, but definitions of *French* ways and means of planning. The difference is not merely semantic. If we agree that there is a rationale for formulating multi-annual global plans for a decentralized economy, then we must also agree that planning, from the indicative plan to the "command economy," can be present in various economic systems—in the same manner, as the philosopher Maurice Merleau-Ponty noted, that one could foresee a generalized political economy in which capitalism and communism are but particular cases.[3]

This "generalized planning" could be defined as a technique by which development is assured and regulated by the acceptance of a common view of the foreseeable pattern of development, as opposed to the market economy where "the decisions to produce and invest are, in general, based on the surveys of the market made by the commercial services of the enterprises—this information often being completed by an observation of the business cycle but generally not being linked with a common hypothesis about the possible long-range patterns of development of the economy."[4]

[2] *Rapport général sur le Premier Plan de modernization et d'équipment* (Paris, Imprimerie Nationale, 1946; new edition, 1963), p. 21. (Italics in the original French text.)

[3] *Les Aventures de la Dialectique* (Gallimard, 1955), p. 303.

[4] Claude Gruson, *La Prévision économique aux Etats-Unis* (Cahiers de l'Institut de Science économique appliquée, 1956, Serie K, No. 2).

Starting with this minimal concept, it is possible to arrive at a definition of "the Plan" which would be valid for France as well as for other cases, even though the plans are very different in scope and degree: an economic plan is a set of coherent figures, characteristic of the economic activity of the country considered and dealing with a terminal year more or less distant. This stresses the two characteristics essential to any plan: consistency (that is, the necessary interdependence of the various figures) and duration (that is, the temporal distance between the drafting period and the terminal year). The four French plans have each been for a four-year period, but they have been framed by longer-term projections and also, during their implementation, divided into annual economic budgets.

Objectives

The figures that are characteristic of economic activity are now set in France, as they are in an increasing number of other countries, within the framework of a national accounts system which, on the principle of double accounting, allows the activity of economic agents that in general exercise the same function, as well as the totality of operations of the same type, to be described and measured. The Second Plan especially relied on such figures, in contrast to the way prevailing scarcities permitted the planner both to define the First Plan's orientation and to choose the priority industries without an accurate knowledge of the domestic output and its prospects of growth. At the very beginning, the plan consisted of an aggregation of sectoral targets of production and investment which supposedly could be implemented without being synthesized in a general study of the problems inherent in the very fact of implementation. By contrast, the establishment of a system of integrated accounts in the early 1950's offered planners a technical instrument to describe economic interdependence, to determine the main economic aggregates, and to test the consistency of the various parts of a plan (as will be discussed later).[5]

That the quantitative elements defining a plan are presented in national accounting terms could suggest that the classic difference between "goals" and "means" is outmoded, because goals and means are interdependent. In the case of the French plan, however, we can note the necessary distinction suggested by Professor Jean Bénard between normative

[5] See Mme. E. Betout-Mossé, "La Comptabilité nationale dans la préparation du IV° Plan," *Etudes et Conjoncture*, No. 4-5, April-May 1963 (Paris, PUF; Imprimerie Nationale).

objectives and "constraining objectives."[6] The normative objectives are "those which express the deliberate choice of the government within the framework of the economic and social constraints and assume therefore a scale of values, regardless of whether this scale of value is explicit or not." This is the case, for example, with the improvement of living standards, the effort to encourage public investment in education or basic research, and the policy of regional development. The constraining objectives are concerned with "the goals which must be attained in order that the general economic balance does not seriously deteriorate and grave social tensions do not arise." We can sum them up by referring to the well-known "magic triangle"—full employment, monetary stability, equilibrium (or overequilibrium) of balance of payments. These objectives determine the framework within which the normative objectives are to be defined; they also in some sense set forth the limits which cannot be transcended.

The French plans have underlined the constraints that must always be respected if the final objectives are to be attained without jeopardizing economic stability, but the priorities have varied from one plan to another, depending on the problems that developed during a plan's preparation. The First Plan vigorously stressed modernization and development of the basic sectors of the economy (energy, railroad transportation, cement, steel, agricultural equipment) aiming to eliminate bottlenecks that could frustrate further expansion. Once this economic infrastructure was reconstituted and modernized, the Second Plan could propose objectives which were conceived in global terms and which put much more stress on productivity and competitiveness.[7] The Third Plan, the beginning of which coincided with the economic slack of 1958 and 1959, announced as its main objectives: (1) re-establishment of monetary stability and balance of payments equilibrium, with a growth rate of 20 percent of GNP within four years; (2) adaptation of the French economy to the Common Market; (3) measures concerning the problem of the increase in the labor force due to the increase in the birth rate since 1945.

So far, one can say that the fundamental objective of the plans had been to push economic growth to the maximum, yet to emphasize at the same time the obstacles to be surmounted in the area of physical and

[6] J. Bénard, Cours sur la programmation économique nationale, à moyen et à long terme dans les pays industrialisés (Paris, 1960), Centre d'Etudes des Programmes Economiques, Fascicule I, pp. 60-61.

[7] Between the First Plan and the Second the Missions concerned with productivity visited the United States and made their important contribution to the propagation of technical innovations in the French economy.

financial balance, as well as the structural adaptations implied by this growth rate (export-mindedness in business circles, interindustrial shifts of production factors, improvement of productivity).

For the Fourth Plan the push toward maximum economic growth continued to be a major objective, but other preoccupations were added, which were directly linked to the problem of wider distribution of the benefits of an expanding economy.[8] For example, how should the benefits be shared between marketable goods and services for private consumption and the services that are rendered by collective (or social overhead) equipment, or between the prosperous regions of the country and the insufficiently developed? And how can more of the benefits go as social allowances to disadvantaged segments of the population—aged people, overlarge families, and workers still paid at the lowest legal wage (SMIG)—without upsetting the stability of the economy?

These preoccupations with the ultimate goals of economic growth were given concrete form in the Fourth Plan through: (1) an increase of the public investment by 50 percent within four years, at a rate twice higher than that of the gross domestic output (24 percent); (2) a "priming" policy in favor of the regions suffering from a serious imbalance between the possibilities of and the demands for employment; and (3) an annual examination of changes in the various categories of income, which would serve as a basis for governmental decisions concerning social allowances and SMIG.

With the Fourth Plan, French planning took on a certain normative character. The term is not misused (if one points out that this normative aspect was not completely new): searching for a maximum growth compatible with the physical and financial constraints judged admissible, or formulating a plan implying the achievement of full employment (or, more precisely, insignificant frictional unemployment) means, in many cases, going against the natural tendency of the economy—notably in the

---

[8] The change in view can be illustrated by comparing the following two excerpts from the Third and Fourth Plans, dealing with objectives in the field of social investments:

The Third Plan (page 10): "The investments that will dominate the future such as those in energy or production or services that contribute to the balance of payments must not be delayed. In return, the rate of growth of other investments will be adapted according to the possibilities."

The Fourth Plan (page 26): "The attainment of the whole of these programmes [in social investment] is an integral part of the objectives of the Plan. But if it should happen that disappointments arose, either as regards the rate of growth, or the maintenance of economic balance, the Government would strive, in making the adjustments which would then become necessary, to safeguard the increase in this category of investments."

opinion of those who believe that economic growth cannot be predetermined and that full employment and monetary stability are incompatible.

It would be more exact, however, to say that the normative aspects
of French planning have varied, depending on the level of development
attained and the degree of maturation of public opinion concerning the
problems. According to the wording of the Fourth Plan, "the social and
regional dimensions" it contains "represent an attempt and a hope" whose
goal is to mark, not a turning, but an inflection which will allow a clarification of the possible alternatives and provoke public debate on the
choices to be made. Going farther would be nearly impossible and actually
not very desirable, first of all because the "civilization of the gadget"
remains for numerous Frenchmen a still unattainable goal, and also because the flexibility of technical, economic, and psychological structures is
not sufficient to permit quick modification of the direction of development.[9]

A plan does not, however, limit itself to the determination of a certain
number of goals relative to the magnitude of the rate of growth and to
its breakdown according to certain national preference. It is equally concerned with production and investments, which, in the vocabulary of a
plan, are defined in terms of programs and of forecasts.

As far as productive enterprises are concerned, the French plan has
been described as "market research on a national scale" (P. Massé), allowing enterprises to buy their inputs and to sell their products on
ex ante balanced markets, each one's production constituting the outlet
for all. But this general scheme is implemented differently from branch
to branch, according to the nature of the economic activity concerned.
In the basic sectors, which are very concentrated and necessitate heavy
investments, the plan has tended toward a definition of programs in
elaborate detail, starting with specific projects of the enterprises and
possibilities for outlets in the internal market and the export market. For
the processing industries, however—because of their great number and
also because of the rapid changes in their markets due to the rapid
progress in technology, the freedom of choice of the consumer, and the
intensity of the competition—the establishment in advance of detailed

---

[9] "In any future situation of reasonably full employment, we can estimate certain
quantities of goods and services that each sector will treat as necessities and will
surely buy if the money is available. For 1970 we estimate that these *basic* purchases
will pre-empt about 85 percent of the GNP. It is only the remaining 15 percent that
we can regard as subject to shifting preferences which may throw more in one sector
or another according to the economic, social, and political considerations of the day."
See National Planning Association, *The American Economy in 1970* (October 1959),
p. 16.

programs is not feasible. The plan has presented, therefore, an aggregation of forecasts, which are consistent with the general growth objective,
projected demand of the internal and external markets, and the technical
relationships between the several branches of industry.

The Search for Consistency

A plan does not constitute an aggregation of partial programs separately formulated. The First Plan for Modernization and Equipment,
in spite of the absence of national accounting (which was a definite handi-
cap), stressed that it was not "simply an aggregation of partial plans,"
but included ". . . objectives and . . . means with a view toward synthesis."
Thus begun, the search for consistency between the projected economic
magnitudes was from then on facilitated, first by the requirement that
each account must show a balance between supply and demand (which
avoids projecting future trends that are incompatible with each other),
then by the knowledge of certain relations which are fairly stable and
can only slowly be modified: structural coefficients (the relationship
between production and intermediary consumption and between production and capital formation, etc.), and behavioral relations (propensity
to consume and the attitude of private enterprises toward the ratio of
indebtedness). Essentially, this search—the practical application of which
we shall discuss later—concerns the physical balance of goods and services,
manpower balance, and financial balance.[10]

In summing up the functional role of French plans, two points should
be stressed:

1. The plans seek to improve the informational basis on which public
and private decisions are made, by estimating possibilities of growth for
a given future period through a quantitative statement of both probable
(for that part of the resources which are decentralized) and desirable (for
that part of the resources which are centrally allocated) proportions that
will prevail in the planning period. In this area, the plan works to reduce
the uncertainty that can be a powerful brake on productive investments—
and therefore on growth itself.

2. The plans also offer a framework for those long-term decisions on
which the market cannot function as a valid guide, either because market

[10] When the relations are not of purely technological order, but bring into play
psychological and institutional factors, as well as others (such as the admissible
budgetary deficit, the ratio of indebtedness of private enterprises, and wage increases),
the search for consistency assumes the aspect of a judgment about verisimilitudes.

indications cannot by themselves correct any developing imbalance (higher wages, for example, cannot correct a paucity in the labor force—they can only rearrange its distribution), or because, for certain goods and services, there is no market where consumers can express their preferences. To the degree that the four-year or five-year periods generally utilized turned out to be too short for certain economic investments (energy, public transportation, urban renewal, education), planners (and not only in France) were forced to integrate medium-term plans with long-term programs of ten to twenty years. This took the form either of quantitative plans or of a more qualitative analysis aimed at identifying the signs of what might be changes of a permanent nature—which one must discover at a very early stage, either to attempt to eliminate them, or, on the contrary, not to thwart them imprudently.[11]

ELABORATION OF THE PLAN: METHODS AND PROCEDURES

During the drafting period of a French plan—that is, the period when the general objectives are determined, as well as the sectoral and regional implications of the objectives—there is a convergence of three processes: the technical process of estimating the possibilities of developing and synthesizing the decentralized studies; the process of consultation with committees of general competence (such as the Economic and Social Council) and specialized committees (such as the Modernization Commissions); and finally the process of decision-making, in which the legislative and executive agencies of the government intervene. (The diagram on page 190 indicates how the three processes meshed with one another for the Fourth Plan; it also indicates the time table of the plan, which will be discussed later.)

The administrative structures of the planning process are uncomplicated and modestly staffed—as deliberately conceived by their creator, Jean Monnet. Established by decree on January 3, 1946, the General Planning Commissariat (CGP) has had a professional staff of no more than fifty people of diverse backgrounds—government officials, economists, engineers, and so on. From 1946 to 1954 it was attached to the Office of the Prime Minister, and from 1954 to 1962 to the Ministry of

---

[11] This qualitative analysis is occasionally called "prospective." See the magazine *Prospective* (Paris), as well as the studies published by the *Bulletin Sedeis* (Paris) under the general title "Futuribles."

Finance and Economic Affairs. Since 1962 it has again been attached to the Prime Minister's Office.

Ever since its inception—and without any written regulation to that effect—the Commissariat has enjoyed authentic intellectual independence. It has also apparently avoided the two classic stumbling blocks in this field: first, the academicism which threatens research organizations not directly connected with the governmental apparatus, and, second, the all-too-possible rivalries with the financial and technical departments of the government.

Undoubtedly it has been aided in this respect by various factors. It is, for instance, not responsible for any investment funds; it operates at a high level of the governmental apparatus; and the small size of its staff has made cooperation with other organizations and services more or less imperative—first of all to study the problems adequately and then (and especially) to implement the solutions. In the formulation of the Fourth Plan, for example, the following organizations were active participants with the Commissariat: the National Institute of Statistics and Economic Studies (INSEE), notably through its Division of Programs; the Economic and Financial Studies Service of the Ministry of Finance (SEEF), in the preparation of the initial projections and the verification of the coherence of the sectoral programs or forecasts; the National Institute for Demographic Studies (INED), in demographic projections of various kinds; the Center for Research and Documentation of Consumption (CREDOC), in long-term projections of consumer demand; the Center for Mathematical Research for Planning (CERMAP); the Center for Long-Term Projections (CEPREL); the "1985 Group"; and, of course, the many technical services of the various relevant ministries.

There are two main phases a French plan must weather before it reaches the stage of publication in the *Journal Officiel*. In describing these phases, we shall use the specific example of the Fourth Plan.

First Phase: Determination of General Objectives

The law of August 4, 1962, by which Parliament gave final approval to the Fourth Plan, officially defined the general objectives of the plan in these terms:

> Expansion of the economy; division of the gross domestic output between consumption and investment; a desirable structure for final consumption; guidelines for development of social policies as well as regional policies.

The determination of this type of objective can scarcely be entrusted to other than policy-making bodies; in France, however, the manner in which responsibility for planning has been divided between Parliament and the Administration has not been a matter of conscious deliberation. Rather, it reflects (1) a current characteristic of French political institutions—described by B. de Jouvenel as a decline of support along geographic and partisan lines in favor of support along occupational and professional lines—and (2) the difficulties French politicians have in approaching the problems of an industrial society.

That the Second and the Fourth Plan were approved by law, and the First and Third by simple decree, was the result of circumstances much more than of intention. (Incidentally, it must be admitted that the unusual and nonimperative legal character of a plan does nothing to facilitate an answer to the question: what governmental body is legally committed to settle the basic options of the plan?) Since 1962, however, the situation has become clearer from an institutional point of view; the terms of the law approving the Fourth Plan committed Parliament to much more active participation in the preparation of future plans.

Whatever the balance of political responsibilities in the determination of a plan's general objectives, the decisions concerning the Fourth Plan were clarified by the preliminary projections for long and medium terms, and by the debates within the Economic and Social Council.

In 1959, the SEEF drew up two projections dealing respectively with the year 1975 (the "horizon" of the plan) and 1965 (the "terminal year" of the plan).[12] The method chosen for the formulation of the projections was not based on a projection of manpower growth rate and productivity trends by branch, but implied an *a priori* selection among three annual rates of growth of the gross domestic output supposed to deal with all the probable situations: 3, 4½, and 6 percent.[13] The projection was made at constant prices, following an analysis which resorted to an increasingly detailed nomenclature (3, 17, 28, and then 65 branches). Finally, the projections were made with a procedure of successive approximations, implying a continuous to-and-fro movement between the initial hypotheses and their consequences, whose clarification influenced in turn the initial hypotheses.

[12] For that distinction, see P. Massé, "Prévision et Prospective," *Prospective,* December 1959.

[13] The 3 percent corresponds to the average and spontaneous growth trend of Western economies; 4½ percent is the average rate of growth in France for the 1950's; 6 percent was the "peak" rate attained in some years by the French economy.

As mentioned, the preliminary projections for 1965 were preceded by long-term studies (1975)—the far-away horizon being chosen to allow for a better recognition of the structural modifications caused or demanded by economic growth. In spite of the increasing uncertainties inherent in an extension of the estimate, this exploration of the future makes sense if certain constraints limit the range of possibilities. This is the case with the demographic constraints, whose study serves as a basis for the forecast of manpower resources, needs for educational and health investments, and so on. It is also possible to determine in general the limits which the national production could not permanently exceed without causing serious imbalances. Finally, there are institutional constraints which exclude vast and rapid changes of the structure of the final demand or of the instruments of governmental policy.[14]

We can say that the implications of alternative rates of growth for gross domestic output are most significant. Depending on whether the French economy progressed by 3 or by 6 percent, the index of GDO for 1975 would be 197 or 284, the individual means of transportation would multiply by 3 or 5, the volume output of the mechanical and electrical industries would multiply by 2.4 or 3.6. Thus, for the 1975 prospective study, the alternative growth rates in the 1965 projections were used.

As part of the procedure for choosing between the growth rate variables, the next step was the formulation of estimated physical balances (compatible with each assumed growth rate) between output and final demand, and between manpower availabilities and requirements. This was followed by a study of the financial balance.

The Output and Manpower Balance. A prospective physical balance for the terminal year of the plan was constructed by starting from the final demand side and working back to the supply side. Household consumption was directly estimated, instead of being treated as a balancing item arrived at by deducting from the gross domestic output the other elements which could be directly appraised. The technical work for this (mainly done by CREDOC) involved applying income

[14] The same basic hypothesis was evidently kept for the formulation of the projections for 1965: "For each one of the rates of growth retained, only one coherent set of needs and means has been studied. In each case its definition took into account the present economic organization and the preference for the solutions which did not affect the existing social structure. With the exception of foreign trade, where interventions of a protective character are as a rule eliminated, the means whose implementation is foreseen are of the same type as those utilized in France during the past decade." See CGP and SÉEF, *Les Perspectives de l'économie francaise en 1965* (February 1963), p. 13.

STAGES OF THE FOURTH PLAN (1962-1965)[a]

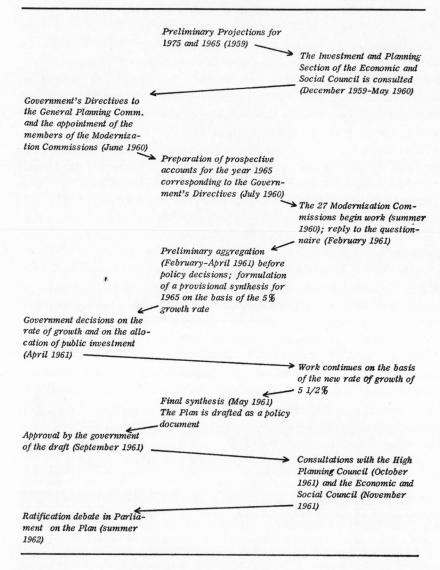

| Political Organs | General Planning Commissariat, National Institute of Statistics and Economic Studies (INSEE), and Economic and Financial Studies Service (SEEF) | Social-Occupational Representation |

Preliminary Projections for
1975 and 1965 (1959)

The Investment and Planning
Section of the Economic and
Social Council is consulted
(December 1959-May 1960)

Government's Directives to
the General Planning Comm.
and the appointment of the
members of the Moderniza-
tion Commissions (June 1960)

Preparation of prospective
accounts for the year 1965
corresponding to the Government's Directives (July 1960)

The 27 Modernization Com-
missions begin work (summer
1960); reply to the questionnaire (February 1961)

Preliminary aggregation
(February-April 1961) before
policy decisions; formulation
of a provisional synthesis for
1965 on the basis of the 5%
growth rate

Government decisions on the
rate of growth and on the allocation of public investment
(April 1961)

Work continues on the basis
of the new rate of growth of
5 1/2%

Final synthesis (May 1961)
The Plan is drafted as a policy
document

Approval by the government
of the draft (September 1961)

Consultations with the High
Planning Council (October
1961) and the Economic and
Social Council (November
1961)

Ratification debate in Parliament on the Plan (summer
1962)

[a]Bernard Cazes, La Planification en France et le IVe Plan (Paris, Editions de l'Epargne,
1962), page 67.

190

elasticity coefficients to the present consumption of individual goods and services, with the assumption that income distribution would be unchanged. For public consumption and investment (including housing, because of the large amount of public funds devoted to financing home construction), projections were made on the basis of (1) data supplied by the ministries and (2) the known long-term policy intentions of the government. The exports projections implied a certain number of hypotheses about the overall growth of foreign markets and the share of French exports in each market. The required level of productive investment was calculated through direct inquiry (for energy, railways, steel, and aluminum) or indirect evaluation (by capital coefficients), with a breakdown of investments, first by branches of productive activity, second by types of product. For intermediate consumption an interindustrial matrix was used by the SEEF, with adjustments to take account of predictable technological changes. Eventually, manpower requirements by sectors were calculated according to projected rates of increase in productivity, and then checked with availabilities, the comparison being made at three levels: nationwide, skills, and regional balance.

The Financial Balance. The projected physical output targets allowed identification of the tensions arising as the rate of growth increases. But the conditions for implementation are not only physical; a study of the financial difficulties which may arise must also be made. Therefore a projection was made of the financial behavior (that is, in relation to income) of households, of enterprises, and of the government, to identify the risks of incompatibility between the saving propensity of the household, the debt-incurring propensity of the enterprises, and the admissible level of the government's budgetary deficit. Tables of prospective financial operations were drafted to find out whether the demands and the financing capacity of the various economic agents resulting from the preceding global projection could be balanced through the action of financial intermediaries.

Although a study of the three growth rate variants did not yield a complete picture of the alternative possibilities of the French economy between the drafting period and 1965, it did permit certain important conclusions to be drawn. From the point of view of the main equilibria, the lowest variant (3 percent) appeared to be relatively easy to achieve; indeed, it allowed a slight slackening of the investment effort. But it would not take care of the most pressing national needs—new jobs for the young, improvement of the standard of living, national defense, economic aid for developing countries—all of which called for a rapid rate of growth. The rapid rate was physically possible, but could jeopardize the foreign trade balance and also would require considerable effort from the steel, metalworking, and electrical industries. Therefore, the Commissariat concluded its preliminary report by recommending a growth rate between 4½ and 5½ percent.

Consultation with the Economic and Social Council. Before reaching a final decision on the plan, the government made an important innovation by submitting the results of the three 1965 projections (the 1975 projections were not made public because of their experimental character) to the Investment and Planning Section of the Economic and Social Council. The Section was asked to appraise the forecasts (especially in the case of foreign trade), the provisional decisions regarding the individual and collective needs that ought to be met and regarding the means of meeting them, and, finally, whether the difficulties to be surmounted had been adequately considered. After several months of hearings and study the Section unanimously recommended to the government that the Fourth Plan adopt a growth rate as close to 6 percent as possible—to speed an increase in collective consumption, and to reduce discrepancies in income levels between regions and between social categories.

The Governmental Directives. After the Economic and Social Council had made its recommendations, the government issued a set of directives to the CGP (and, through it, to the Modernization Commissions), prefaced as follows:

> This document is intended to define the direction that the Government—in the light of surveys submitted to it by the General Planning Commissariat and by the Investment and Planning Section of the Economic Council—has decided to give to the work of elaborating the Fourth Plan (January 1, 1962/December 31, 1965). It will enable the General Planning Commissariat to furnish the Planning Commissions, responsible for working out the detailed programmes of the different branches, with a common view of the general lines of development within which their individual work will be contained and its coherence assured.

The directives made the following four main points in defining the policy orientation of the Fourth Plan.

1. The twofold general objective of the plan was defined as "fulfillment of the grand national tasks" and "improvement of the living conditions of the population." The first referred to the development of Al-

geria and the overseas territories, aid to the member states of the French Communauté, and national defense. The second point stressed the immensity of the needs that must be satisfied, and the necessity of insuring full employment and of giving a larger role than before to the social investments that help to counteract the numerous shortcomings of an industrial civilization.

2. The overall rate of growth decided upon as the basis for the work of the Modernization Commissions was an increase of approximately 22 percent of the gross domestic output—or an annual average of 5 percent—but the directives did not exclude a higher rate (5½ percent) if further studies showed it to be a possibility. Considering the demographic situation that would prevail during the period covered by the plan, and particularly the slow rate of increase of the working population until 1965, such an output objective implied that there could be no general reduction in working hours. Its fulfillment also implied a vigorous effort in the areas of exports and investments, and "a discipline of prices and wages to avoid reviving inflation by the distribution of unearned incomes."

3. Specific guidelines for the main sectors of the economy were suggested for the Commissions' consideration in their detailed studies. These dealt with productive activity in the fields of agriculture, energy, industry (both heavy and processing), transport, communication, commerce, and tourism.

4. Conditions for implementing a basic equilibrium were stressed because the chosen rate of growth was ambitious and had not been achieved (except sporadically) since the end of World War II. The Commissions were therefore asked to make an extremely careful study of equilibrium regarding employment, foreign exchange, sources of and needs for savings, and regions. Regional balance especially would become the object of more detailed study than in earlier plans: the Commissions were charged with proceeding, as much as possible, toward "regionalization"—that is, evaluating their estimates of investment and employment according to the distribution in the twenty-two regions of France.

Second Phase: Detailed Formulation of the Plan

After the governmental directives were issued, the three variants that had been studied during the first phase were combined into one, corresponding to a growth rate of 5 percent. This coherent but schematic outline would serve as a basis for the work of the Modernization Commissions, and would be translated in terms of programs or forecasts by sectors.

The Modernization Commissions. The thirty to fifty persons who made up each Modernization Commission for the Fourth Plan served (without compensation) from June 1960 to September 1961. Appointed by decision of the Minister of Finance, having been proposed by the Commissariat, they were representative of the following groups: high-level civil servants; producers (heads of private or nationalized enterprises and farmers); leaders of business associations; trade unionists; and university economists and other independent experts.

From one plan to another, new Commissions had been added as a consequence of demands made by private enterprises or public agencies that wished to participate in the process of formulating a plan—either because it would give them a better knowledge of their markets or because it would provide a more solid basis for decisions about their own investments, as well as for budgetary discussions with the Ministry of Finance. Thus, not only has the number of Commissions increased with each new plan, but the total personnel (including ex officio members) serving on them has increased even more: for the First Plan, Commission members totaled 494; for the Second and Third, 730 and 892; for the Fourth, 1,336. (A listing of the Fourth Plan Commissions and the composition of their membership is provided at the end of this paper.)

Each Commission creates, according to its needs, a variable number of "working parties" which include many people who are not Commission members.[15] Their activities are widely varied. For the Steel Commission on the Fourth Plan, for example, one working party studied outlets for the year 1965 in the domestic and foreign markets by calculating the correlation between the gross domestic output and the consumption of steel, then cross-checking it with a direct examination of the demand, consumer by consumer. Another concerned itself with investment programs, through analyzing replies to questionnaires sent to the steel firms.

The specific composition of the Commissions is not designed according to any given pattern, and there is no proportional representation of each enterprise interest. If unanimity cannot be achieved within a Commission, the opinions of the minority are expressly mentioned in the eventual reports. Experience over the years has revealed one especially difficult functional problem: consumers and users of public services are represented on the Commissions only by trade union members, but political

---

[15] For the elaboration of the Fourth Plan, the working party members (most of whom are civil servants) totaled over 2,000.

considerations and lack of financial and human resources hamper the union members' representational effectiveness. A solution of the problem based on parity of representation would be illusory, since the Commissions have no voting procedures. And the appointment of a union representative as *rapporteur* or chairman of a Commission or working group would not be easily compatible with his representation of his own union. Apparently the wisest solution to the problem is to increase the economic expertise of union members.

The Modernization Commissions are grouped in two categories: those described as "vertical" (of which there were twenty-two for the Fourth Plan), each of which studies all the problems involved in the development of a specific sector of economic or social activity, and those described as "horizontal" (five for the Fourth Plan), which are charged with synthesizing the information furnished by the vertical commissions about a general problem—for instance, financing, growth of the labor force, research, productivity, or regional development. The horizontal Commissions are one of the means, though not the only one, whereby the work of all the vertical Commissions results in a plan in which all parts fit correctly.

The Problems of Synthesis. The consistency of a plan is jeopardized by the corrections made by the Commissions (for example, corrections in the provisory economic equilibrium for 1965 in the Fourth Plan), but is looked for, even so, through the singleness of the basic hypotheses on which the Commissions are working, the homogeneity of the forecasting methods used, and eventually the general coordination to which all the evaluations are submitted.

The basic hypotheses for the Fourth Plan furnished by the government directives to the Commissions were supplemented by the provisional national accounts for 1965, which showed prospective estimates for production, employment, and investment for twenty-eight branches of the economy. Each "vertical" Commission studied the estimates for the specific branch it was analyzing (especially the development of domestic and foreign outlets) and made explicit the resulting production figures for the final year of the plan. Each one also determined the various means whereby the production figures might be realized. The results of the work were cast in two forms: quantitative replies to the common questionnaire which had been sent to each Commission, and later reports dealing with the current situation and the projections of the branches analyzed.

The figures supplied in the questionnaire were of course provisional, and the Commissions could modify them, either at their own discretion or at the request of the CGP, when varying estimates needed to be reconciled. Questionnaire answers were to be completed before February 1961, so that the Equilibrium Working Party[16] and the Manpower Commission could proceed during the first quarter of 1961 with a "first" (provisional) synthesis of the Plan—in other words, formulate a balanced economic perspective for 1965 on the basis of the 5 percent growth rate.

This provisional synthesis was another innovation (during formulation of the Third Plan a synthesis was not made until after the Commissions had finished their work). It served to inform the Modernization Commissions of the hypotheses formulated by the groups that dealt respectively with "upstream" and "downstream" sectors and to check their compatibility. It also facilitated a comparison between the information furnished by the Commissions and the opinions of the experts within the technical services of the Ministries, the SEEF, and the CGP, and brought to the attention of each "vertical" Commission (before its report was made) the general questions that the "horizontal" Commissions considered important—such as the impact of the Common Market, regional balance, and the problems of financing investments. Finally—and possibly most important—it was a kind of "breathing space for consideration" which made it possible to see whether the draft of the plan conformed to the governmental directives, especially those concerning economic growth and public investment. For example, the decision made by the government in April 1961 to have the work on the plan continue on the basis of a 5½ percent annual growth rate rather than 5 percent, for the four years of the plan, was in part motivated by the fact that the synthesis revealed frictional unemployment to be higher than had been calculated during the preliminary projections.

The Equilibrium Working Party then went on (May 1961) to make the definitive synthesis of the Commissions' studies. First of all, it verified whether the production estimates of each branch corresponded with the outlets created by the purchases made by the other branches, and conversely, whether the purchases made by each branch corresponded with the production estimates of the branches that furnished them, in such a manner as to avoid bottlenecks or excess production. Then a study of consistency in the flows of funds took place: balance between savings and investments, between resources and utilization of foreign currency. Finally,

[16] A key working party (of the "horizontal" General Economic and Financial Commission) charged with the tasks of checking the compatibility of the propositions coming from the Modernization Commissions and of laying down an overall economic balance in conformity with the government's directives.

the synthesis took into consideration the government's decisions concerning publicly financed investment (in railroad transportation, highways, public education, etc.), according to the priorities set in the directives.

Such governmental decisions indicate that the plan is not determined solely by an aggregation of consistent forecasts, but is also an instrument of orientation of the economy. It proposes certain directions of action for the public powers (the Administration), the business organizations, and the heads of enterprises. In conformity with the spirit of French planning, the Commissions and the working parties participate in the formulation of these guidelines, which suggest a systematic study of fresh ideas. There is, however, a distinction between the *recommendations* made by the Commissions in their reports and the *official orientation* retained in the plan itself.

The Reports of the Modernization Commissions. The studies made, the conclusions reached, and the figures assembled all became the subject of a report from each Commission. These reports, once synthesized, were the essential elements of the Fourth Plan. They furnished in effect an aggregation of the objectives which each branch has to reach, and the means to attain them. At the same time, they were reference material for the government and instruments of orientation for the heads of enterprises, who can find in them information more detailed—and therefore more usable—than in the overall plan.

Each report described the current situation in the branch analyzed, from the point of view of production, employment, relationships with the other branches of the national economy and with foreign trade, referring especially to the objectives and the achievements of the plan. The perspectives of each branch, and especially the development of domestic and foreign outlets, were studied within the global framework of the plan and of the hypotheses made for the economy after 1965.

The implementation of the Treaty of Rome—the main dispositions of which will have been applied by 1965—made it particularly difficult to determine the volume of foreign trade, because the branches, at the time of the Fourth Plan's preparation, had only a limited experience with the effects of a large liberalization of foreign trade. Meanwhile, the Commissions tried to make their evaluation on the basis of the information they could gather on the comparison of production costs in France and abroad, taking into consideration the effects a drastic change in the outlets could have on the structure of their own needs.

The Commissions also defined the means that were implied if the targets were to be fulfilled, notably:

1. The volume and the nature of investments for the branches. In addition, all possible information had been gathered on the location of these investments among the various regions, and the most important operations were examined separately.

2. The consumption of raw materials and intermediate products by each branch.

3. The amount of manpower required, and its distribution among the regions. Particular attention was paid to the needs of each branch for skilled workers, and to means of providing these skills through training.

The Commissions and their working parties also studied various factors that could increase productivity: improvement of management methods, agreements for specialization, projects in the field of technical research, and so on. Without pretending to define norms, the Commissions provided information on the types of equipment or techniques that could aid development, as well as on useful changes in the structure of the branches or of the production units. Ways in which the distribution of products might be improved were also examined. Finally, in the areas of credits, taxes, price policy, and government purchasing policy, modifications were suggested which each Commission believed would assist its specific branch in achieving the objectives.

The kind of examination to which the Commissions subject both their branches and themselves is obviously not completely disinterested, and on occasion has given business groups opportunities to voice criticism of the government or to lay claim to credit or tariff policy advantages. Nevertheless, such an examination makes it possible for those members of the Commissions who are farseeing and capable of objectivity to be heard and to influence their possibly less objective and farsighted colleagues. And it is a matter of record that the *rapporteurs* (most of whom are civil servants) of the Commissions and of the working parties are often able to dispose of demagogic and unrealistic proposals and to retain only the constructive proposals, which then are studied by the competent "horizontal" Commission. In the last analysis, however, the report of a Commission, which is the synthesis of the individual reports of its working parties, is only the responsibility of its authors and of the Commission which approved it. It is not binding on the General Planning Commissariat and even less on the government.

Approval of the Plan

After the Commissions had submitted their reports, the CGP undertook the final elaboration of the plan. This draft version was then submitted as a policy document for approval to the government and for consultative advice to representatives of the socio-professional agencies.

A preliminary consultation was held in October 1961 with the High Planning Council (which was established by decree in July 1961 as a replacement for two successive earlier agencies, and which is presided over by the Prime Minister; its sixty members include representatives from business organizations, trade unions, regional development committees, and the Economic and Social Council). The Council is kept informed of the plan's successive phases and makes a report on the final version drafted by the CGP before the version is submitted to the government and the Economic and Social Council. Every year it must examine reports on the implementation of the plan—comparing results with the objectives set for the main productive activities and the various economic regions, and suggesting to the government any further measures needed to implement the plan, especially the social objectives.

When the High Planning Council was consulted, only the "Introduction" to the plan was ready to be submitted for its advice. By November, however, the whole draft was ready to submit to the Economic and Social Council, as required by the Constitution of 1958 (Article 70).

The last step before the Fourth Plan could take official effect was the ratification debate in Parliament. Although a plan is not part of the legislative competence, legislative sanction has been deemed necessary. The Fourth Plan received this sanction through the law of August 4, 1962.

IMPLEMENTATION OF THE PLAN

"The French Plan is a plan by branches, sometimes highly aggregated, and not a plan by firms or by products."[17] As our earlier example of the processing industries indicated, estimates must be sufficiently detailed to be workable, but the synthesis of the Fourth Plan was made for only sixty-five groups of products, on the basis of figures gathered by approximately three hundred working groups. The plan thus presents a framework in which each enterprise can evaluate its own development, and try to achieve "more" or "less" than the average trend at its own risk. Therefore, divergence is possible between what the plan indicates and the actual behavior of the enterprises. At the same time, the phenomenon of

[17] Pierre Massé, remarks in a symposium on Democratic Planning, reprinted in *Les Cahiers de la République*, July 1962.

collective psychology must also be considered. It is clear that decentralized planning does benefit from what the sociologists call "self-fulfilling prophecy," according to which a belief is verified to the degree to which it is held by a sufficient number of people.[18] On this theory, within certain limits, the confidence in economic growth which a dynamic plan creates makes the growth more of a foregone conclusion.

That this phenomenon will play a bigger role if representatives of the most relevant economic and social forces are closely associated with the determination of a plan's objectives was the fruitful idea of Jean Monnet, the first General Commissioner of Planning, and led to the establishment of the Modernization Commissions.

During the preparation of the Fourth Plan, all the reports made by the Commissions and a certain part of those made by the working groups were printed and widely distributed. The Commissions have met yearly since 1962 to appraise the fulfillment of the plan and the difficulties encountered, and to suggest corrective measures that may be necessary to modify the plan. The recommendations, suggestions, and criticisms resulting from these periodic meetings are scheduled to be systematically analyzed by the General Planning Commissariat and the various other competent agencies.

Finally, despite what the formula "indicative planning" might lead one to believe, the government's attitude toward the goals proposed by the plan is not purely contemplative. All available means are made use of to reduce to a minimum the gaps between the plan and the reality. However, these means are not particularly different from those that are used in other Western nations to give impetus to private investments through public investments. If there is anything novel in the French approach to planning, it may be the use of these incentive instruments, not solely for short-term considerations, but also to stimulate economic growth and to reduce the cost of this growth.[19]

The real problem arising from the intervention of a government in the implementation of a plan is not that of state control (because, as P. Uri has pointed out, there can be state control without a plan), but rather the marginal character of the means utilized. Financial incentives offer the

[18] This phenomenon was first mentioned by the Belgian sociologist H. Janne, during the Brussels colloquy of January 1962 dealing with planning; see Institute for Sociology of Brussels, Les Problèmes de planification (Brussels, 1963).
[19] A detailed description of the means used by the government to give impetus to the French plan can be found in a publication of the Ministry of Finance, Les modes de crédit utilisable pour le financement des investissements dans les entreprises industrielles et commerciales (Imprimerie Nationale, January 1963).

advantage of minimal impact and do not distort economic calculations, but they also have one main drawback: their scope is too limited to embrace certain structural problems, such as the deep regional imbalances. Does not the true rationale for government intervention, therefore, consist in acknowledging that a productive investment (whether private or public) cannot constitute the only instrumental variable, but must be integrated within a general policy in which investments in the economic infrastructure (roads, airports, railroads) and in the social infrastructure (schools, housing, recreational facilities) also intervene, following the principle adopted in the Fourth Plan for regional "priming"?[20]

As far as the government is concerned, the Fourth Plan did not represent a four-year budget in which the global amount and the allocation of public expenditures are determined *ne varietur*. Nevertheless, over time the articulation between the government budget and the plan has been strengthened. As we have noted, priority for social investments was explicitly stated in the plan. Further, the creation of the Specialized Committees for the Economic and Social Development Fund and of the "Comité interministeriel du Plan" (made up of the various Ministers responsible for following, at the government level, the plan's preparation and implementation) made for a more fruitful liaison between administrative action and the guidelines for economic and social policy included in the plan.

Finally, the plan's implementation requires that household consumption should neither brake nor accelerate expansion unduly. The plan presents a plausible balanced accounting between production and the income spent and saved, but does not guarantee the achievement of this balance. Such a guarantee would imply an income policy which has so far been nonexistent in French planning, but which is being drafted now. This search for an income policy is a response to two preoccupying problems: (1) how to achieve a growth of total income rapid enough to insure an expanding production with sufficient outlets, yet moderate enough not

[20] Which evidently does not exclude attempts to maximize the efficacy of the incentive policy in terms of production investments induced by public assistance. The following figures give some indication of the size of the work implied by the consultations of the Planning Commissariat: medium-term loans, 25 files every month; long-term loans, 80 files each year; debentures, 15 files each year; plus 4 to 5 "*emprunts groupés*" (firms in the same branch which group together to issue debentures) every year.

However, although the CGP scrutinizes a considerable amount of the investment projects under the plan, its direct advice concerns the sources of funds of only about 15 percent of all of the projects. The total of private investments actually surveyed by the CGP is about 10 billion F., but of this total only 1.5 billion are required to be submitted to CGP examination.

to produce inflationary tendencies; (2) how to take selective measures in favor of certain disadvantaged categories of the population—very elderly people, the lowest-paid workers, and so on—without endangering the economic stability without which the measures could not be achieved.[21]

The implementation of an income policy must be applied not only to wages but to all types of income, and take into account tax payments, private savings, and fringe benefits. The policy will be formulated, discussed, and applied in relation to the degree of fulfillment of the plan, as delineated each year in the consistent and comprehensive framework supplied by the national economic accounts. The Fourth Plan stated:

> The free discussions which will remain the rule shall, nevertheless, be clarified by studies undertaken within the framework of the national accounts and submitted to public argument. The Government anticipates that the betterment of information, the consciousness of economic interrelations, and the feeling about the importance of the stake will increasingly tend to distill from life itself the elements of an income policy. The competent agencies which will follow up the implementation of the Plan will have a very important role to play in the formulation of this policy.[22]

Inasmuch as French statistics are currently not perfectly adapted for a periodic survey of the changes in the various categories of income, a working group was created in the summer of 1962, headed by General Planning Commissioner Pierre Massé and comprised of upper-level civil servants and experts from employers' and employees' organizations. The group was instructed to determine the kind of data necessary for such a survey. At the same time, the Service for Economic and Financial Studies of the Ministry of Finance was asked to gather all the figures available in this field. The results, in regard to the year 1962, were presented at the October 1962 session of the High Planning Council. It was decided that the statistical working group should keep on with its technical studies and try to make the information concerning the evolution of income distribution as complete and as rapidly available as possible.

AN EXAMINATION OF THE IMPLEMENTATION of the Fourth Plan would be neither complete nor realistic if it did not consider the problems arising from the inclusion of France in a market area which is becoming more and more open. One of the ambitions of the plan is to reduce un-

---

[21] See Pierre Massé's report on national income policy (Documentation Française, 1964).

[22] *The Fourth Plan*, pp. 32-33.

certainty. But isn't uncertainty increased by the reduction in tariffs and quotas and by the freedom of movement for capital and manpower? The Fourth Plan's answer to this challenge is built around the ideas of "export strategy" and "European programming." Indeed, from one point of view, the intensified international competition will force planners more and more to develop alternative policies depending on the modifications of the external factors, and to insist on competition by innovation, "that is, the application of scientific and technical research to the production of consumer goods and equipment qualitatively superior to that available on the market."[23] On the other hand, the recent expansion of economic planning in several nations of Western Europe (Belgium, Britain, Italy) and the desire shown by the Common Market Commission in its Memorandum of October 1962 to introduce certain forms of economic planning at the European Community level, suggest that the habit of collective consideration of the problems of economic and social development will be spreading more widely and will make possible the introduction of consistency and rationality in growth policies.

THE FIFTH PLAN

When the Fourth Plan was discussed in the National Assembly, the Prime Minister declared (during the May 22, 1962, session) that the government "in preparing the Fifth Plan, was proposing to submit to the Assembly a choice of major objectives and major options even before the Plan would be drafted."

This decision was made concrete in the law (August 4, 1962) that gave approval to the Fourth Plan, by the insertion of Article 2, which states:

> The Government will submit to Parliament, before sending its directives to the General Planning Commissariat, a draft law approving a report on the principal options necessary to prepare the [Fifth] Plan within the framework of the regional development policy, and notably those concerning: the expansion of the economy; the distribution of output between investment and consumption; the desired structure of the final demand; the general orientation of the social policies, as well as the orientation of the regional policies.

This change in procedure will modify the methods used so far, as well as the time table of the drafting work.

[23] *Ibid.*, p. 21.

Methods of Elaboration

Certain criticisms were raised concerning the use of the method of successive approximations to determine the aggregative objectives of the Fifth Plan, which should serve as a basis for the detailed work of the Modernization Commissions. Although the method was necessary because of the absence of a global econometric model defining in advance the proportions and relations between the different variables to be considered in the formulation of a plan, it has definite drawbacks. In the preparation of the Fourth Plan these drawbacks became visible, and they would be even more evident for the Fifth Plan. It is true that the "discretionary" character of the procedure prevents the planner from becoming the slave of the calculating machine and allows him to retain the right to modify the obtained figures through intuition and common sense; thus he can himself realize the moment when he has evaded reality—and can then introduce the necessary corrections.

Nevertheless, the procedure constitutes a very serious impediment to any discussion of the options of a plan. From the beginning, it prevents the hypotheses and the conditions for implementation—which dictate the choice of the objectives and bring them close to reality—from being made explicit. This lack of explicitness manifested itself notably when the Investments and Planning Section of the Economic and Social Council discussed the variants in the rate of growth for the Fourth Plan. The Section pronounced itself unanimously in favor of the maximum variant of 6 percent without complete awareness of the conditions which must be satisfied—such as price and income disciplines, industrial dynamism, and technical innovations.

It is to the interest of formalized planning to have all the assumptions made explicit at the very beginning of the resolution process (the rest of the process—that is, the processing of the data in order to calculate the unknowns—can thereby take on an automatic character). The risk of misunderstanding is reduced to a minimum, and a realistic discussion of the hypotheses and of the options is more feasible. The rapid exploration of a great number of variants, due to the use of electronic computers, is also made possible.

The methodological changes in the elaboration of the Fifth Plan can be explained in comparison with the Fourth Plan as follows:

1. For the Fourth Plan, the first procedure was the simultaneous study of the conditions of realizing each of the three rates of growth that were supposed to cover all possible developments and that constituted *a priori*

hypotheses whose consequences on the demand and production structures could be studied without first investigating the factors of productivity which would make them possible. For the Fifth Plan the approach has been quite the reverse. The rate of growth is no longer the starting hypothesis, but a result deduced from a set of hypotheses on the factors of production within the framework of a growth model; thus, it is possible to discuss the soundness of these hypotheses.

2. The projection thus arrived at is a conditional image of the future French economy, i.e., it is based on a set of assumptions, and the situation described by the projection will prevail only if these assumptions are fulfilled. Some of them are "given," when they deal with economic magnitudes the spontaneous evolution of which it is possible to forecast, or which will not vary, or which are deemed outside of the planners' (and the government's) control. Conversely, other assumptions are "targets," if and when they correspond to deliberate choices in fields open to the policy-makers' influence.[24] One of the growth schemes, formulated according to the most probable trends and the government's preferences, will provide a referential economic equilibrium; it is called "central sketch" (esquisse centrale), and will be supported by the Administration before Parliament. Parallel with this central sketch, a number of variants, arrived at by modifying the starting assumptions, are drafted.

The contents of the variants were not made public until the autumn of 1964, but some indications about them were available at the time of writing. Two types of variants have been hammered out for a discussion in Parliament: some of them deal with the rate of growth, and others with the distribution of the benefits of expansion. For every level of achievement in terms of rate of growth, various types of "subchoices" will be presented, concerning the respective proportions of private consumption and collective needs and, within private consumption, of direct income and social transfer payments. The planners are seeking to make as explicit as possible the economic and financial implications of every choice, especially in terms of government instruments and price and income increases.

The Time Table of the Drafting Work

For the Fourth Plan, as we have seen, the various phases—ending with the studies of the Modernization Commissions—took place as follows. The medium-term projections (1956-65) and the long-term projec-

---

[24] For example, housing and other types of social overhead capital, full employment, industrialization of backward areas of France.

tions (1956-75) were prepared during 1959 on the basis of three growth rate variants of the gross domestic output; the results of the 1965 projection were then submitted for advice to the Investments and Planning Section of the Economic and Social Council, at the beginning of 1960. Then, in view of the preliminary studies made by the General Planning Commissariat and the Service for Economic and Financial Studies of the Finance Ministry, and the results of the consultation with the Economic and Social Council, the government, in June 1960, issued directives to the CGP stating the major objectives of the Fourth Plan. The implications of the objectives at the sectoral and regional levels and the conditions for their implementation were then studied by the Modernization Commissions, starting in the summer of 1960; the Commission reports were generally available in the summer of 1961.

For the Fifth Plan, the decision to submit the central sketch to parliamentary debate before the elaboration of the governmental directives—and the time it will take to prepare the variants to be submitted with it—necessitated not only some lengthening of the working time table but also led to extending the period of the Fifth Plan to five years, instead of four.

Progress Made in Methods and in Gathering Information

Since the fall of 1963 the CGP, in cooperation with the INSEE, has been preparing the elements of the central sketch and the variants. This work has benefited from the progress made (since the Third and the Fourth Plans were prepared) in the areas of information gathering and of method.

The formulation of the sketch for the Fifth Plan is being made through the usual successive approximations, but these have been manipulated much more strictly on the basis of experience gained during preparation of the Third Plan and the Fourth. They are supported by a better knowledge of the correlations between output, employment, and investment in the main sectors of the economy—agriculture, industry, services—and, thanks especially to the work of certain Commissions of the Fourth Plan, by a larger amount of information about the production conditions in the twenty-eight branches the central sketch will be dealing with.

The formulation of the variants of the central sketch is being done cooperatively by the National Institute of Statistics and the Center for Mathematics Applied to Planning (recently created under the CGP). The attempt is to formulate an econometric model that will make possible an immediate identification of the conditions and consequences of all envisaged combinations of variants.[25]

The research being done by the SEEF on the financial balance and constraints corresponding to the principal economic choices will make it possible to set forth, during this phase of the formulation, the problems of financial balance created by the fulfillment of the Fifth Plan.

Finally, a prospective study of the economic horizon of the year 1985 through two methods has been undertaken by the Group of Prospective Research, created within the CGP. The first method is the classical approach by long-range projections of past trends under a set of explicit assumptions; the second is more qualitative, and bears some relation to what Olaf Helmer (of the Rand Corporation) calls "a controlled opinion feedback in which a panel of experts exchanges reasoned opinions anonymously and through an intermediary." (In the French case, however, both anonymity and the intermediary were lacking.) The aim of the "1985 Group" which is composed of independent experts from various backgrounds, is to derive from the available data "the facts which are carriers of the future" (P. Massé), such as the process of urbanization, the growing importance of imported raw materials for the French processing industries, and the impact of medical breakthroughs. This study has provided useful information about potential structural changes to be taken into consideration in preparing the Fifth Plan.[26]

[25] See Annex No. 8 of the *Report on the General Orientations of the Fifth Plan* (Imprimerie de Journaux Officiels, Paris, 1965).
[26] See P. Massé, "L'esprit prospectif et l'application," *Prospective*, October 1963; also see the *"1985 Group" Report* (Documentation Française, 1964).

THE PLANNING COMMISSIONS*

HORIZONTAL COMMISSIONS

General Economic and Financial:
Chairman, Governor of the Bank of France; vice-Chairman, the director general of the Caisse des Dépôts et Consignations; general rapporteur, a senior member of the staff of the General Planning Commissariat; three rapporteurs; 40 members (four trade unionists). The Chairmen of the vertical sections attend when questions concerning their branch are discussed.

Manpower:
Chairman, a University professor and economist; vice-Chairman, a director of the Ministry of Labour; general rapporteur, a member of the staff of the Economic and Social Council; two rapporteurs; 13 *ex-officio* members; 26 members (four trade unionists).

National Productivity Committee:
Chairman *ex-officio,* the Commissaire General of the General Planning Commissariat; 14 members; eight observers.

Regional Planning:
Chairman, the deputy Commissaire of the General Planning Commissariat; vice-Chairman, a senior official of the Ministry of Construction; 13 members.

Scientific and Technical Research:
This Commission is in fact the permanent Consultative Committee of the same name with a certain number of additional members.

VERTICAL COMMISSIONS

Agriculture:
Chairman, a Counsellor of State and member of the Agricultural Academy; three vice-Chairmen, all senior civil servants; one general rapporteur, a senior civil servant, and six rapporteurs; 21 members *ex-officio;* 55 members of whom four are trade unionists.

Agricultural and Food Industries:
Chairman, a Counsellor of State; vice-Chairman, two senior civil servants; general rapporteur, an engineer, member of the General Planning Commissariat staff; two rapporteurs, 24 *ex-officio* members; 64 members (four trade unionists).

* For the Fourth Plan. From John Hackett and Anne-Marie Hackett, *Economic Planning in France* (George Allen & Unwin, 1963), Appendix III.

208

Artisans:
Chairman, a Professor of Economics at the University of Paris and member of
the Economic and Social Council; vice-Chairman, a senior civil servant; two
general rapporteurs, a professor of economics and a senior civil servant from the
Ministry of Industry; 10 *ex officio* members; 24 members (three trade unionists).

Building and Public Works:
Chairman, a Counsellor of State; vice-Chairman, a member of the professional
association; general rapporteur, an engineer; 27 *ex-officio* members; 13 members (four trade unionists) of the first section (Building) and 13 members (four
trade unionists) of the second (Public Works).

Chemicals:
Chairman, the Chairman of the Board of Directors of Kodak-Pathé Ltd. and
vice-Chairman of the Union of Chemical Industries; two vice-Chairmen, senior
civil servants from the Ministry of Industry and the Ministry of the Army; three
general rapporteurs, the secretary-general of the Union of Chemical Industries,
two senior civil servants from the Ministry of Industry; 10 *ex-officio* members;
35 members (four trade unionists).

Culture and Arts:
Chairman, a Counsellor of State; vice-Chairman, the director of the French
archives; general rapporteur, a member of the Council of State; two rapporteurs;
19 *ex-officio* members; 54 members (four trade unionists).

Energy:
Chairman, a senior civil servant at the Ministry of Industry; vice-Chairman,
two senior civil servants from the same ministry and a representative of the
Atomic Energy Commissariat; general rapporteur, a mining engineer and five
rapporteurs; nine *ex-officio* members; 32 members (eight trade unionists).

Housing:
Chairman, an Inspecteur des Finances; two vice-Chairmen, the governor of the
Crédit Foncier de France and a director from the Ministry of Construction;
general rapporteur, an engineer; 13 *ex-officio* members; 26 members (four trade
unionists).

Non-ferrous Mines and Metals:
Chairman, the head of the École Nationale Supérieure des Mines; vice-Chairman, a director at the Ministry of Industry; general rapporteur, the deputy
head of the École Nationale Supérieure des Mines; nine *ex-officio* members;
20 members (four trade unionists).

Overseas Territories:
Chairman and general rapporteur, senior civil servants at the Ministry for
Overseas Territories; vice-Chairman, an Inspecteur des Finances; a number of
ex-officio members; 36 members (four trade unionists).

Petrol (collaborating with the Energy Commission):
Chairman, an engineer; vice-Chairman and general rapporteur, senior civil servants; 10 *ex-officio* members; 29 members (four trade unionists).

Post Office and Telecommunications:
Chairman, an engineer and senior post office official; vice-Chairman, the secretary-general of the Ministry of Posts and Telecommunications; rapporteur, a senior post office engineer; nine *ex-officio* members; 14 members (four trade unionists).

Radio and Television:
Chairman, an engineer; vice-Chairman, the director-general of the Radio Television Française; rapporteur, an engineer from the RTF; six *ex-officio* members; 14 members (four trade unionists).

Sanitary and Social Equipment (Public Health):
Chairman, a Counsellor of State; vice-Chairmen, the general directors of health and population of the Ministry of Health; general rapporteur, a member of the Council of State; 13 *ex-officio* members; 34 members (four trade unionists).

School, University and Sport Equipment:
Chairman, a Counsellor of State; vice-Chairman, a director of the Ministry of Education; general rapporteur, a member of the Council of State; 15 *ex-officio* members; 24 members (five trade unionists).

Sea Fisheries:
Chairman, a Counsellor of State; vice-Chairman, a director at the Ministry of Fisheries; rapporteurs, two senior civil servants; nine *ex-officio* members; 25 members (two trade unionists).

Steel:
Chairman, the Chairman of the board of the Société Métallurgique de Knutange Ltd.; vice-Chairman, a senior official from the Ministry of Industry; general rapporteur, an engineer; eight rapporteurs; eight *ex-officio* members; 40 members (four trade unionists).

Trade:
Chairman, a Counsellor at the Court of Audit; vice-Chairman, a senior civil servant from the Ministry of Trade; general rapporteur, the Chairman of the Committee for Economic Expansion of Bourgogne; nine *ex-officio* members; 35 members (four trade unionists).

Manufacturing Industries:
Chairman, the Chairman of the board of directors of Papeteries Navarre Ltd.; two vice-Chairmen, directors at the Ministry of Industry; one general rapporteur, a senior civil servant at the Ministry of Industry and two deputies; nine *ex-officio* members; 61 members (eight trade unionists) divided into two sections—mechanical and electrical and textiles and others.

Transport:

Chairman, an engineer and senior civil servant; six vice-Chairmen, senior officials representing aviation, railways, ports, roads, shipping, public works; two general rapporteurs, two engineers; nine *ex-officio* members; 70 members (12 trade unionists) divided into three sections (internal, sea, air transport).

Tourism:

Chairman, the chairman of the Crédit Populaire de France; vice-Chairman, a senior civil servant; general rapporteur, an Inspecteur des Finances; 16 *ex-officio* members; 30 members (four trade unionists).

Urban Equipment:

Chairman, the general director of the Caisse des Dépôts et Consignations; vice-Chairmen, two directors from the Ministries of the Interior and Construction; general rapporteur, an engineering member of the staff of the General Planning Commissariat; seven rapporteurs; 22 *ex-officio* members; 37 members (three trade unionists). This commission has a permanent mission.

9

Japanese Experience with Long-Term Economic Planning

SHUNTARO SHISHIDO[1]

As BACKGROUND FOR MY DISCUSSION of present economic planning in Japan, a brief review of developments in the economy since 1945, especially as they relate to economic policy, will be useful. The developments can be grouped roughly into four periods, and their line of evolvement as a whole is, in a sense, a history of growth of the earning capacity of foreign exchange, the most limiting factor for Japan's economic growth.

The period from 1946 to 1950 was characterized by war-damage reconstruction and the institutional reforms initiated under the "economic democratization" and decentralization policy of the American occupation authorities. A serious inflationary trend, due to extreme shortages of food and raw materials and to the enormous government expenditures for reconstruction, forced the government to impose strict controls over foods, strategic materials, investment funds, and foreign exchange. Economic aid from the United States, totaling $1.8 billion, served substantially to assist recovery during the period; nevertheless, although production of important goods increased rapidly, a kind of economic disorder prevailed in many fields for several years. Particularly for large industries, the serious war damage to plants and equipment remained a deterrent to recovery until 1949. In that year the program of decreased government expenditure, suggested by Joseph M. Dodge at the request of the

[1] Senior Planning Officer, Planning Bureau, Economic Planning Agency. (The author is indebted to M. Sakisaka, Director of the Planning Bureau, and Professor T. Watanabe, of the Economic Research Institute, for their useful comments, and to T. Tanaka, of the Planning Bureau, for much assistance. The views expressed in this paper are entirely personal and do not represent any view of the government.)

Occupation Authorities, was implemented, and the chronic postwar inflation finally came to an end. The result, however, was a deflationary trend.

The outbreak of hostilities in Korea in 1950 marked the beginning of a new period and a turning point in economic recovery. The substantial "special procurement demand" made on Japan by the United Nations forces for goods and services for the conflict was a great stimulus to industrial expansion and international competitiveness, and considerably raised total employment and national income. (It should be noted that the fairly rapid economic recovery at this time was more or less attributable to unused capacity and substantial disguised unemployment; thus the ratio of fixed investment to gross national product was fairly low.) With the restoration of sovereignty in the spring of 1952, Japan could once again formulate its own economic policies. Various government controls were gradually removed, and the role of the private sector as a driving force for economic growth came to be widely recognized. In 1954 the per capita income attained a level not reached since the mid 1930's.[2]

This transitional period led into a new development stage in Japan's economic history. Beginning in 1955 and stimulated by a new expansion in world trade, there was a remarkable increase in Japanese exports, with ships, radios, and steel heading the list. Many new products appeared, related to new strides in technology. The declining tendency of import prices for raw materials was favorable to the terms of trade. Thus, gradually, the pessimism about Japan's capacity for economic self-support that had prevailed early in the transition period was replaced by a mild optimism.

This change in general economic conditions was accompanied by structural changes in the pattern of economic growth (see Table 9-1). An increasing shortage of labor led industrial firms to adopt more capital-using or labor-saving techniques. New industrial sites began to be constructed near large cities during this period, requiring substantial amounts of indirect capital expenditure, such as land reclamation, port and harbor construction, and so on. A remarkable industrial growth, particularly in the chemical, metal, and engineering industries, was also in process. On the other hand, the growing shortage of social overhead capital was becoming a serious impediment to further expansion of the private sector. The period was therefore characterized by the govern-

[2] See M. Sakisaka, *Postwar Development of the Japanese Economy* (1962: mimeographed).

ment's more liberalized policy toward private business at the same time that greater emphasis was placed on public investment.

TABLE 9-1. *Annual Rates of Increase of GNP, Labor, and Capital Stock in Japan, 1953-61*[a]

	GNP	Labor Man-Hours	Capital Stock
1953	8.70%	3.27%	5.62%
1954	8.15	3.23	5.61
1955	7.81	3.27	5.86
1956	7.22	2.90	6.56
1957	7.73	2.49	7.39
1958	9.58	2.21	8.48
1959	11.30	1.77	10.17
1960	12.22	1.37	11.99
1961	10.68	1.45	13.08

[a] Data on GNP and capital stock are in 1955 prices. The basic data were adjusted by a four-year moving average to remove cyclical fluctuations.

The fourth (and present) period, starting in 1960, has been characterized by a more open and internationalized economy. Restrictions on imports were substantially removed, and, as of late 1963, the degree of liberalization was 92 percent of the total. Japan now belongs to the group of Contracting Party countries to the General Agreement on Tariffs and Trade (GATT) which, under Article XI of the Agreement, has eliminated quantitative restrictions on imports; as of late 1963 Japan also joined the group of countries that are members of the International Monetary Fund and maintain convertibility of their currencies under Article VIII of the IMF Agreement.

Because of the still high rate of increase in exports, no serious balance of payment deficit has resulted from the increased liberalization of foreign trade. On the average, the economy has kept the high growth rate of 9 percent since 1961. Another favorable factor has been the increasing inflow of foreign capital, followed by the gradual lifting of restrictions, all of which may offset the expected future declining tendency in the rate of growth. In 1963, Japan applied for membership in the OECD, and restrictions on invisible trade and capital transaction items were to be abolished shortly.[3]

On the domestic side, the structural shift to a more heavily industrialized economy is still underway. The shift has entailed a continuous

[3] Subsequent to the writing of this paper, Japan became an OECD member. In the spring of 1964 trade and transaction restrictions were lifted.

shortage of labor and fast-rising wage rates. The recent rapid increase in consumer prices is partly attributable to these factors.

The period is possibly most notable for furnishing the base year—1960—for the present Ten-Year Plan for Doubling National Income, which is the main focus of my discussion. Before going into the details of the plan, however, some background on earlier planning will be useful.

A BRIEF HISTORY OF JAPANESE ECONOMIC PLANNING

The economic plans produced since the end of World War II can be classified into three groups, related to the development periods mentioned above: planning for the reconstruction program (1946-49); planning for economic self-support (1950-54); planning for long-term growth (1955-60 and 1960-present).[4]

The most important of the various plans in the first group was the "Economic Rehabilitation Plan, 1949-53" drafted in 1949 under the Socialist Cabinet of Tetsu Katayama. Although the plan was not officially adopted (because of the shift of power from the Socialist Party to the Liberal Party in 1950), it served to provide basic information on the possibility of regaining the 1930-1934 standard of living by the end of 1953, and on the policy measures that would be needed. In view of the extreme shortage of energy resources, the plan laid special emphasis on the details of demand and supply of these items.

In contrast to the strict deflation and austerity policies of the Dodge program, which was proposed a little later, the plan aimed at a moderate disinflation policy and the gradual removal of price subsidies to large industrial firms through higher productivity and modernization. Although a free-market mechanism was sought as an ultimate end, various direct controls on price and quantity of raw materials and foods and restrictions on private investment and imports were still regarded as effective measures for economic reconstruction. Annual planning targets were specified for national income and expenditure, production and foreign trade, balance between supply and demand for investment funds, and government revenues and expenditures. The plan also emphasized United States aid and foreign capital inflow for reconstruction.

The first officially adopted economic plan was formulated under the Hatoyama Cabinet in 1955. This "Five-Year Plan for Economic Self-

[4] S. Ohkita, *Economic Planning in Japan* (Shiseido, 1962; in Japanese).

Support, 1956-1960" had two basic objectives: economic self-support and full employment. Because the economy was in transition, the first objective was the most crucial current problem, and in view of the decline of procurement revenues after the Korean armistice and the rather gloomy export outlook at this time, it seemed vital to gain a clear vision of Japan's economic development for the next five years. The threat of increasing underemployment, with an extremely high rate of increase expected in the working-age population, was another factor calling for strong planning of long-term economic policy.

The plan assumed an average 5 percent growth rate of GNP during the planning period on the basis of the so-called "Colm Approach," in which the projection was made on the assumption of labor availability and labor productivity for the future.[5] In the case of Japan, the annual rate of increase in the labor force was assumed at approximately 2 percent (which was considered desirable from the point of view of employment policy), and the annual rate of increase in labor productivity at 3 percent.

In regard to the international balance of payments, the plan's import requirement was first estimated by means of the ratio of imports to GNP; then the export target was derived on the basis of the world trade growth rate and the elasticity of Japanese exports to world trade. Although detailed estimates were made on this broad assumption for major components of national accounts, for commodity production, for employment, etc., the plan was faulty in taking labor as the most limiting factor of economic growth at that time, ignoring other more important limiting factors such as capital and foreign exchange. (This methodological shortcoming was remedied in the next five-year plan.) In regard to the private sector, the plan favored controls through fiscal and monetary policy rather than the more direct controls relied on heavily by the 1949-53 plan.

Shortly after the preparation of the 1956-60 plan, the economy began expanding at a rapid pace, and an unexpectedly high rate of increase in exports followed. Because the growth rates of GNP and of exports were almost double the planned targets, the plan had to be replaced by another one.

The "New Long-Range Economic Plan," drafted in late 1958 (under the Kishi Cabinet) for the period of 1958-62, emphasized the role of the private economy as a driving force in economic growth and the impor-

[5] Gerhard Colm, *The American Economy in 1960* (National Planning Association, *Staff Report* No. 81, 1952).

tance of indirect controls through fiscal, monetary, and foreign exchange policy. It also stressed achieving a welfare state through full employment and a high standard of living.

When quantitative targets for 1962 were being formulated, a method called "Alternative Growth Rates Approach" (suggested by Professor K. Okawa of Hitotsubashi University) was adopted. The method aims at selecting among several alternatives an optimal rate of growth consistent with the constraints of a reasonable employment level, equilibrium in the international balance of payments, and availability of domestic saving. After experiments with several GNP growth rates, 6.5 percent was taken as the most reasonable target—even though it was considered a little too ambitious, since at that time the economy happened to be in recession.

Not enough serious consideration was given to the strong upward trend that had been prevailing since around 1955 in such basic conditions as production, investment, and exports. Thus, there were some serious underestimations. The assumed exports target of 10.5 percent growth annually was not seriously divergent from the actual performance of 12 percent, but the 4 percent assumption for the private investment target was far off from the actual 17.4 percent. And the actual growth rate of 10.5 percent of GNP in constant prices was so divergent from the assumed rate that this replacement plan was itself destined to be quickly replaced. Although very detailed commodity budgets had been built up for key products, specifying domestic output, imports, exports, and domestic consumption, the failure to take sufficient account of the basic economic growth potential in this period had made the detailed commodity analysis almost meaningless.

THE TEN-YEAR PLAN FOR DOUBLING NATIONAL INCOME[6]

In 1959 the Economic Planning Agency established a special committee of the Economic Deliberation Council to draw up an unofficial long-term projection which could serve as an approximate basis for the contemplated ten-year plan. The committee first analyzed the growth potentiality for 1980 at five-year intervals by examining limiting factors such as labor, energy, foreign exchange, and domestic savings. The supply and demand balance of key commodities was also projected. After

[6] *New Long-Range Economic Plan (Plan for Doubling National Income), 1961-1970* (Economic Planning Agency, 1961).

experimenting with various growth rates (according to the Okawa method) the committee projected the rate of 7 percent for 1961-70 and 5 percent for 1971-80.[7]

The formulation of the present Ten-Year Plan for Doubling National Income began in June 1960, when four additional committees were established in the Economic Deliberation Council: the Overall Policy Committee, in charge of coordinating the general planning, the Public Sector Committee, with ten subcommittees, the Private Sector Committee, with seven subcommittees, and the Committee for Quantitative Analysis.[8] These groups examined and revised the preliminary draft of the plan that had been prepared by the Planning Bureau of the Economic Planning Agency.[9]

The new plan differs in several ways from all of the preceding plans. First, the distinction between planning for the public sector and for the private sector was more clearly drawn: targets for various public sectors were more clearly specified, and "guide posts" for private industry were simplified. Cumulative investment funds for 1961 to 1970 were indicated and classified according to purpose, while projections of production, exports, and imports for the private sector were simplified in terms of number of commodities and of industrial groups. In short, the plan emphasized that the government's intent was, not to exert control over private industries (as was more or less true of earlier plans), but to provide information which would help them draw up their own long-term projections in accordance with the long-term government policy.

Second, the need for long-term policy considerations was stressed much more than in earlier plans. Various direct policy recommendations to promote economic growth and social stability were made.

[7] Economic Planning Agency, *Long-Range Outlook of the Japanese Economy for 1980* (1962).

[8] The ten subcommittees for the Public Sector Committee were identified with: Distribution of Investment; Industrial Location; Transportation System; Housing and Living Conditions; Use of Land and Water; Energy; Science and Technology; Education and Training; Social Security; Finance and Banking. The seven subcommittees for the Private Sector Committee were: Private Sector, General; Advancement of Industrial Structure; Foreign Trade; Modernization of Agriculture; Small Business; Wages and Employment; Living Standards.

[9] Career personnel constitute about one fourth of the Agency's total staff; the other three fourths includes representatives from various ministries, from semi-governmental organizations, and from leading banks and business firms. Only the career members can be said to be permanent staff; the others serve for one year or two. Although the system of recruiting members from a number of relevant sources is necessary for the proper performance of the Agency's coordinating function, such excessive dependence on temporary staff weakens the Agency somewhat and makes consistent long-term projection difficult.

Third, such human factors of economic development as the need for general education, for training in science and technology, and for social security were emphasized strongly. Preceding plans had treated such problems as somewhat external to economic planning. Also emphasized was the need to mitigate wage, productivity, income, and regional disparities, a matter that previous plans had not explicitly treated in quantitative terms.

Objectives of the Plan

The following five items are indicated as the objectives of the plan. (Major target figures are shown in Table 9-2.)

1. *To strengthen social overhead capital.* The rapid expansion of private sectors after 1955 had resulted in a serious shortage in such social overhead facilities as roads, harbors, railways, and water supply, and it became essential for the government to restore a balance between private and public investment by strengthening the public sector through strong policies based on a longer economic perspective—say, at least ten years. Further, from the welfare point of view, city planning, sewage systems, low-rent housing, and so on were strongly emphasized. According to the plan, the 1970 ratio of public investment to GNP for general government is 7.9 percent, compared to 5.6 percent in 1956-58, and that for public enterprises is 2.9 percent, compared to 2.6 percent in 1956-58.

2. *To provide inducements whereby a highly industrialized economic structure could be realized.* The plan assumes a higher growth rate for the industrial sector than for other sectors, with special emphasis on the machinery and the chemical industries. The average rate of growth assumed for the industrial sector as a whole is 11 percent, with 14.6 percent for machinery, 10.4 percent for steel, and 11.9 percent for chemicals. Although attainment of these targets is expected to depend chiefly on private initiative and market price mechanisms, the plan includes various government policies to promote such initiative—among them, tax provisions, supplementary investment through government financial institutions, and special legal provisions to assist in developing new industrial sites.

3. *To promote export trade and strengthen economic cooperation with the less-developed countries.* The plan assumes that exports are to grow at an annual rate of 10 percent, to meet the need for increasing imports. Behind this assumption is the expectation that the annual rate of increase for world trade will be 4.5 percent; the elasticity of Japanese export

trade to this is estimated as around 2.2. And two important assumptions were made regarding the balance of payments: (1) that the trade liberalization policy which affects the increase of imports, particularly of machineries and consumption goods, will continue; (2) that the special procurement revenues from United States forces in Japan will be greatly reduced. Regarding imports, the plan assumed a gradual increase from

TABLE 9-2. *Principal Economic Indicators*

Economic Indicators	Base Year (fiscal 1956–58, average)	Target Year (fiscal 1970)	Target as Per- cent of Base Year	Projected Annual Rate
Total population (1,000 persons)	91,118	102,218	112.2	0.9
Population over 15 years old (1,000 persons)	62,174ᶜ	79,019	127.1	1.9
Gross national product (1958 prices) (1,000 million yen)	9,743	26,000	266.8	7.8
National income (1,000 million yen)	7,993	21,323	266.8	7.8
National income, per capita (1 yen)	87,736	208,601	237.8	6.9
Personal consumption (1,000 million yen)	5,797	15,116	260.7	7.6
Personal consumption per capita (1 yen)	63,636	147,883	232.4	6.7
Gross capital formation (1,000 million yen)	2,947	8,283	281.1	8.2
Industrial production index	100.0	431.7	431.7	11.9
Agricultural, forestry, and fishery production index	100.0	144.1	144.1	2.8
Number of population at work (1,000 persons)	41.540	48,690	117.2	1.2
Number of employees (1,000 persons)	19,240	32,350	168.1	4.1
Exportsᵇ ($1 million)	2,701	9,320	345.1	10.1
Importsᵇ ($1 million)	3,126	9,891	316.4	9.3
Domestic freight transportation (1,000 million ton/km)	97.5ᵃ	217.3	222.9	6.9
Domestic passenger transportation (1,000 million person/km)	210.9ᵇ	508.2	241.0	7.6
Total energy demand (1,000 tons in terms of 7,000 cal. coal)	131,815ᶜ	302,760	230.0	7.8

ᵃ Based on custom clearance statistics.
ᵇ For 1958.
ᶜ For 1959.

the present 14.1 percent of the national income to 16.7 in 1970. In view of the increasing share of the machinery and the chemical industries in the economy, the plan expects a similar trend in the components of Japanese exports; thus it assumes that the share of machinery and transport equipment in total exports will rise from 24 percent to 37 by 1970.

As for the composition of Japan's export market, the plan expects an increase in the share of the developed countries and a relative decrease in the share of the less-developed countries, on the assumption that in the latter the shortage of foreign exchange will continue. The plan stresses economic cooperation with these less-developed nations, through the expansion of financial and technical assistance to them and the promotion of imports from them. In 1970 the share of such economic assistance in GNP is expected to be 1.4 percent.

4. *To aid the development of human abilities and the advancement of science and technology.* In view of the increasing importance of technological progress for further economic growth, the plan expects: (1) to raise the expenditures for research from 0.9 percent of GNP to 2.0 percent by 1970; (2) to increase the annual number of university graduates of science and engineering schools by 16,000 over the present figure of 29,000 in the ten-year period; (3) to increase the annual number of engineering high school graduates by about 85,000 over the present level of 95,000 in the same period; (4) to promote the policy of "secondary education for all" and to raise the proportion of junior high school graduates who go on to senior high school from the present 59.8 percent to 72 percent by 1970.

5. *To mitigate effects of the dual economic structure and to increase social stability.* The dual economic structure and various differentials of wage and income are old problems of the Japanese economy. Although the rapid economic growth since 1955 has indicated some decline of dual economic factors and disguised unemployment, the plan states that a further decline cannot be expected without adequate and positive policy measures that will, for example, promote labor mobility, modernize employment practices, and provide financial and technical assistance to raise the productivity of small-scale industries and agriculture.

Among these measures, promotion of labor mobility, especially from the traditional sectors to the modern industrial sector, is considered essential for further economic growth, because the rate of increase of the working-age population is expected to fall drastically after about 1965. (A kind of wage-push inflation now underway in consumer prices is the first warning sign of this fall.) And as a basis for assistance to agriculture, the plan suggests a "Fundamental Law for Agriculture," which would aim at modernizing agriculture to accord with the new circumstances of trade liberalization and the rapidly changing pattern of the population's eating habits.

Quantitative Planning Method

Determination of the plan's quantitative targets began with the adoption of an "Alternative Growth Rate Approach" (similar to but more detailed than the one used in the unofficial projection). After several experiments the rate of 7.2 percent was selected, on the assumption that with this rate GNP would double in ten years. However, because of a demand from a political pressure group, the original rate was changed to an increase of 9 percent for 1961-63, which implied a rate of 6.4 percent for the remaining period to attain 7.2 percent on the average for the ten years. In view of various future uncertainties, the plan stated that "the doubling of national income should be attained *in and around ten years*." (Italics added by the present author.) Thus the growth target was made more flexible—and also somewhat ambiguous—but there was little attempt to relate the other targets to this political revision.

Before summing up the mathematical framework of the macro-model used for the plan, certain explanations are necessary. First, it should be noted that the model has three phases of national accounts—final products (or final expenditures), income originated, and income distributed—and that all figures are stated in constant 1958 prices. The original model (which was called "Framework Model," as it provided a quantitative basis for various sectoral or detailed side analyses) includes all transactions in the conventional national accounts, and thus needed to be simplified for our purposes of illustration here.

The most important simplification is the integration of the household and private enterprise sectors, which were indicated separately in the original model. (The original model has about fifty equations, if all minor structural relations are counted.) The items for current government expenditure, capital expenditure of general government, and capital expenditure of government enterprises, which are separately treated in the original model, are also integrated here into the single item "government purchases of goods and services." The symbols listed below differ from those used in the original model but accord with the equations of the simplified model. (Exogenous variables are indicated by a bar above the letter; policy variables are indicated in Greek letters.)

Simplified Model for the Ten-Year Plan

$$(1) \quad \overline{V}_1 + V_2 + V_3 = \overline{V}$$

$$(2) \quad \overline{V} = C + G + I + E - M$$

$$(3) \quad W + R = \overline{V} - T_i$$

$$(4) \quad C + T_d + S_p = W + R + A$$

$$(5) \quad G + A + \overline{S}_g = T_i + T_d$$

$$(6) \quad E - M = B$$

$$(7) \quad V_2 = f_1(\overline{V})$$

$$(8) \quad I = f_2(K)$$

$$(9) \quad K = f_3(\overline{V})$$

$$(10) \quad M = f_4(\overline{V})$$

$$(11) \quad E = f_5(\overline{F})$$

$$(12) \quad W = f_6(\overline{V}_1, V_2, V_3)$$

$$(13) \quad S_p = f_7(W, R, T_d, A)$$

$$(14) \quad G = \alpha\overline{V}$$

$$(15) \quad A = \beta\overline{V}$$

$$(16) \quad T_i = \gamma\overline{V}$$

$$(17) \quad T_d = \delta W + \epsilon R$$

$$(18) \quad L = L_1 + L_2 + L_3$$

$$(19) \quad L = f_8(\overline{N})$$

$$(20) \quad L_2 = f_9(V_2)$$

$$(21) \quad L_3 = f_{10}(V_3)$$

Explanation of Symbols

$\overline{V}$ gross national product
$\overline{V}_1$ gross value added in primary industry
V_2 gross value added in secondary industry
V_3 gross value added in tertiary industry
C private consumption
G government purchases of goods and services (including government investment)
I private investment
K private capital stock at the end of year
E exports

M	imports
$\overline{F}$	world trade
W	wages and salaries
R	nonwage income
T_i	indirect taxes
T_d	direct taxes
A	transfer payments
S_p	private saving
B	net exports
$\overline{S}_g$	government surplus (government current saving minus government investment)
α	share of government purchases in GNP
β	share of transfer payments in GNP
γ	indirect tax ratio
δ	direct tax ratio of wage income
ϵ	direct tax ratio of nonwage income
L	total labor force
L_1	labor force in primary industry
L_2	labor force in secondary industry
L_3	labor force in tertiary industry
$\overline{N}$	total population

Here we have twenty-one equations, nineteen endogenous variables, five exogenous variables, and five policy variables. Since letter f stands for a structural or behavioral relationship, there are ten structural equations in this system. Equations (1) to (6) refer to accounting identities of national accounts; the left side of the equations relates to the expenditure side of the account, the right side to the receipt side of the account. As there are twenty-one equations, two out of five policy variables must be converted to endogenous variables to obtain a solution of the system. Therefore, tax ratios δ and ϵ are treated as endogenous variables, and government expenditure ratios α and β and indirect tax ratio γ are treated as exogenous variables, so that the system can be solved on the basis of eight exogenous variables. Since some of the equations take nonlinear form, it is not possible to derive the general solution, but the system is still workable for various types of experimentation by simply changing the pattern of exogenous variables.

Equations (1) and (2) deal with the net output and final products of the economy, and equations (3) and (4) relate to income distribution and expenditures of the private sector. Equation (5) relates to the account of general government, equation (6) to the international balance of payments in the current account before adjustments of international transfers. In view of budgetary considerations, the government surplus, $\overline{S}_g$, reflects the traditional policy of a balanced budget; however, as will be discussed later, by changing the amount of this variable, we can assess the fiscal and financial implications of budgetary operations. Equation (7) relates to the growth elasticity of the secondary sector. The estimation of the secondary sector provided a basis for further elaborate projection of industrial output of key products. Value added in the primary sector was fixed as an exogenous variable from the employment and social point of view.

Equations (8) and (9) are important because they relate to the efficiency of total productive capital, which can greatly influence the rate of growth of the economy. Actually, the estimation of capital stock was also made on the sectoral basis, but the results were adjusted at the final stage to the overall estimate of capital requirement—equation (9).

Equation (12) relates to total payroll, which is based on sectoral distribution of GNP. Therefore, the relatively faster growth of secondary industry, which usually has a higher labor share than primary industry, tends to raise the total labor share of the economy. Equation (13)— private saving function—is assumed to be influenced by income distribution, direct tax policy, and social security schemes of the government. As mentioned earlier, parameters α and β deal with the direct government decision on expenditures; they were adjusted, however, after several experiments on the amounts of δ and ε. Equation (19) is the function for labor participation, and the labor force in primary industry is assumed to be determined as a residue or a balance between labor demand from secondary and tertiary industry and total labor supply, as indicated in equations (18) to (21).

The merit of this model is its flexibility for experimenting with various quantitative assumptions concerning external conditions, limiting factors, and political decisions. Provided that an ambitiously high rate of growth of GNP is expected to be attained, the investment requirement—and in particular its share of GNP—would also tend to increase substantially in view of the Harrod-Domar type assumption. Increased imports affected by such a high rate of growth might adversely affect the balance of payment position of the economy and also produce an extreme labor shortage.

Such considerations appear to indicate that the planned target of GNP should be lowered. There is, however, another way to test feasibility— the test from the fiscal and financial point of view by means of the saving function and policy variables on expenditures. If the private sector is not able to provide sufficient voluntary saving for investment under the ordinary tax burden, the government would be obliged to lower the tax rate and to cut down its expenditures on investment and social security.

If this tax reduction policy is not effective, the government surplus, $\bar{S}_g$, which has been fixed before, would have to be raised by reducing government expenditure or by increasing the tax burden.[10] In this case the government would be expected to use this surplus to finance investment in the private sector to make up for the lack of private saving. If, however, even such an increase in government surplus could not meet the shortage of private saving for business investment, the planners must either expect a general price increase or lower their growth target of GNP.[11] In any case, the above discussion illustrates the model's potential for planning and its flexibility for changing situations.

Simplicity of structure is another merit of the model. Since almost all variables are connected with gross national product, $\bar{V}$, the economic effects of alternative growth rates and their policy implications are readily obtained. The model may not be very helpful in obtaining a rigorous solution regarding the optimal level of GNP for a given target year, but it still retains a practical usefulness in deriving approximate levels of GNP and other variables.

As noted, the model we have outlined above is simplified. The original "Framework Model" is far more complicated, since it contains all transactions of the conventional national accounting, including enterprise, government, household, external, and capital accounts. Various quantitative analyses—such as foreign trade projection by region and commodity group, output projection of key commodities, energy balance, labor balance, technological and engineering study on transport demand and public investment requirements—are all linked to the "Framework Model" and coordinated into a single economic system. To complete the quantitative targets took about one year.

Criticisms of the Model

Although the model has many merits, its method has also stimulated a variety of critical comments, as noted below.

1. The model is elaborately specific on the basis of national accounts, but the predictability of its key structural parameters has been questioned, especially when compared with actual performance. Outstanding in this respect is the underestimation of capital-output ratio and saving

[10] Another alternative would be to keep government expenditures as they are and to reduce tax burdens to promote private saving. This policy of deficit budgeting (i.e., the reduction of $\bar{S}_g$) is strongly contrary to the traditional fiscal policy and was therefore not seriously considered in the present plan.

[11] Even in this case the introduction of foreign capital or aid might help to keep the high rate of growth. This device, however, was almost ignored in the present plan.

ratio, which eventually led to the shortage in social overhead facilities relative to the present level of private investment and GNP. The insufficiency of the statistical method in estimating these parameters has been pointed out.

2. The lack of price mechanism analysis has also been repeatedly criticized. Although the model is equipped with various fiscal policy variables, the presentation of all variables in constant prices has made fiscal planners reluctant to follow the planned targets, as the annual budgeting is always carried out in current prices. Yet if price mechanisms were included, along with the many fiscal policy variables, the model would be extremely complicated and call for sophisticated statistical estimation techniques.

3. The degree of the model's consistency has been another target for criticism.[12] Although an effort was made to give the model as much internal consistency as possible, consistency between macro and sectoral targets was not firmly established because an up-to-date interindustry table was not available at the time. This raises a question about the imbalance of relatively low demand and high supply targets for the machinery and the chemical industries on which the plan placed one of its highest priorities. More recent study, based on the new interindustry data, has revealed substantial scope for readjustment, especially in regard to capital goods.

4. The lack of an intermediate plan has been attacked by many critics, since this lack obscures the intention of the government in implementing the long-term plan. Large private firms desire intermediate target figures for their own projections, even on selected items. The critics also point out that the lack of intermediate planning has made it difficult for users of the plan to tie in with the government's annual budgeting system. In short, the enforced use of an intermediate target of 9 percent growth of GNP for the first three years of the plan, without concurrent adjustment of any of the other targets, was too simple a step to serve users as a guide post or a basis for policy decisions.

Binding Force of the Plan

Although the plan was not presented to the Diet, it was officially approved by the Cabinet, and therefore each ministry has the obligation to gear its long-term policy to it. This obligation is particularly important for the public sector. One of the plan's features is specification of de-

[12] T. Watanabe's paper, which follows mine, discusses the consistency problem in some detail.

tailed public investment targets up to 1970. Although intermediate targets are not indicated, the planning elements for the public sector are significant, especially for such key sectors as roads, ports and harbors, agriculture and fishery, housing, sewage, flood control, and water resources.

As noted before, the figures for the private sector production targets are regarded in principle as guides for the sector's long-term planning. One problem, however, is the degree to which private firms may be willing to cooperate with the principles of the plan in formulating their own long-term growth targets. Many business leaders were members of the committees or subcommittees attached to the Economic Deliberation Council; further, each ministry concerned with the preparation of the plan organized private groups under its charge to consider the draft of the sectoral plans prepared by the Economic Planning Agency. Thus, representatives of most of the leading business organizations did participate to a considerable extent in formulating the plan. Nevertheless, whether or not an individual industry follows the plan in preparing and implementing its own plans is entirely its own decision. The government can give warnings, or suggest certain investment plans as part of an anticyclical policy, but its control over the private sector is now, in principle, quite indirect. That private industry can easily be stimulated by long-term government planning was seen after the release of the ten-year plan; on the other hand, to restrict individual industries to investment policies that accord with the plan has become increasingly difficult for the government.

IMPLEMENTATION AND DEVIATIONS

Private industry responded with much greater enthusiasm to the present plan than it had to the previous one. Toward the latter part of 1960, the prevailing high growth rate of the economy was leveling off somewhat, and many business men were beginning to fear that this was the consequence of the government's increased trade liberalization policy. But the release of the long-term plan encouraged long-term perspectives again and greatly stimulated investment. Indeed, in some industries—particularly steel and heavy machinery—this enthusiasm resulted in excessive fixed investment.[13] Nevertheless, the plan's great merit was to give confidence

[13] One group of economists and business leaders, who regarded the planned targets as underestimates in view of the traditional underbias in preceding plans, responded to the targets with overoptimistic investment behavior. The result was excessive capacity in some industries.

to industry as a whole, at a time when the economy was entering a more liberalized and open system.

The pace of expansion for public investment was also accelerated after the release of the plan, but the effect was less conspicuous than for private investment. In other words, even this large increase in social overhead facilities has not been sufficient to meet the still rapidly increasing present demands.

Statistical indicators have revealed that the plan's initial goal of a 9 percent rate of growth up to 1963 was almost attained, despite the wide fluctuations of the growth rate of GNP—i.e., about 14 percent in 1961, 5 percent in 1962, 8 percent (expected) in 1963. The rate of increase of exports has been slightly above the assumed rate, mostly owing to a higher-than-expected rate of increase of world trade. Imports have also been above the expected level, and payments for international freight transport have increased at a faster-than-expected rate. The expected balance in current accounts of international balance of payments appeared (as of late 1963) to be unlikely for the time being, but the larger amount of capital inflow tended to make up for the gap. Industrial production is expanding above the expected rate, and, surprisingly enough, private investment in plant and equipment is already at the level the plan expected for 1970. On the other hand, due to the higher industrial expansion, the shortage in social overhead facilities is again increasing, although the actual investment in this field, after price adjustment, is almost on schedule. But underestimation of transport demand has resulted in a serious shortage in the road and harbor sector, a situation that demonstrates a pressing need for certain revisions of the plan.

A rise in consumer prices is now becoming one of the most serious obstacles to further economic growth. It is largely a consequence of the higher-than-expected increase in wage rates resulting from the growing labor shortage, which in its turn is due to an inherent factor of Japan's traditional lifetime employment system—low mobility of the labor force.

Japan's international relationships have been changing at a far faster rate than was expected. The shift to Article VIII nations of the IMF and membership in the OECD are destined to expedite the liberalization of commodity trade, invisible trade, and capital transactions to a greater extent than originally assumed in the plan.

In view of the deviations and the many new factors arising during implementation of the plan, the Economic Planning Agency established a committee (attached to the Economic Deliberation Council) to review the implementation. The committee organized ten subcommittees, each of which was specialized for each relevant field and made up of business leaders, economists, and scholars. These groups were to analyze the deviations from the plan and the reasons for them, as well as the new factors that the plan could not have foreseen.

For the macroeconomic targets, including some related sectoral targets, the Planning Bureau took the following approach. First, the parameters of the "Framework Model" were re-examined in the light of newly available statistical materials. Second, deviations of exogenous variables from expected values were studied. Third, deviations of policy variables were analyzed in connection with changes in other exogenous variables. Fourth, the deviations were classified as to changes of structural parameters, policy variables, and exogenous variables. Generally speaking, the deviations of the global capital-output ratio and saving-propensity were found to be the most influential in effecting wide differences of the endogenous variables.

CONCLUDING REMARKS

What we have learned from our past experiences of quantitative planning of economic policy is summarized below.

1. Japanese economic planning has shifted its emphasis from the direct controls of the postwar emergency period to the more indirect controls of an economy that has been widening its perspective—that is, from five to ten years. The growing shortage of social overhead capital (due to the rapid growth of the private sector) and the increasing importance of market mechanisms in the private economy have been major factors behind this tendency. In the present ten-year plan, however, the lessened emphasis on projections for the private sector has tended to cause inconsistency between macro and sectoral projections, especially for capital goods industries. This shortcoming could have been avoided had there been sufficient data and had more adequate projection techniques been employed.

Preparatory work for a revision of the plan, now underway in the Planning Bureau, is making extensive use of an interindustry analysis which takes account of likely changes in technical coefficients, import coefficients, and levels of final demands for the target year. Since private business also demands information on the detailed components of future demand and supply for its own use, the government's projection on the basis of an interindustry analysis will be of great assistance to business projections and also prevent excessive overinvestment or underinvestment.

2. It is difficult to make long-term projections for a fast-growing country like Japan, where rapid structural changes are always taking place. The difficulty is particularly emphasized in projections of private fixed investment. Various earlier projections failed to grasp the exact movement of future investment demand, because of the wide structural change in capital-output relationship and capital-labor substitutions. The Economic Planning Agency is now experimenting with models taking account of labor-capital substitutions and technological progress on sectoral as well as macroeconomic levels. So far, this approach seems more promising than the conventional approach by capital-output ratio.

A new difficulty arising from an increasing disparity between consumer prices and wholesale prices requires the inclusion of wage-cost relationships in the macroeconomic model. An econometric approach is now being made by the Economic Research Institute within the framework of national accounts, with the aim of deriving a consistent set of wage rates, return to capital, and price indexes of imports, exports, investment goods, and consumer goods and services.

3. Interest in projection techniques by econometric models is growing among government officials, economists, and leaders in private business. A model that is simplified but well-grounded by reliable parameters would be more persuasive for such practical decision-makers than a sophisticated model which has a great number of equations. Furthermore, it is dangerous to rely too much on the results of a single model; various alternatives ought to be used until the policy implications of the analysis are thoroughly clear.

4. Three types of models are being studied by the Planning Bureau: a quarterly (or annual) model, a long-term model, and a perspective model. The long-term model relates to some five to ten years, the perspective model to a longer period—say ten to twenty years, with a very limited number of equations. The price indexes of products and factors are included in the quarterly (or annual) model and will be included in the long-term model, in view of the importance of a current value series for fiscal and monetary analysis. As noted, the lack of intermediate targets in the present ten-year plan has been criticized by many economists, since it obscures the course of implementation. The long-term model, therefore, will indicate the intermediate growth path by a limited number of indicators up to the target year, and will be closely linked with the annual model to carry out an effective anticyclical policy. In this respect, the concept of capacity is the most important link between short-term and long-term models.

5. Unlike the situation in a socialistic economy, quantitative planning in a mixed economy is characterized by "conditional projection," since the economy is geared mostly by indirect government controls through fiscal and monetary policy. In Japan the various restrictions on imports and foreign exchange are now being rapidly removed; long-term projection is therefore becoming somewhat more difficult. Nevertheless, if a high rate of growth and a high standard of welfare are to be achieved without too much effect on the balance of payments and the general price level, formulation of an effective long-term plan and of a flexible countercyclical policy is becoming increasingly important.

In regard to Japan's long-term planning the most crucial items of the government's fiscal and monetary policy are (1) the creation of additional savings to further economic growth and (2) the provision of adequate social facilities. The first item relates to the continuing scarcity of domestic capital and the importance of maintaining a high rate of saving. (The suggestion made by a group of economists for a spending policy to counteract the so-called "coming of chronic stagnation as a result of the excessive private investment in recent years" seems unrealistic in view of the long-term perspective of increasing capital intensity and labor shortage.) The second item, since public investment is now taking a most active role in economic growth, is expected to raise the efficiency of private investment substantially.

Thus the government today in Japan, no matter how indirect its leadership of the private sector, is increasing the significance of its role, especially because of the strong interdependence of the public and private sectors.

Stronger measures for countercyclical policy are also being demanded by many people, as the economy becomes more liberalized and open. These demands imply that long-range and intermediate quantitative targets should be prepared more carefully—and in closer cooperation with private business—by means of advanced projection techniques. If this is done, private business can be expected to conform more closely to government intentions, thus preventing unduly wide fluctuations in the rate of economic growth. In this case, as stressed before, a consistent projection of demand and supply for individual private sectors will serve as an effective tool for a long-term investment policy.

10

National Planning
and Economic Growth in Japan

TSUNEHIKO WATANABE[1]

"ECONOMIC PLANNING" has become a familiar term in nearly every country of the world since the end of World War II, but the nature of planning may differ significantly from country to country. Japan, for example, differs from a number of other nations in the multiplicity of its plans: since 1946, more than a dozen overall (or national) plans have been drafted (not counting annual projections, which are closely related to the government's annual budget). Since, on the average, this means almost a national plan a year, planners in other nations may well raise the following questions. (1) Why so many? (2) Have the plans been effective in realizing economic growth during the postwar period? And (3)—if the answer to the preceding question is in the affirmative—is the effectiveness expected to continue into the future?

Our discussion here is primarily concerned with the second question—the effectiveness of the plans during the postwar period—but the first and third questions will not be entirely neglected. Six main national plans have been selected for detailed discussion:[2]

    I. "Draft Plan for Economic Rehabilitation" (authorized in May 1948)
    II. "Economic Rehabilitation Plan" (May 1949)
    III. "Economic Self-Support Plan" (January 1951)
    IV. "Five-Year Plan for Economic Self-Support" (December 1955)
    V. "New Long-Range Economic Plan" (December 1958)
    VI. "Plan for Doubling National Income" (November 1960)

[1] Associate Director, Economic Research Institute, Economic Planning Agency, and Professor of Economics, Gakushuin University. (This paper was prepared in cooperation with S. Shishido. The author is indebted to Professor S. Tsuru, who unpublished paper, "Rapid Growth with Formal Planning Divorced from Action: Japan," was of assistance to him.)
[2] Plans prior to 1948 were omitted here because they were drafted by agencies other than the Japanese government and also because most of the economic problems

TABLE 10-1. *A Comparison Between Actual and Planned Levels of National Income*[a]

(in billions of yen)

Year	Actual	Plan I	Plan II	Plan III	Plan IV	Plan V	Plan VI
1947	968	968					
1948	1,962	1,142	1,962				
1949	2,737	1,279	2,197	2,737			
1950	3,382	1,416	2,374	3,110			
1951	4,525	1,565	2,550	3,573			
1952	5,085	1,671	2,727	3,761			
1953	5,748		2,923	3,964			
1954	6,022				6,022		
1955	6,719				↓		
1956	7,628					7,628	
1957	8,286				6,937		
1958	8,519				↓	↓	
1959	10,037				↓		
1960	11,937				8,072		11,904
1961	14,196					↓	12,995
1962	15,782					11,129	14,191

[a] Figures for actual national income are from Economic Planning Agency *National Income Report* (Tokyo, 1964). The planned series are adjusted to a level of starting year or the base year, for comparability.

A comparison between actual levels of national income and the levels assumed in the six plans from 1947 to 1962 is shown in Table 10-1. As can be seen, the discrepancies between actual and planned levels of national income have been significant, particularly in the direction of underestimation. However, the *number* of discrepancies may be misleading, since no price adjustments are made in this comparison. In Table 10-2, therefore, a comparison is made of the growth rate of GNP in real terms. Discrepancies still exist in considerable number, especially during the last six years; nevertheless, the actual growth rates of 1958 and 1962 are the only ones that did not meet or exceed the planned targets.

From these rather superficial observations, one might conclude that national planning in Japan has been useful in assisting rapid growth (although a reservation must be made about the skillfulness of the planning technique). This conclusion, however, would only follow if Japan had a centrally planned economy. The fact is that the Japanese economy is not now, and never has been, centrally planned; it is a mixed economy.

confronted at that period were war-caused and completely irregular. The above-stated six plans, and especially the last three, were much more directly concerned with the rapid economic growth of Japan in the postwar years.

TABLE 10-2. *A Comparison of the Growth Rate of GNP in Real Terms* *(Base Year, 1955)*[a]

Year	Actual	Plan I	Plan II	Plan III	Plan IV	Plan V	Plan VI
1947							
1948	17.2%	17.0%					
1949	15.7	12.0	12.0%				
1950	12.2	10.7	8.0				
1951	13.5	10.5	7.4	4.3%			
1952	10.5	8.0	6.9	5.3			
1953	8.4		7.2	5.4			
1954	3.3						
1955	10.3				4.8%		
1056	9.0				4.8		
1957	7.9				4.9	6.5%	
1958	3.2				5.2	6.5	
1959	17.9				5.2	6.5	
1960	13.2					6.5	9.0%
1961	14.0					6.5	9.0
1962	5.6						9.0

[a] The series of actual rate of growth are reported in Economic Planning Agency, *National Income Report* (Tokyo, 1964), and the planned series are compiled from the report of each of the plans.

This being so, the above discrepancies must be interpreted in one of two ways: either national planning has not influenced the pattern of economic growth, or the underestimations have themselves been part of a successful planning policy.

The interpretations of the discrepancies will be discussed in detail later. There are, however, several direct causes of the discrepancies that should be mentioned briefly here. Two important miscalculations were made in the quantitative projections, the first one concerning the balance of payments level (and mainly due to underestimation of the effects of changes in the trade situation), the second concerning underestimation of investment activities in the private sectors. Thus, we have an indication that the quantitative projections in the plans were insufficient. This point will be the first one discussed below.

But even when the original quantitative projections are reasonably sufficient, the reactions of the private sectors to the plans can be quite different from what the planners had assumed—and if they are, discrepancies between actual and planned levels, may be large. Thus, the relationships between the public and private sectors are very important to the effectiveness of planning. The second section below will be concerned with this aspect.

The third possible cause of discrepancies in the national plans has to do with the reality that policy implementations in Japan have been, in general, adjusted and executed mostly within the framework of the annual government budget. The third section below will consider the relationship of long-term planning to the annual budget.

Finally, the principles of economic planning in Japan have changed significantly since 1948. This fact is also important when we are considering the overall effectiveness of national planning, and will be part of a final discussion of effectiveness as viewed from the vantage point of late 1963.

INSUFFICIENCIES OF QUANTITATIVE PROJECTION

It is reasonable to say that a mixed type of economy, such as Japan's, requires much more reliable projection for quantitative planning than a centrally planned economy does. In the former case, government agencies cannot use overall direct controls, except in emergencies (such as war or acute economic depression). Thus, in drawing up a national plan in a mixed economy, the construction of reliable longer-term projections must be given first priority. ("Longer-term" is used here to connote periods of ten years or more.) In Japan, this procedure was first explicitly introduced for the "Ten-Year Plan for Doubling National Income" (Plan VI), which was drafted after a twenty-year projection had been drawn up by the Economic Deliberation Council. Without this kind of longer-term projection, it is hardly possible to make a rational selection of suitable economic policies for promoting economic growth during the specified planning period, since some of the policies, especially those which are designed to change institutional factors, may become effective only in the long run.

Viewed from this aspect, Japan's national plans, except for Plan VI, have been insufficient. Plan IV, for example ("Five-Year Plan for Economic Self-Support"), projected a 5 percent GNP growth rate as the yearly average from 1955 to 1959, where the basic assumption was that the future economic trend would be a return to the prewar level (4.5 percent GNP growth and 3 percent annual increase in labor productivity, for instance), simply because of the disappearance of elements that had played a role in economic recovery. The prewar level was introduced rather conventionally into the projection scheme as a normal standard for the future Japanese economy, without detailed study of the long-run impacts of structural changes which had accumulated in the postwar period—such as changes in the rate of technological progress, or changes from an economy of military preparation to one of peacetime uses of resources (including human assets). Three years after Plan IV was announced, the Economic Deliberation Council reported that a 5 percent GNP growth rate would be a pessimistic projection until the 1970's. The lack of a longer-term projection that would have taken account of the structural changes had created confusion at the policy implementation stage; as a result, a revision of the plan had already been initiated in 1956.

Nevertheless, the necessity for the longer-term projection was still not sufficiently recognized, partly because the main defect of Plan IV was considered at the time to be the adoption of an unrealistic policy target —the achievement of full employment.

Although the preparations for Plan VI recognized the projection's insufficiency and overcame it to some extent, another type of difficulty appeared—a lack of internal consistency. The most important requirement in a mixed type of economy is consistency between the aggregate and sectoral projections; otherwise the planned policies will not be effective. This sectoral consistency check was not systematically examined at the time of the preparation of Plan VI, although the possible values of the production index were projected for fourteen manufacturing industries, as well as agriculture, mining, public utilities, trade and transportation, and services. The plan envisaged a rapid growth of industrialization with a special emphasis on heavy industries, but the projected rate of growth in manufacturing industries disclosed a very moderate pattern of industrialization, as compared with the international average obtained by Chenery.[3]

As Table 10-3 shows, the projected rates of growth in Plan VI were, in general, slightly lower than the international averages, but the differences were rather insignificant, except in iron and steel. This could be interpreted as indicating that the industrial growth projected in Plan VI represented a reasonably balanced structure on the production side, except for iron and steel.

The important question, however, is the relationship between supply and demand, as given in the aggregate national account. When the plan was being prepared in 1959-60, no sectoral consistency check was undertaken, mainly because a suitable framework and associated figures for the

[3] See Hollis B. Chenery, "Patterns of Industrial Growth," *American Economic Review*, Vol. 50 (September 1960); and United Nations Secretariat, Department of Economic and Social Affairs, *A Study of Industrial Growth* (1963).

TABLE 10-3. *Sectoral Projection in Plan VI*[a]

Industry	(1) Planned Increases (percent)	(2) Standard Increases (percent)	(3) Planned Projections (billion yen)	(4) Consistent Estimates (billion yen)
1. Agriculture	137	144	3,943	4,379
2. Coal Mining	115	}135	173	157
3. Other Mining	165		259	339
4. Processed Food	185	197	3,674	3,785
5. Textile	213	231	4,228	4,381
6. Chemicals	310	293	4,062	3,320
7. Iron & Steel	258	}398	7,155	5,828
8. Nonferrous Metals	223		1,206	1,141
9. Machinery	}	}	4,669	2,035
10. Electric Machinery	}352	}394	4,128	2,387
11. Transport Machinery	}	}	3,011	2,283
12. Nonmetallic Mineral Products	239	223	1,149	939
13. Misc. Mfg. (I)	}277	}368	4,714	4,277
14. Misc. Mfg. (II)			2,256	2,050
15. Building Construction	233	}221	2,179	2,082
16. Other Construction	297		3,829	2,874
17. Public Utilities	263	—	1,256	1,247
18. Trade & Transport	245	242	8,866	8,200
19. Services	238	210	11,212	12,198
20. Unallocated	221	—	2,236	4,138
21. Import (noncompetitive)	235	—	1,061	1,180
Total			75,263	69,218

[a] The figures in Column 1 are compiled from the official report of Plan VI, Economic Planning Agency, *The Long-Range Economic Plan, 1961–1970* (Nippon Times Co., 1961), p. 176; in column 2 from Hollis B. Chenery, "Patterns of Industrial Growth," *American Economic Review*, Vol. 50 (September 1960), p. 634, Table 3 (for sectors 1, 2, 3, 15, 16, 18, and 19), and U.N. Secretariat, Dept. of Economic and Social Affairs, *A Study of Industrial Growth* (1963), p. 39, Table I-4 (for the remaining sectors); in both columns it is assumed that per capita income will double within ten years from 1961. Column 3 is derived from the official report of Plan VI, p. 176. Column 4 is computed by the formula given in our footnote 6 on page 239, using corresponding figures from Plan VI.

purpose were lacking. The input-output table of 1955, for example, was not ready for use at that time. (Although the input-output table of 1951 and the partially revised table of 1954 were available, the irregularities of 1951, mainly due to the Korean war, were considered to be quite significant.) After several trial tests of the input-output table of 1955, which was officially released in the middle of 1960,[4] the tentative conclusion was that

[4] Ministry of International Trade and Industry, *Input-Output Analyses in the Japanese Economy* (1962; in Japanese).

the input-output framework would be applicable for checking the consistency of sectoral projections with some modifications in individual coefficients.[5]

As the first step of preparatory work on the input-output table of 1960 (started in the middle of 1961), the tentative table of 1959 was compiled. After price adjustments were made (since Plan VI was presented in 1958 prices and the input-output table of 1959 was in 1955 prices), the basic model for sectoral consistency check was formulated with the input-output table of 1959, taking into consideration possible technological changes in individual sectors.[6] As columns (3) and (4) of Table 10-3 show, there were many significant discrepancies between Plan VI's sectoral output projections and the computed estimates that were derived by the interation method (see footnote 6), assuming the given final demand bill in Plan VI. There were particularly large differences in those sectors which were considered to be essential for the growth of industrialization. For example, overestimation was significant for machinery, construction, metals, and nonmetallic mineral products, where the latter two sectors are closely interrelated with the former two. On the other hand, the levels of agriculture and mining were underestimated.

The inconsistency between the aggregate and the sectoral projections may be a serious problem, depending on which projections—the aggregate or the sectoral—the private sectors accept as their guide posts. Ac-

---

[5] S. Shishido, "Interindustry Analysis and Plan for Doubling National Income" (1961, unpublished manuscript; in Japanese).

[6] Define the marginal technological change as a ratio of (actual intermediate demand minus estimated intermediate demand) to the increase in estimated intermediate demand, or in symbols:

$$t_i = \frac{\sum (a_{ij}^{T_o} - a_{ij}^{T.})x_j^{T_o}}{\sum_j a_{ij}^{T.}(x_j^{T_o} - x_j^{T.})}$$

where a_{ij} = input-output coefficient in the $i - j$ cell

x_j = output in the j-th sector

T_o : indicating the base year (in the case 1951)

$T.$: indicating the last available year (here, 1959)

t_i : marginal technological change in the i-th sector.

Further, by defining the diagonal matrix T, whose elements are t_i's, the expansion series were computed:

$Ax_1 + T(Ax_1 - A\bar{x}) + (y - m) = x_2$

$Ax_2 + T(Ax_2 - A\bar{x}) + (y - m) = x_3$

$Ax_3 + T(Ax_3 - A\bar{x}) + (y - m) = x_4. \ldots$

where x_1 = projected output in 1970 (vector); $\bar{x}$ = actual output in 1959 (vector); A = input-output matrix in 1959; y = projected final demand in 1970 (vector), given in Plan VI; m = projected import in 1970 (vector), given in Plan VI.

ceptance of the sectoral projections by private enterprises, however, is almost certain since the sectoral figures are much easier to use than the totals. This would lead to a significant increase in production, together with proportional increases in imported raw materials; as a consequence, a distortion in the balance of payments would appear much faster than expected. The tight-money policy, which was introduced in September 1961 and continued until October 1962, can, in fact, be partly explained by this consequence of the plan's inconsistencies.

The existence of internal inconsistency in a plan can become a crucial disturbance in the long run, because of the relationships between public and private sectors, which are discussed below.

RELATIONSHIPS OF THE PUBLIC AND PRIVATE SECTORS

From 1946 until about 1952, Japanese economic policy was tied to recovery from war damages and to stabilization of inflationary tendencies. To pursue these policy targets effectively, extensive and direct government controls prevailed, especially in the production of basic commodities, such as rice, coal, electricity, steel, and transportation facilities; the attitude of the private sectors was completely passive.[7]

Strong power configurations were created in several government agencies, particularly the Ministry of Finance, through controls over monetary institutions, including the creation of several semi-governmental banks; the Ministry of International Trade and Industry (MITI), through import quotas and capital allocations; and the Ministry of Agriculture, through heavy subsidies for rice production. Curiously enough, the Economic Planning Agency did not achieve similar power during this period. (This point, which is closely related to the special nature of executive procedure in Japan's national plan—i.e., the role of the government's annual budget—will be discussed in the next section.)

Under these circumstances, the planned targets of this early period were, to a considerable degree, actually directives to the private sectors. And even after 1952 (and indeed, even today) passivity remained a characteristic of the private sectors, although it has been gradually declining.

---

[7] This passive attitude was not solely due to the above-stated factors, since it was a traditional matter originating in the Meiji era. Even after this era, the top-ranking graduates of national universities tended to join government agencies, and, especially in the postwar period, attached themselves to the Ministry of Finance and MITI.

Consideration of and arrangements regarding relations between the public and private sectors were first made an explicit part of Japanese policy planning during the preparation stage of Plan VI. Briefly, this problem was handled by providing concrete plans for public sectors and general guide posts for private sectors.

A brief description of the nature and role of planning in the public sectors will be helpful here. The most continuously important strategic factor in the public sectors has been "administrative investment."[8] This connotes government investment minus that of public corporations. Investments in Japan National Railway Corporation, Japan Telephone and Telegraph Corporation, Japan Housing Corporation, Japan Highway Corporation, and the Nuclear Power Research Institute are treated as non-administrative.

Traditionally, the share of administrative investment in GNP has been higher in Japan than in other countries; in 1957, for example, it was about 6 percent in Japan, and 1.6, 2.5, and 3.5 percent in the United Kingdom, the United States, and Sweden, respectively. The ratio to gross domestic capital formation has been over 20 percent on the average during the last seven years and is gradually increasing. Another important aspect of administrative investment is its composition. Since 1955, at least 25 percent of the total has been allocated to the "creation of external economies," while the allocation to improvement of living standards has been continuously less than 10 percent. According to Plan VI, the ratio of administrative investments to GNP would increase from 6.7 percent in 1960 to 7.9 percent in 1970, and 35.1 percent of total administrative investment would be allocated to roads, ports, and agricultural facilities in 1970.

Within the public sectors of any country there are several other alternatives for planned spending—such as current government expenditure, military outlays, and social security. In the case of Japanese planning, these alternatives are handled mostly through the annual plan, rather than the long-term plans. (However, some constraints are placed on such items; in Plan VI, for example, the amount of transfer payments is projected at 6.1 percent of total national income in 1970.)

In the strictest sense of planning, among the individual items of administrative investments, those for roads, port facilities, public housing,

---

[8] "Administrative investment" is subdivided into four categories: (1) creation of economies external to industries, e.g., roads, ports, and agricultural facilities; (2) improvement of general living conditions, e.g., housing, sanitary facilities, and other welfare facilities; (3) rehabilitation, e.g., from war damage in the early period and from damages due to typhoon, earthquakes, etc.; and (4) all others, e.g., education facilities, regional development facilities, and so on.

and conservation and development of forests and rivers are completely under the plan—ie., the amounts to be invested in them within a specific period, usually five years, are determined by law. (They represent about half of the total administrative investment.) For other items, the amounts to be invested during the planning period are also determined in the plan but must be negotiated with the Ministry of Finance every year to become effective. It appears, therefore, that the influence of long-term planning in the public sector is small in the quantitative sense, in view of the planning roles of other government agencies and of the annual budget.

As mentioned above, several governmental agencies, especially the Ministry of Finance and MITI, have had strong influence on the execution of the national plan. Here we will focus on the role of MITI, since the task of the Ministry of Finance is more or less limited to short-run financial and monetary policies. In principle, the legal responsibility for drafting the national plan is in the hands of the Economic Planning Agency (and more specifically in the hands of the Planning Bureau); nevertheless, the plans for industrial sectors were almost wholly prepared by MITI. (The plans for rapid industrialization, for example, as discussed in the previous section, were worked out by MITI's staff.) Furthermore, MITI's influence in the execution stage of the plan has been even larger than in the preparation stage. Importation of goods and services—especially raw materials and large-scale machinery and equipment—has been, until very recently, fully controlled by MITI, although the strict quota system for commodities was abandoned in the early 1950's.[9] MITI also has a tool in its intervention in allocations of long-term capital funds for individual industries, especially loans from the semi-governmental banks.[10]

By using these two tools, together with other administrative directives, MITI has strongly promoted policies for rapid industrialization, with special emphasis on heavy industries. This promotion was sometimes out of step with the national plan, despite the fact that consistency in formulating national plans is necessarily one of the most important conditions. (It should, however, be noted here, that MITI's power has been gradually declining, especially in recent years as international trade policies have been liberalized.)

[9] In the early reconstruction period, almost all commodities were under the quota system. After about 1951 this system was replaced by a combination of a "foreign currency allocation" system (which requires the permission of MITI with regard to the needed amount of foreign currency for importing each individual commodity), an "automatic fund allocation" system (which requires no permission until the amount of foreign currency reaches the limit specified in the budget for each commodity), and "an automatic approval" system (in which the limit is set up globally).

[10] S. Ohkita, *Economic Planning in Japan* (Shiseido, 1962; in Japanese).

The private sectors, particularly the manufacturing industries, have been inclined to behave as if a close connection with MITI is the most profitable policy for them. For example, many of the big firms have been hiring higher-ranking officials retired from MITI for their top executive staffs. And it is a rare firm that does not feel compelled to obey the MITI directives, even though they are informal.

On the other hand, optimism about the growth of the Japanese economy has prevailed among private firms ever since the Korean war, and especially after 1955. It is not possible here to analyze extensively the reasons for this optimism, but several of the factors that have contributed importantly to Japan's rapid economic growth can be mentioned: (1) aggressive use of imported technologies,[11] which is considered to be one of the most important reasons for the relatively abundant and well-educated labor force;[12] (2) continuation of the higher rate of saving, or investment; (3) drastic reduction of military expenses—6 percent of GNP in 1934-36 compared to 1.1 or 1.2 percent in the postwar period—which created a favorable condition for rapid expansion of public investment (from about 3 percent of GNP in the prewar period to about 8 percent of GNP in the postwar period); and (4) progress of import substitution technologies.

Being supported by this favorable setting, competition between individual firms for expanding the market-share has been so keen that the target rate set by long-term national planning has been interpreted almost always as the minimum attainable level. Thus, if a plan stated that expansion in a specific sector during the next ten years would be 300 percent, a firm would not only automatically triple its current rate of production but also probably add some further amount of production.[13]

[11] According to a recent survey by MITI, the ratios of production achieved by imported technologies were about 5 percent in 1955 and about 11 percent in 1960, respectively, of total production in manufacturing industries. Furthermore, the use of imported technologies was heavily biased to the larger firms; about two thirds of the firms with over 1 billion yen of paid-in capital used the imported technologies, compared to only about 2 percent of the firms with less than 50 million yen of paid-in capital.

[12] T. Watanabe, "Economic Roles of the Dualistic Natures in the Industrial Development of Japan" (paper read at the Sao Paulo meeting of the United Nations Seminar on Industrial Programming, March 1963; unpublished).

[13] The strong competition among private enterprises has created some serious difficulties for both the national economy and the private sectors. With respect to the national economy, there has been an excess demand for import of raw materials and also for heavy machinery and equipment. Although this sharp increase in imports has been offset to some degree by an increase in exports, cyclical deficits in the balance of payments have emerged. So far, the government has adopted relatively drastic policies in such cases, and cyclical fluctuations have subsequently been

After some fifteen years of experience with national planning, private firms have recognized the importance of long-term business planning. In 1961, for example, among 200 representative firms only 13 percent had no plans; in 1952 close to 100 percent had no plans. In addition, of the firms which have been formulating long-term plans, 84 percent use the government plan as an important basis for them. This attitude of private firms, in short, reflects two things: on the one hand, the traditional passive reaction to government leadership; on the other hand, initiative to undertake, either on their own or through the use of the guide posts of the government's plan, long-term business planning.

In any case, the influence of the national plan can be said to be growing, in the sense that the initial purpose stated by the Economic Planning Agency—concrete planning for public sectors and provision of a general guide post for private sectors—is penetrating into private industry. This increasing influence does not, however, mean that Japan's national planning has achieved complete success as an economic policy. Although relationships between government and private industry have improved in recent years, the actual performance of the Japanese economy is still not satisfactory. In the private sector, institutional obstacles still remain which reduce efficiency—for example, the lifetime employment contracts, and price determination based on the income-parity principle. On the government side, there are still insufficiencies in the quantitative projections, both for the long run and the short run.

Overall, the real success of Japan's national planning in the quantitative sense is heavily dependent upon the validity of the long-term projection and its consistency.

LONG-TERM PLANNING AND
THE ANNUAL GOVERNMENT BUDGET

In Japan's long-term planning, quantitative targets are generally given for the final year of the planning. Plan VI, for example, provides the 1970 levels of GNP and its components and other important indicators. Exceptions to this are found only in the public sectors, where the cumulative amounts to be invested within the planning period are given. Since (as noted earlier) economic activities in Japan are, in principle,

---

amplified. With respect to the private sectors, the actual capacity of production has grown much faster than the desirable levels, and thus the effects of technological inventions have been discounted.

based primarily on private enterprise, short-term adjustments in economic policies become very important. Therefore, a projection of important indicators is made each year. In January 1963, for example, the Economic Planning Agency (whose Coordination Bureau does the actual work on the projections) announced the projected values of important economic indicators, such as the rate of GNP growth (6.1 percent in real terms and 8.1 percent in current terms), estimated exports and imports ($5.2 billion of exports and $5.0 billion of imports), and so on.

The determination of this annual projection has two especially important aspects. First, the government revenues expected from taxes and other sources are estimated from the projection, and so are government expenditures.[14] Second, the projection has a strong effect on private enterprises, since it contains a detailed production projection for mining and manufacturing industries, as a reference table.

Before discussing the actual effectiveness of the annual projection, several points regarding the projections and the annual government budgets should be mentioned: (1) the annual projections have always been underestimated; (2) since 1951 there have been tax reductions every year, except in 1960; (3) the "balanced principle"—i.e., that the sum of government purchases of goods and services and investment expenditures should be equal to or less than government revenues, including the surplus of government enterprises—has been firmly held by the Ministry of Finance; and (4) at least about 40 percent of government expenditure has been allocated to investment since 1951, and the growth rate of government investment was much higher than that of government purchases of goods and services. (In 1961 the indexes of government investment, purchases of goods and services, and GNP were 296.6, 155.6 and 184.7, respectively, at constant 1955 prices where the base year was 1955.)

In combination, the underestimation of the annual growth rate and the adherence to the balanced budget principle have created a government surplus every year, in spite of the continual tax reductions. Compared with the operation of an accurate estimate, this implies a negative stimulant to economic growth or a check on the inflationary impact of government

[14] In practice, the projected rate of economic growth is determined through hard negotiations—sometimes including political negotiations—between the Coordination Bureau and the Tax Agency. Generally speaking, the Tax Agency has constantly tried to push down the projected rate of economic growth, since the lower the projected level, the easier is the administrative effort to collect tax revenues. Furthermore, the lower rate of projected growth has been strategically important for government budget control. The Coordination Bureau, on the other hand, has attempted to make the projections reliable.

expenditures. (As a matter of fact, this policy has so far been purposely adopted.) On the other hand, the relatively high ratio of government investment seems to be useful in stimulating Japanese economic growth (as noted in the previous section). Thus both the annual projections and the annual government budgets have played important roles in stabilization.

The annual projection also plays a role in the policies of the monetary authorities in the Ministry of Finance and the Bank of Japan. Though the government's fiscal budget, which is closely related to the annual projection, is on the whole relatively conservative, capital funds needed to attain the production target must be financed. The monetary policies extensively used for this purpose have had the consequence that the amount needed for investment in private sectors has been almost fully financed by commercial banks. The policy in this sense has created the so-called "over-loan" situation in the accounts of the commercial banks and the "over-borrowing" situation in the private firms.[15] This has produced a favorable condition for short-term adjustments—i.e., the changes in the discount rate were very effective for controlling the investment behavior of private enterprises.[16]

The relationship between the long-term plans and the annual projections (including the determination of the annual government budget) is a specific part of the problem of how the annual projection will be made, in the quantitative sense. As an administrative procedure, the Coordination Bureau of the Economic Planning Agency has the responsibility for formulating the annual projection. The fundamental difference between the quantitative framework of the long-term plan and that of the annual projection is the criterion for evaluating the experience of the previous two years. The annual projection for 1963, for example, was formulated with the basic assumption that the policy for slowing down the growth rate (which was adopted in September 1961 to overcome the

---

[15] "Over-loan," as used here, means that the ratio of loans to deposits is extremely high, sometimes exceeding 100 percent. Since the discount rate has been lower than the call rate (with some exceptions), the usual policy of commercial banks has been to finance the needed short-term funds through the Central Bank in the form of rediscounts. On the other hand, the liquidity of corporate bonds has been extremely low; thus borrowing from commercial banks was the most suitable way to finance private enterprises—which is called "over-borrowing." Under these circumstances, the composition of liabilities in private enterprises depended heavily upon outside borrowing; e.g., in 1958 the ratio of net worth to total assets was around 30 percent in Japan, compared to 40, 65, and 60 percent in West Germany, the United Kingdom, and the United States, respectively.

[16] The so-called "window control" (which means quantitative regulations of loans from the Bank of Japan to commercial banks) has usually been adopted, together with the changes in the discount rate.

increased deficits in the balance of payments) had achieved its objective, and that, to avoid an "over-heating" situation (i.e., the chain of extremely high rates of growth and induced deficits in the balance of payments), the orderly growth rate should be preferred. Consequently, the growth rate was projected as 6.1 percent. Plan VI, when announced, had set out the average rate of growth for 1960-62 as 9 percent.[17] During 1961 to 1963 the actual growth rates were 14, 5.1, and 12.3 percent.

The most significant deviation between planned and actual levels was found in the amount of private fixed capital formation: the 1970 level in the plan was actually achieved in 1961, the first year of Plan VI. This inaccuracy meant that estimates in the long-term projection were not applicable to the subsequent short-term plans. Unfortunately the repetitions of faulty estimates (as exemplified in Tables 10-1 and 10-2) has created a feeling of distrust toward projections—whether long-run or short-run.

The last question to be examined in this section is the role and effectiveness of the government budget as a complement to long-term national planning. As is generally true in most countries based on a free-enterprise system, the government budget in Japan is used both to direct the action of government bodies and to affect the behavior of economic units outside the government sector. Needless to say, the possibility of effectiveness is much greater within the government than outside. Within the government, the budget entries can be used as directives; outside the government, the specific estimates must be depended on to have the power of persuasion.

To maintain the effectiveness of the national plan, it is therefore necessary for the government to allocate reasonable amounts of funds for the main policy proposals in the annual plan. In Plan VI, for example, the annual rate of increase in administrative investment was assumed at 10.5 percent for the first five years. The actual rate during the fiscal years 1960 to 1962 was about 20 percent per annum at constant 1958 prices.[18] Also, the cumulative amount of this investment was about 10

[17] Because of the extremely favorable performances of economic activities during 1959 and 1960 (in those two years the rate of GNP growth was 17.9 and 13.2 percent, respectively) and also because of political pressure (the Ikeda Cabinet used Plan VI as its most important slogan for the general election in 1960), the original 7.2 percent target rate of economic growth, on the average, for the next ten years, was modified to 9 percent for the first three years of the plan. It is almost impossible to provide rational explanations, from the aspect of national planning, for this modification.

[18] The planned rate of 10.5 percent was set for the 7.2 percent rate of GNP growth, while the actual GNP growth was about 11.7 percent per annum during this period.

percent over the original plan. The ratio of administrative investment to fixed capital formation was expected at 1:2 in the final year, compared with the ratio of 1:3 in the base period, but it actually became wider— 1:3.8 in 1961, for example.[19] On the other hand, both the planned and actual rates of increase of transfer payments were about 12 percent per year.

From these observations, one may draw the following tentative conclusions: (1) to determine Japan's annual government budget without both long-run and short-run projections is at present almost impossible; (2) the relative importance of the annual projection has been increasing, both because of the greater ease of modifying an annual plan, and because of the past history of miscarriages in the long-term quantitative projections; and (3) the government budget in its main policy proposals has been trying to be a good complement of the long-term plan, even though, on the whole, the proposals are conservative.

EFFECTIVENESS OF NATIONAL PLANNING IN JAPAN

In the sense that the planned targets, without being coercive, were met or exceeded in almost every field before the termination of a plan, the past fifteen years of Japan's experience with national planning may be considered as rather exceptional, when compared to the experience of other countries in which actual economic performance lagged behind the targets. An analysis of the experience may explain how Japan, with its mixed economy, a relatively poor endowment of natural resources, and a high population density, has accelerated its economic growth without sharp increases in price levels, without excessive deficits in the balance of payments, and without severe controls over private activities.

The characteristics of Japan's national plans can be summarized as follows: (1) there has been underestimation of important economic activities in every quantitative projection; (2) revisions of national plans have been frequent; (3) the annual projections and the government's annual budgets have played aggressive roles; (4) the strong power configurations of various government agencies have exerted greater influence than the Economic Planning Agency has; (5) many inconsistencies in the quantitative projections have occurred; and (6) changes in policy principles have been frequent.

---

[19] "Fixed capital formation" as used here includes both private and government enterprises.

From this summary, one might easily conclude that the effectiveness of national quantitative planning has so far been small. Structural changes due to the rapid economic growth have been large, and it may be true that long-term quantitative projections cannot be successful without being geared to cover all possible changes in the economic structure. Nevertheless, the recent history of Japanese planning could have been much worse than it actually has been, considering that the very necessary condition of internal consistency has not been fulfilled.

On the other hand, it may also be true that rapid economic growth in Japan could not have been achieved without the national plans, since the power configurations of several governmental agencies might have been strong enough to prevent the economy from achieving a reasonably balanced growth.[20] From this point of view, one may say that a kind of coordination between mutually conflicting interests has been implemented by the overall national plan and, for that purpose, the quantitative projections have been very necessary, even though the coordination realized might not be the most desirable one.

Before we make further judgments, one further problem is worth mentioning—the changes in policy principles that Japan has experienced in the past fifteen years. Broadly speaking, there have been five changes: (1) principles used by the American occupation authorities (1945-48); (2) overall direct controls by government (1949-51); (3) transitions from direct to indirect controls (1952-55); (4) adoption of the principle of competition, domestically (1956-now), and (5) an extension of the competition principle to international relations (1962-now). The most significant of the changes is the principle of competition (both domestic and international), which was explicitly introduced in Plan VI, and which affected the nature of the plan considerably.

During the early period of reconstruction, most of Japan's economists were not opposed to overall direct government controls based on national planning. The validity of the plans during this period, therefore, could be judged primarily by levels of realized performance. In other words, the plan which achieved higher levels of specific economic activities, *ex post*, than those assumed in the plan was considered to be effective, even though the discrepancies between the planned and the

[20] The concept of "balanced growth" used here is slightly different from the usual meaning, since we mostly relate it to the fact that excessive expansions in specified sectors may create disturbing (and sometimes fatal) bottlenecks, which may considerably reduce the rate of economic growth. In other words, the concept does not deny that unbalanced growth may be a desirable incentive for economic development.

realized levels were large. In this sense, therefore, one can say that almost all plans during the period of reconstruction were effective. The longer-term quantitative projection was not considered to be a necessary condition, since the levels of important economic indicators in 1934-36 were the immediate objectives.

Plan IV was one of the most ineffective plans. It had three serious defects: (1) its policy principles were confused, so that the role of government was not clearly defined and the longer-term projection did not exist; (2) the target was either extremely unrealistic or too politically oriented—i.e., an achievement of full employment for five years was presupposed; and (3) most of the model's parameters that were used for the quantitative projection were biased toward the prewar pattern—the annual increase in labor productivity, for example, was assumed to be 3 percent, which was the average of the prewar period.

In 1956 an economic white paper was published which stated that "the recovery period from war is now over." This was accepted by planners and economists as a starting point for new versions of planning and of policy principles. Plans V and VI, therefore, need to be evaluated in the light of that circumstance. Plan V was still ambiguous in several ways—for instance, the relationships between the public and private sectors were not clearly defined. Plan VI was formulated with a much clearer understanding of the problems, and our final discussion will thus be concerned only with it.

There are two crucial points to be examined here in evaluating Plan VI: (1) is it effective as a guide post for private activities; (2) are its plans within the public sector sufficiently realistic? According to the three years of experience since Plan VI was announced, the answer for the first question is partly "yes," for the second, mostly "no."

As noted earlier, the private sectors still maintain a somewhat passive attitude toward planning, and thus they interpret the planning guide posts as semiofficial requirements. Nevertheless, the optimism in private business circles that had resulted from the higher rate of economic growth in 1959-60 was further confirmed by Plan VI. The announcement of the plan, therefore, was in itself a strong stimulant for further economic growth. (This effect was further strengthened by the aggressive plan of industrialization, even though it was unfortunately inconsistent with the aggregate projections, as mentioned above.) In this sense, we can say that Plan VI has so far been very effective as a tool for economic policies.

However, the acceptance of the projected levels by private enterprise

—especially the levels given in the projection on industrialization—led to a situation that produced unforeseen deficits in the balance of payments through sharp increases of imported raw materials and heavy machinery. In this sense, Plan VI was effective, but not satisfactory.

Furthermore, from a technical point of view, the plan contained a serious mistake. Originally, the plans for the public sector were formulated with special reference to the industrial activities assumed in the industrialization plan. In the final stage, however, they were adjusted to the level of aggregate production; in the adjustment process the relationship between private fixed capital formation and public investment was distorted. Consequently, the plans for the public sector, in their final stage, cannot be regarded as having been realistic.

IN CONCLUSION, let me consider the possible lines of future national planning in Japan. First, from a technical point of view, the preparation of longer-term projections and the maintenance of their internal consistency will become increasingly important, especially in quantitative terms. Second, the effects of price movement will have to be incorporated into the projections, since price increases in consumer goods and services within the first three years of Plan VI are already much larger than the plan expected. (Introduction of prices into quantitative projections in a national economy will of course be extremely difficult, theoretically and statistically.) Third, the role of planning within the public sector will become much more important. However, if planning is to be useful as both a positive stimulant for economic growth and a stabilizing force, increased coordination between the long-term plan and the annual plans (together with the annual government budget) is required in the future.

11

Quantitative Decision Analysis and National Policy: How Can We Bridge the Gap?

CHARLES C. HOLT[1]

THE MOST CASUAL OBSERVATION of the process by which governments formulate their economic policies reveals an extremely sharp contrast with the quantitative decision analysis approach; in the United States there is relatively little contact between the people working in these two areas. However, such contact does occur to some degree in the Department of Defense, and in the more progressive corporations where quantitative decision methods are being introduced. In various countries in Europe and Asia, as the papers in this volume indicate, efforts have been made to use mathematical models of economic relationships in the political decision-making process, but again virtually no use is made of quantitative decision analyses. The presence of this tremendous gap should stimulate us to examine both the methods that are currently used in choosing national economic policies, and the present status of formal decision analysis, with a view to determining whether it would be desirable to try to close this gap, and, if so, how it might be achieved.

This paper is oriented toward the United States, but most of its points are applicable also to other countries. First, the decision methods now used in formulating national economic policy are considered briefly. Second, the areas where most quantitative economists are concentrating their efforts are surveyed, and what direction this might take in the future is considered. Third, the problem of determining suitable welfare objectives is examined. Fourth, certain questions that arise in the estimation of eco-

[1] Professor of Economics and Director of Center for Research on Policy and Operations, Social Systems Research Institute, University of Wisconsin.

nomic relationships are touched on. Fifth, the quantitative decision analyses currently available are characterized. Sixth, some of the problems of relating to the political decision process are briefly surveyed. Finally, directions are suggested in which research is needed, if we are to move toward closing the gap. The objective is to give a broad nontechnical view of important questions that constitute a challenge for future research effort. Unfortunately, in the space available, adequate recognition cannot be given to the past work that serves as the basis of this paper, but some basic references are provided at the end of the paper.

CURRENT DECISION METHODS

Any brief summary of the process by which the President, the Congress, and the electorate of the United States reach decisions on national economic policy is necessarily a crude caricature. Nevertheless, if we are to discuss some of the basic elements in the process, some such simplified picture as the following is needed: first, a problem is recognized which requires attention; second, alternative courses of action are formulated; third, the outcome associated with each of the alternatives is predicted; fourth, the outcomes are evaluated to determine their relative desirabilities; fifth, a choice is made in the context of conflicting political and constituency interests. The actual process is, of course, a complicated successive approximation procedure: for example, one of the political choices may be to redefine the problem—thereby starting the whole process from the beginning again.

Several observations can be drawn from this simple scheme. The process proceeds from the immediate and concrete (problems and alternatives) to the distant in time and abstraction (predictions and evaluations). The arrangement is logical, workable, and probably serves for most of the work-a-day world's decision-making. The choice process is so closely associated with the evaluation process that explicit evaluation statements are required only as arguments for particular courses of action. Making a choice of one action as better than another precludes the necessity of saying how *much* better one set of outcomes is than another or of considering outcomes not associated with the particular alternatives. The formulation of action alternatives tends to be reduced to the art of finding legislation that stands a chance of passage in Congress, and, again, comprehensive statements of objectives are largely avoided.

If we examine the American process for making economic policy choices, we are struck with the tremendous dispersion of political power among various agencies, committees, and chairmen, as well as the Senate, the House, and the President. The whole process, from problem formulation to choice, may occur simultaneously in different agencies on the same problem and on different problems in the same agency, so that the final choice is often some global political compromise involving a number of otherwise unrelated problems. Thus the difficulties of achieving a coherent and timely set of economic policies are formidable, to say the least.

And how do quantitatively oriented economists contribute to this decision process?

ECONOMISTS AND THE DECISION PROCESS

Economists make contributions to the decision process at all of the levels designated above (now and then even by being elected to office), but they would probably agree that their greatest contributions, based on professional competence, are the unconditional and conditional forecasts they may make of the outcomes of alternative courses of action. The drive to study economic relationships quantitatively is oriented in large part toward efforts to foresee the changes that are taking place in the economy, so that preventive action, if it appears called for, may be advised. When alternative actions are proposed, economists are called upon to make conditional forecasts of the outcomes. We have reason to expect that econometric models will be increasingly useful in predicting the outcomes when several instrument variables are used together.

As useful—even indispensable—as forecasts are in facilitating policy decisions, quantitative economists recognize that the decision process involves a great deal more to which they could contribute. They have, for instance, often formulated courses of action, and supplied the value judgments needed to evaluate the outcomes. But if they are to make even greater contributions, they will need a framework for thinking about the decision process that is less simplified than the one discussed above. This implies, not a change in the process itself, but a different way of relating the work of economists to it. *If* the values which are sought by the citizenry and the responsible elected officials can be determined— that is, if the most abstract ingredient in the decision-making process can somehow be subjected to objective study and quantitative estimation—the economists can take an entirely different approach in their contributions to the decision-making process.

The problem of maximizing the accomplishment of a welfare function subject to the constraint of economic relationships can then be posed. And when the problem is stated in mathematical language it can be solved by formal methods to determine the action alternatives that are efficient—that is, effective in achieving the desired ends. Because of our limited knowledge and the genuine differences between the objectives of various groups, the conclusion of the formal analysis will be, not a single "best" action alternative, but rather several "good" alternatives depending upon the assumptions that are made.

This approach would enable economists to contribute on a professional level to the formulation of action alternatives, and thus the political debate on economic policy could *start* with a set of alternatives, each of which is in some sense efficient. This general approach has proved feasible in operations research on business and military decision problems, and it has the potential to tremendously increase the contributions of economists to national economic policy. We are *not*, however, visualizing a benevolent dictatorial technocracy run by professional economists; rather, we are foreseeing a day when economists will be better able to offer sound advice on a professional level to politically responsible decision-makers.

Welfare functions would need to be empirically based on the preferences of the elected officials and the citizenry, and not merely reflect the economists' preferences. To the extent that economists can discover what objectives are desired, they may be able to supply counsel in formulating good alternatives, forecasting outcomes, evaluating the strong and weak points of the outcomes, and, finally, interpreting the concepts of optimum strategy that enter decision problems when uncertainty is involved—particularly in the dynamic case where a time sequence of actions is required. The role of the welfare function and its successful empirical treatment is of primal importance in this development.

It is often argued that economic policy problems are much too complicated and subtle to be amenable to quantitative approaches. The complexity is granted, but one may question the conclusion. Would it not be more convincing to argue that the admitted complexity, if it is really to be treated, requires the use of quantitative methods that can simultaneously take into account variables that are too numerous for human capabilities when judgmental methods alone are used? Certain oil companies, for example, are now using computer methods to seek the optimum solution to cost and profit problems involving several hundred thousand variables. The power of computers to handle very large problems makes it possible to seek optimal answers to very difficult decision problems which cannot even be formulated, much less solved, without the compact and efficient language of mathematics.

Some people may feel that such an approach to national economic policy is an unnecessarily "fancy" one. Perhaps so; but the economy is an exceedingly complicated mechanism even when we are considering only those variables that are the most obviously relevant to national policy deliberations. It seems likely that economists, in trying to contribute to national economic policy-making, will ultimately need mathematical decision analyses, involving the use of electronic computers. If we grant for the moment that it may be desirable to move in this direction, how well equipped are we with the quantitative tools and knowledge necessary to cope with the difficult problems of national economic policy?

DETERMINATION OF WELFARE OBJECTIVES

In spite of (or perhaps because of) the long history of utility analysis, economists are inclined to be skeptical of the utility function as a workable concept. But the fact remains that the goal structures of most societies are sufficiently cohesive to keep the societies from falling apart. Since a welfare function is only a language for expressing this reality, it seems more constructive for economists to ask *how* this formulation can be made usable rather than to continue to ask whether or not such a function exists. There is without doubt a body of shared values that are relevant to economic policy choices, and they *can* be studied empirically.

The utility function concept is not only unpopular with economists but is also almost unknown in some of the other social science disciplines. The well-known problems of volatility and inconsistency are often used to discredit the concept, but in a fundamental sense there is no alternative, if a man or a society is to organize coherent goal-oriented activity. The concept should be interpreted with sufficient breadth to be consistent with satisficing as well as optimization, and attention should be paid to uncertainty and lack of knowledge as they relate to preferences.

To develop quantitative knowledge about objectives relating to economic stability, it is clear that skills, research techniques, and theory from various disciplines—particularly economics, sociology, social psychology, political science, and law—will need to be brought to bear. We need not only to determine direct and indirect impacts on social welfare of such basic variables as unemployment and the rate of inflation, but also to study preferences which, for example, attach directly to such instrument measures as tax-rate changes.

Hopefully, study can provide a rough picture of relative preferences and also some quantitative information on how the marginal trade-offs between objectives change with their levels of attainment. Questions of consistency and uniformity of preferences should be studied across individuals and officials, at different points of time, and between different political groupings. Questionnaire methods would probably be used intensively, but considerable effort would need to be devoted to making the questions meaningful, relevant, and answerable. Novel methods undoubtedly will be needed.

It simply is not true that elected officials *know all* the interests and desires of their constituencies. Although a member of the U.S. House of Representatives, for example, is extensively exposed to pressures from politically active minority groups and organized commercial interests, he may have only the vaguest knowledge of where his own constituency stands on many of the issues on which he must vote. Objective study of this area would help elected officials to perform that part of their jobs that relates to economic policy.

Preference structures are not innate. They rise out of the experience of living in a complex world—and much more basic research is needed on the process by which people develop them. A substantive creative effort will also be required to achieve a meaningful formulation of preferences; we need to invent abstractions that will help people and researchers think about their value judgments.

The fact that people need to express preferences about situations that a given generation of Americans may never have experienced—a high rate of inflation, for example—means that the formulation of a welfare function involves a strong element of prediction whose solution may necessitate recourse to the experience of other people, times, and places. We need to know how a situation would be liked (or not liked) *if* it ever happened.

Talcott Parsons' emphasis on the means-end chain makes clear the inherent complexity of "ends." In a sense, the researcher needs to build a social utility function that did not previously exist. To do this responsibly and objectively is a challenge of high order. In contrast to the evaluation of particular outcomes associated with particular action alternatives (as occurs with current decision methods), a welfare function is inherently more comprehensive in covering, at least conceptually, all possible outcomes.

Consider the problem of determining the percent unemployment which would be the most desirable level to maintain. Rather than treating this as a simple *a priori* value judgment in which the Republican party members might come up with a larger number than the Democratic party members, a careful cost-benefit analysis could be made that would indicate in concrete terms the consequences about which value judgments are required. For example, when unemployment becomes very low, the labor turnover rate rises markedly, raising the cost to business firms of training and recruitment. On the other hand, a plentiful supply of job opportunities may stimulate labor mobility, thereby increasing economic efficiency, and may be an important source of satisfaction and security even to those workers who do not enter the job market to make a change. At increased levels of unemployment the average duration of unemployment increases, as does the percentage of unemployed workers who suffer long-term unemployment. As the term of unemployment extends for individual workers, families are subjected to ever increasing stress: financial reserves and unemployment benefits are exhausted and emotional fatigue accumulates. Health, marital, and crime problems may follow.

By careful study, many of these effects can be measured and the seriousness of the economic and noneconomic consequences determined. Value judgments must of course ultimately be made, but they can be tied to concrete consequences about which people have a better basis for judgment than they do for such an abstract quantity as percent of unemployment. Similar studies could be made of the welfare consequences associated with other variables and instruments.

I have stressed the welfare function here, because up to now it has received very little attention and because it is essential to the full development of quantitative decision analyses.

THE ESTIMATION OF ECONOMIC RELATIONS

The urgent need for better knowledge of economic relationships is recognized by those economists who are content with present decision methods as well as by those who would like to see greater emphasis put on quantitative decision analyses. As a consequence, nearly all of the quantitative research being done is currently directed to this area.

However, we still need quantitative estimates of the relationships that determine the dependent (endogenous) variables in the economy, and estimates of the relationships that can be used to forecast the (exogenous) variables that influence the economy but are not to an appreciable extent influenced by it. It is increasingly recognized that we need comprehensive sets of equations if we are to study the economy as a complete system, but most of the research is still organized on a piecemeal basis.

One problem that has received little attention to date will become of greater importance as models are increasingly used for policy analyses. Historical data reflect not only the relationships in the economy that may be expected to continue in the future but also the policy actions that were taken in the past. When a new policy strategy is being studied, it is important to delete from the model of the economy the effects of the old strategies which may be supplanted. To do this we need to separate statistically the effects of the old policies from the other relationships in the economy. This poses a problem of identifying and estimating the *structure* of these relationships, and this may be difficult. And where structural relationships are to be changed by policy measures, the problem of estimating them arises. However, where policy actions are intended primarily to influence the values of economic variables rather than the parameters of the system, it may suffice to know the relationships between variables without having to know the exact path by which one variable influences another. In this case it is not necessary to estimate the economic structure.

Even though the emphasis that economic research is presently putting on empirical data is healthy, we often go too far in expecting the data to suggest and test structural hypotheses, as well as to be used in estimating the parameters of the relationships. This is asking too much of the relatively small amount of historical data ordinarily available. As powerful as regression analyses and other statistical methods are, they require other inputs besides quantitative data. We increasingly need to bring to the data all the institutional and theoretical insight that we can muster. We also badly need sets of data that are richer than the highly aggregated numbers which the United States government so profusely supplies, and more research on the statistical problems of estimating relationships within a complex interacting system that is not subject to experimental manipulation.

But since these problems are all more or less well recognized, what we need most at this point are resources and talent to carry their exploration forward. Yet, despite the tremendous practical importance of this research for national economic policy—and the stress given it by economists—the federal government has put a relatively small amount of money into this field of study. More on this point later.

STATISTICAL DECISION ANALYSIS

Imagine that someone presented economists with an accurate quantitative model of the economy, and a social welfare function relevant to national economic policies. What could we do with this embarrassment of riches? This is hardly a likely predicament but it should make us think about the decision problem itself.

Normative analyses that indicate what actions ought to be taken are not new. Economists have been assuming for years that business firms and consumers somehow could manage to equate marginal costs and marginal benefits in all directions; at the same time, they made few serious contributions toward showing how this might, in fact, be done. In recent years, however, economists have increasingly become involved in cost-benefit analyses of various government projects, largely with local impacts, and the operations of business firms and military organizations. Some have had the humbling experience of discovering that an optimum decision depends on the solution of an infinite set of equations, or that certain decision problems, which are conceptually straightforward, saturate the largest electronic computers available.

We are not implying here that decision problems are insoluble, but we do assert that they are of serious magnitude. Difficult problems in mathematics, probability theory, and statistics are involved, not to mention the economic and political issues that may be raised. How well are we currently equipped to handle decision problems—to find, that is, a course of action, or a strategy for determining actions, which maximizes a welfare function subject to the constraint of the economic relationships? This involves finding the optimum trade-offs between different variables, across different time periods, while taking into account uncertainty through the introduction of random variables.

In the static case under certainty, a decision poses the pure allocation problem with which economists have long been familiar. Where the functions are continuous, local optimum conditions may be obtained by using calculus; where the functions are discontinuous, linear programming is a flexible and powerful tool. If time is introduced without introducing uncertainty, we have a larger but conceptually identical problem. In some cases analytical solutions are available; other cases will require resort to numerical methods and machine computation. In this category we are fairly well equipped to solve the problems.

When uncertainty enters the static problem, the decision needs somehow to take into account the unknown conditions that interact with the action that is taken. The best decision action must be some sort of compromise that is not likely to be the best action for any of the alternative sets of circumstances considered individually. Stated differently, an action that is optimal when the choice has to be made is unlikely to be the action that would have been taken if the values of the random variables had been known at the time. The static uncertainty case involves optimizing a probability weighted average, an operation that often can be performed without undue difficulty but is surely more complex than the certainty case.

Under dynamic uncertainty, knowledge gradually becomes available as time passes. An event that is an unknown random variable before the time period is reached becomes known after the period has passed, and forecasts that are still in the future may need to be revised in light of the new information. The optimum decision analysis under these circumstances requires response to unknown random variables in the future (feed forward) and response to events that have already happened (feed back). Optimum decisions for this case are made by conditional strategies whose determination requires the analysis of a complex process that takes place through time.

In general, we are not yet in a very good position to handle this problem. If we face a relatively simple situation with a small number of instrument variables, solutions can be numerically calculated, using the dynamic programming techniques. Where a large number of instrument variables are involved, the problem can be handled only in the case of special simple mathematical forms such as are treated by linear decision rules, or chance constrained programming. Where the decision-maker's environment is purposeful—for example, in a game situation—we can treat some classes of simple mathematical functions usually involving discrete alternatives.

For decisions that must be made in an economic environment in which not only the variables but also the structural relationships themselves change through time, so that the relationships must be continually re-estimated, we are only beginning to develop adaptive estimation and forecasting methods. The circumstances of such an economic environment are, of course, exactly what we face in many decision problems of national economic policy.

In short, many of the decision situations that are of practical importance cannot be treated adequately by existing techniques. We have not even tried to discuss the additional problems which are involved in decision-making in the context of political and administrative organizations. The delegation of authority, continuing collection of performance data, monitoring of administrative organizations, etc., relate to the policy decisions and ultimately should be taken into account, because the preferred choices clearly depend in part upon the administrative structures available. The conclusion is clear that a great deal more work is required in building the decision analyses for the specific classes of problems that are important in national economic policy.

RELATING TO THE POLITICAL DECISION PROCESS

It is often said by researchers that half of an Operations Research job is finding the answer to a decision problem, and the other half is convincing the responsible decision-maker that he should act on the basis of the analysis. In the American arena of national political decision-making, where the decisions are made by an organization of carefully contrived checks and balances designed to be tyranny-proof, the effort proportions may shift so that two thirds of the job is convincing the responsible officials that they should take action on the basis of the analysis. Although many people from various fields have a good practical feel for this problem of being effective in a governmental organization, few would claim that a sizable body of tested knowledge is available.

Thus even if economists had surmounted the hurdles discussed above —concerning the welfare function, the economic model, and the statistical decision analysis—so that preferable courses of action had been determined, the problem would remain of convincing the responsible elected officials that a sound professional job had been done, and that a basis had been laid for an action choice. Situations in which a professional has advice to offer to governmental decision-makers are hardly novel. Scientists, for example, have made important recommendations for action in the fields of atomic energy, medicine, and space exploration. But the economist faces a unique problem: political leaders often consider themselves to be expert in his subject matter.

While we do not know very much about how to relate to the political decision process, certain broad outlines can be suggested. It is vital that good communications be established. The techniques that will be used for decision analysis should probably be left in the background, since they are not likely to be understood by either elected officials or the public. Communications can be established through two-way discussions of the problem to be solved, the alternatives being proposed, and the pros and cons of each alternative. The fact that the economist's decision analysis may work backward from the objectives to obtain the preferred alternatives that are being presented is quite incidental and should not be stressed.

If the assistance which economists can offer in limiting the range of decision alternatives is actually to be used by elected representatives, a slow process of gradually building confidence will be required. Help will only be accepted if the officials are convinced that the economists are solving the problems that the officials *think* are problems. Getting the right answer to the wrong problem is a common trap; to avoid it, the economists must be willing to accept, at least initially, the definition of the problems as they are seen by the officials. Later, when a clearer picture of the problems is available, they may be redefined by agreement.

The role of the economist is to help elected officials achieve their objectives, and understand fully the implications of the actions that they are taking. An extended two-way education process is clearly indicated. Economists must learn to understand the officials and the constraints on them. The officials ultimately must obtain a basic, but not necessarily technical, understanding of the economist and his tools, and to some extent the public must do the same, if the economist's skills are to be put to effective social use. With the increasingly technical nature of the economist's knowledge and tools and, hopefully, with the gradual demonstration of professional accomplishment, elected officials may come to rely on the economist's contribution.

The closer economists get to the actual decisions made by the political process, the more they will become involved in the conflicts of political power and the greater will be their need to understand the workings of the political process. We hope that parallel research will be pursued in the sister social sciences—and especially in political science—to surmount the undoubtedly very difficult problems of relating effectively to the political decision process. Economists should certainly avoid the naive assumption that, simply because they recommend certain courses of action, even if they do so unanimously, elected officials will necessarily choose accordingly. For example, even though frequent changes in tax rates prove to be indicated to achieve the desired degree of economic stability, this may prove politically difficult to attain with sufficiently short time lags.

IN CONCLUSION

Not everyone will agree that quantitative decision analyses should be applied to national economic policy. In the present state of our knowledge, it is not clear how great a contribution can be made by developments in this direction. The more concrete and structured the decision problem, the easier it is to formulize it, subject it to quantitative analysis, and solve it; the more nebulous the problem, the more we may have to guess at the relationships, the objectives, and the decision solution. Many high-level national policy problems are so unstructured that quantitative methods could turn out to depend mostly on judgments after all.

Just because many business firms have halved their inventory holdings while improving customer service, it does not follow, for instance, that we can halve the national unemployment rate while decreasing inflation. Nevertheless, solid accomplishments have been achieved by developments of this kind, and the man who argues that it cannot be done is always in a risky position. On the other hand, extravagant claims of quick solutions are to be avoided, since a great deal of effort will clearly be required before practical results can be routinely expected.

Since any new direction in science or technology usually brings with it changes that threaten people and jobs, resistance is to be anticipated. Yet weavers and miners have learned to coexist with machines and to control them to their own ends; business managers and elected officials can gradually do likewise. It is important to emphasize that the choice is *not* between a wise man and an electronic computer: we can have a mixture of both, each making the contribution it is qualified to make. From here on in, both are likely to be essential.

Through simulation testing we can compensate, at least partially, for the fact that the laboratory for these decision problems is the national economy where any errors will necessarily be large. We can set up an economic model on a computer and perform experiments with various alternative actions. An extensive testing program of this type is strongly to be recommended to validate the model, the welfare function, and the decision analysis.

Accelerated research effort is needed in all of the fields discussed above, but, whereas the estimation of economic relationships is receiving considerable attention, the other three areas have received much less attention. To say that these areas have been "neglected" is perhaps too strong, but one can at least list the areas in the order of decreasing effort put into them: statistical decision analysis, social welfare objectives, and relations with the political process. Simulation testing has generated a great deal of interest, but relatively little has yet been done.

The increased stress on quantitative measurement in economics, the effort to predict indirect impacts of changes in complex systems, and finally the attempt to determine optimum courses of action—all reflect rising research goals that are difficult of attainment. Such research demands not only more and better-trained economists but also large and expensive data-collection programs, sizable computer programming efforts, and substantial amounts of time on large-scale electronic computers. There is little question that increased financial support is needed.

Against the background of work needed that we have sketched above, and in view of the practical importance of economic research for the successful operation of our national economy, it is interesting to examine the governmental and private contributions to such research at a time when support for all research fields has been tremendously increased.

In fiscal year 1963 the United States government spent approximately $35 million on economics research. Of this, $11.3 million went to what was considered basic research.[2] These two figures are 0.8 percent and 0.3 percent, respectively, of the corresponding total federal expenditures in all research fields. The $35 million was in large part devoted to economic research activities within government agencies. It is also approximately one one-thousandth of the estimated $35 billion economic waste that the recent (1964) tax cut is expected to eradicate by stimulating the economy to a higher production level closer to its full employment potential.

One of the large supporters of university research through the federal government is the National Science Foundation, whose research grants in fiscal 1963, when classified by academic discipline, show economics receiving $2.2 million.[3] This is third from the smallest amount of grants in twenty-one fields and represents 1.89 percent of the NSF total. In biological and medical sciences, nine fields are listed, eight of which receive more research support than economics.

A summary of the scientific research grants made by private foundations in 1962 shows that economics received $1.2 million—3 percent of the total for all sciences.[4] However, some support of economics research certainly is listed under other headings.

[2] National Science Foundation, *Federal Funds for Research, Development, and Other Scientific Activities*, Vol. XII (1964), pp. 136-137.
[3] National Science Foundation, *Thirteenth Annual Report, 1963*, p. 83.
[4] Ann D. Walton and Marianna O. Lewis, eds., *The Foundation Directory* (Foundation Library Center, 1964), p. 39. "Business" and "labor" received $1.2 million in grants. It is probable that part of this amount should be classified under economics.

Since it is admittedly difficult to classify problem-oriented research accurately by academic field, all of the above figures must be considered tentative. Nevertheless, they certainly suggest a modest level of support for quantitative economic analysis, especially in view of the some $16 billion being spent nationally in a year on research and development in all scientific fields.

My purpose here is not, of course, to suggest that other research efforts should receive less support. I am, however, very positively questioning whether the federal government and private funding sources are supporting basic and applied economic research in a manner that is commensurate with the complexity and importance of national economic policy. There is no doubt that, supported or not, the quantitative approach to economic policy problems will continue at an accelerating rate, but an increase in support would hasten the day when this approach will become thoroughly practicable.

However, financial hurdles are not the only ones to be surmounted in the pursuit of this research. Unfortunately, the economists who can move flexibly back and forth between mathematical and statistical tools, economic theory, and policy problems are still relatively few in number. Hence there is a sharp conflict between the short-range research objectives of the here-and-now work to be done, and the long-run objective of educating more researchers. Further, as more comprehensive research objectives are set that involve analyses of systems of relationships, the traditional academic research unit composed of a professor and one or two graduate students is inexorably revealed as inadequate. Yet the coordination of such units into a larger team effort is not easy. Perhaps such an organizational form as the research institute, which so far has been little used in economics, should be explored. The interuniversity research team concept also holds some promise. In any case, these problems all deserve serious consideration by the government and the profession.

Economists can and do (and will continue to) make contributions to the formulation of national economic policies, whatever methods they use. The purpose of this paper has been to point a direction of possible development and to sketch, in general terms, what would be involved in such development. Hopefully, this picture of the possibilities will stimulate many of us to undertake the large amount of work that will be involved in reducing the possibilities to actualities. And as our discussion has tried to make clear, contributions from other social science fields are urgently needed.

REFERENCES

Adelman, I. A., and F. L. Adelman, "The Dynamic Properties of the Klein-Goldberger Model," *Econometrica*, Vol. 27 (October 1959), pp. 596-625.

Bellman, Richard, *Adaptive Control Processes: A Guided Tour* (Princeton University Press, 1961).

——, ed., *Dynamic Programming* (Princeton University Press, 1957).

——, ed., *Mathematical Optimization Techniques* (University of California Press, 1963).

Braybrooke, David, and Charles E. Lindblom, *A Strategy of Decision: Policy Evaluation as a Social Process* (Free Press, 1963).

Buchanan, James M., and Gordon Tullock, *The Calculus of Consent* (University of Michigan Press, 1962).

Chang, Sheldon S. L., *Synthesis of Optimum Control Systems* (McGraw-Hill, 1961).

Cohen, K. J., and R. M. Cyert, "Computer Models in Dynamic Economics," *Quarterly Journal of Economics*, Vol. 75 (February 1961), pp. 112-27.

Duesenberry, James S., Otto Eckstein, and Gary Fromm, "A Simulation of the United States Economy in Recession," *Econometrica*, Vol. 28 (October 1960), pp. 749-809.

Duesenberry, J. S., G. Fromm, L. R. Klein, and E. Kuh, eds., *The Brookings-SSRC Quarterly Econometric Model of the United States* (Rand McNally and North-Holland, 1965).

Eckman, Donald P., *Systems: Research and Design* (Wiley, 1961).

Fox, Karl A., *Econometric Analysis for Public Policy* (Iowa State University Press, 1958).

Goode, Harry H., and Robert E. Machal, *System Engineering* (McGraw-Hill, 1957).

Hoggatt, Austin C., and Frederick E. Balderston, eds., *Symposium on Simulation Models: Methodology and Applications to the Behavioral Sciences* (South-Western Publishing Co., 1963).

Holt, C. C., "Linear Decision Rules for Economic Stabilization and Growth," *Quarterly Journal of Economics*, Vol. 76 (February 1962), pp. 20-45.

Holt, C. C., F. Modigliani, J. F. Muth, and H. A. Simon, *Planning Production, Inventories, and Work Force* (Prentice-Hall, 1960).

Howard, Ronald A., *Dynamic Programming and Markov Processes* (Wiley, 1960).

Huitt, Ralph K., "Congressional Organization and Operations in the Field of Money and Credit," in Commission on Money and Credit, *Fiscal and Debt Management Policies* (Prentice-Hall, 1963), pp. 399-495.

Kijsinisk, Walerian, *Dynamic Optimization and Control: A Variational Approach* (Wiley, 1961).

Klein, Lawrence R., *Economic Fluctuations in the United States, 1921-1941* (Wiley, 1950).

——, "A Postwar Quarterly Model: Description and Applications," in National Bureau of Economic Research, *Models of Income Determination,* Vol. 28 (Princeton University Press, 1964), pp. 11-58.

Klein, L. R., and A. S. Goldberger, *An Econometric Model of the United States, 1929-1952* (North-Holland, 1955).

Koopmans, T. C., ed., *Statistical Inference in Dynamic Economic Models* (Cowles Commission Monograph No. 10; Wiley, 1950).

LaSalle, Joseph, and Solomon Lefschetz, *Stability by Liapanov's Direct Method* (Academic Press, 1961).

Madansky, A., "Methods of Solution of Linear Programming Under Uncertainty," *Operations Research,* Vol. 10 (1962), pp. 463-470.

Musgrave, Richard A., *The Theory of Public Finance* (McGraw-Hill, 1959).

Orcutt, Guy H., Martin Shubik, G. P. E. Clarkson, Herbert A. Simon, "Simulation: A Symposium," *American Economic Review,* Vol. 50 (December 1960), pp. 893-932.

Parsons, Talcott, and Edward A. Shals, *Toward a General Theory of Action* (Harvard University Press, 1951).

Phillips, A. W., "Stabilisation Policy in a Closed Economy," *Economic Journal,* Vol. 64 (June 1954), pp. 290-323.

Popov, E. P., *The Dynamics of Automatic Control Systems* (translated from the Russian edition; Addison-Wesley, 1962).

Radner, Roy, *Notes on the Theory of Econmic Planning* (Center of Economic Research, Athens, Greece, 1963).

Raiffa, Howard, and R. O. Schlaifer, *Applied Statistical Decision Theory* (Harvard University Graduate School of Business Administration, 1961).

Rothenberg, Jerome, *The Measurement of Social Welfare* (Prentice-Hall, 1961).

Suits, D. B., "Forecasting and Analysis with an Econometric Model," *American Economic Review,* Vol. 52 (March 1962), pp. 104-132.

Theil, H., *Economic Forecasts and Policy,* 2d rev. ed. (North-Holland, 1961).

——, "On the Theory of Economic Policy," *American Economic Review,* Vol. 46 (May 1956), *Papers and Proceedings of the 68th Annual Meeting,* pp. 360-366.

——, *Optimal Decision Rules for Government and Industry* (North-Holland, 1964).

Thrall, R. M., C. H. Coombs, and R. L. Davis, eds., *Decision Processes* (Wiley, 1954).

Tinbergen, Jan, *On the Theory of Economic Policy* (North-Holland, 1952).

——, *Economic Policy: Principles and Design* (North-Holland, 1956).

Tustin, A., *The Mechanism of Economic Systems* (Heinemann, 1953).

van den Bogaard, P. J. M., and A. P. Barten, "Macroeconomic Decision Rules for the Netherlands, 1957-1959" (Report 5915 of the Econometric Institute of the Netherlands School of Economics, June 15, 1959).

van den Bogaard, P. J. M., and H. Theil, "Macrodynamic Policy-Making: An Application of Strategy and Certainty Equivalence Concepts to the

Economy of the United States, 1933-36," *Metroeconomica*, Vol. 11 (1959), pp. 149-167.

van Eijk, C. J., and J. Sandee, "Quantitative Determination of an Optimum Economic Policy," *Econometrica*, Vol. 27 (January 1959), pp. 1-13.

Van Trees, Harry L., *Synthesis of Optimum Nonlinear Control Systems* (MIT Press, 1962).

Vickrey, William S., *Metastatics and Macroeconomics* (Harcourt, Brace & World, 1964).

Westcott, John H., ed., *An Exposition of Adaptive Control* (Pergamon Press, 1962).

Conference Participants[*]

Irma Adelman
Professor of Economics
The Johns Hopkins University

Jack Alterman
Chief, Division of Economic Growth
Bureau of Labor Statistics
Department of Labor

W. Locke Anderson
Senior Staff
Council of Economic Advisers
(on leave, University of Michigan)

P. Bauchet
Director of Studies
National School of Administration
France

C. A. van den Beld
Netherlands Central Planning Bureau

Murray Brown
Research Staff
Office of Business Economics
Department of Commerce

Robert D. Calkins
President
The Brookings Institution

Bernard Cazes
Special Assistant to the General Commissioner of Planning
France

Hollis B. Chenery
Assistant Administrator for Program
Agency for International Development (on leave, Stanford University)

Gerhard Colm
Chief Economist
National Planning Association

Edward F. Denison
Senior Staff
The Brookings Institution

Karl A. Fox
Head, Department of Economics and Sociology
Iowa State University

Gary Fromm
Senior Staff
The Brookings Institution

W. Hessel
Director of Scientific Bureau
Netherlands Federal Trade Unions

Bert G. Hickman
Senior Staff
The Brookings Institution

Charles C. Holt
Professor of Economics
University of Wisconsin

Peter E. de Janosi
Program Associate
Ford Foundation

Hyman Kaitz
Assistant Chief, Division of Economic Growth
Bureau of Labor Statistics
Department of Labor

Maurice Liebenberg
Research Staff
Office of Business Economics
Department of Commerce

Herman Liebling
Chief Business Economist
Office of Financial Analysis
Treasury Department

* Affiliations are those at the time of the conference.

271

George W. Mitchell
Board of Governors of the Federal
  Reserve System

Lucien Morissens
Senior Research Worker
Department of Applied Economics
Free University of Brussels

Joseph A. Pechman
Director of Economic Studies
The Brookings Institution

Roy Radner
Professor of Economics
University of California (Berkeley)

Jati K. Sengupta
Associate Professor of Economics
Iowa State University

Shuntaro Shishido
Senior Planning Officer
Economic Planning Agency
Japanese Government

Herbert Stein
Director of Research
Committee for Economic Develop-
  ment

Alan Strout
International Economist
Planning Assistance Division
Agency for International Develop-
  ment

Henri Theil
Director, Econometric Institute
Netherlands School of Economics

Erik Thorbecke
Professor of Economics
Iowa State University

Tsunehiko Watanabe
Professor of Economics
Gakushuin University;
Associate Director
Japanese Economic Research Institute

John Wood
Research Division
Board of Governors of the Federal
  Reserve System

Index[1]

---

[1] Index entries for planning bodies—bureaus, commissions, committees, ministries, etc.—and for planning techniques, economic policy matters, and use of economic models in France, Japan, The Netherlands, and the United States will be found under the specific name of the body or item rather than under the country name.

273